The Political Economy of Turkey

Third World in Global Politics
Series Editor: Dr Ray Bush (University of Leeds)

The Third World in Global Politics series examines the character of politics and economic transformation in the Global South. It does so by interrogating contemporary theory and practice of policy makers, planners and academics. It offers a radical and innovative insight into theories of development and country case study analysis. The series illustrates the importance of analysing the character of economic and political internationalisation of capital and national strategies of capital accumulation in the Global South. It highlights the political, social and class forces that are shaped by internationalisation of capital and which in turn help shape the character of uneven and combined capitalist development in the South. The series questions neo-liberal theories of development and modernisation, and in highlighting the poverty of the mainstream offers critical insight into the theoretical perspectives that help explain global injustice and the political and social forces that are available across the globe providing alternatives to economic and political orthodoxy of the advocates of globalisation.

Also available:

The End of Development
Modernity, Post-Modernity and Development
Trevor Parfitt

The Political Economy of Turkey

Zülküf Aydın

Pluto Press

LONDON • ANN ARBOR, MI

First published 2005 by Pluto Press
345 Archway Road, London N6 5AA
and 839 Greene Street, Ann Arbor, MI 48106

www.plutobooks.com

British Library Cataloguing in Publication Data
A catalogue record for this book is available from the British Library

ISBN 0 7453 1827 4 hardback
ISBN 0 7453 1826 6 paperback

Library of Congress Cataloging in Publication Data applied for

10 9 8 7 6 5 4 3 2 1

Designed and produced for Pluto Press by
Chase Publishing Services, Fortescue, Sidmouth, EX10 9QG, England
Typeset from disk by Newgen Imaging Systems (P) Ltd, India
Printed and bound in the European Union by
Antony Rowe Ltd, Chippenham and Eastbourne, England

*Dedicated to the memory of a dear friend
Carolyn Baylies.
To Vehbi, Müzeyyen, Gülsevin, Esma, Ela
and Sena.*

Contents

Acknowledgements

I would like to thank the School of Politics and International Studies at the University of Leeds for granting me research leave for the preparation of this book, the Department of Politics and Public Administration at the Middle East Technical University and the Department of Politics at Bilkent University in Turkey for providing me with a wonderful working atmosphere. I would like to express my deep appreciation to Ray Bush, Gordon Crawford, Ruth Pearson, Galip Yalman, Nurdan Yalman, Fuat Keyman and Gülsevin Aydın for their encouragement and intellectual support. I am also thankful to Emma Smith for her help keeping my arguments clear and my grammar correct.

Introduction: Globalisation, capitalist crises and Turkey

The last few decades have witnessed a vast array of the most serious crises in Turkey since the establishment of the Republic in 1923. Social unrest, political and ethnic violence, paralysis of the state bureaucracy and other institutions, foreign exchange problems, increasing foreign debt, a decreasing rate of economic growth, astronomical rates of inflation, an alarming trade and balance of payments deficit, uneven urbanisation, increasing unemployment and inefficient social services have all been part of everyday life in the recent history of Turkey.

This book is intended to contribute to both current discussions amongst the social scientists on the political and socio-economic problems faced by Turkey in recent decades and the process of Turkey's integration into the global economy. In so doing it concentrates on various aspects of the current political and socio-economic crisis facing Turkey. The main contention is that current problems in Turkey are the result of the specific way in which political, economic and social forces are shaped by both the internal and external dynamics at work. Turkey's further integration into the world economy as a result of increasing globalisation has meant that upheavals in the world economy are deeply felt in Turkish society. With the turmoil in the world economy in the last few decades generating the collapse of commodity prices for agricultural products, minerals, oil and gas, the crisis in Turkey, along with a number of less economically developed countries, has intensified. This book aims to analyse the internal and external dynamics of the socio-economic crisis in Turkey.

The prevalence of the economic crisis in Turkey has forced governments since the 1980s to give in to international pressures to open up the economy. This has meant the abandonment of nationalistic Import Substituting Industrialisation (ISI) policies in favour of more export-oriented policies. The clash of interests generated between protected manufacturing industries and their underlying

1

nationalist ideology, together with the international capital and its free market economy ideology, have posed a major dilemma for policy makers. Current fiscal, monetary, political and social crises facing Turkey have led many governments to try to develop survival strategies, which have necessitated major changes in economic and social policies. By looking at state policies on agriculture, industry and social services, this book intends to show the multi-dimensional nature of the crisis and explore its roots in their national and international contexts. Furthermore, it will also show that people are not passive sponges absorbing whatever is thrown at them by the state. In doing so, popular reactions to state policies in the form of ethnic, religious and class protests and mobilisations will be concentrated upon.

In the last four decades the economy, state, class structure and external relations in Turkey have been fundamentally transformed. Most studies of the Turkish transformation have concentrated on various dimensions of change, such as economic structuring under the influence of Structural Adjustment Policies (SAPs), the rise of militant Islam, the process of democratisation, ethnic conflict, etc. while ignoring the deeper structural forces that play a determinant role in shaping these historico-specific conjunctural changes. A deeper understanding of these changes requires a wider perspective which provides a spectrum to reveal interconnections between factors appearing to be unrelated.

INTERPRETATIONS OF GLOBALISATION

Such a wide perspective is provided by globalisation, which is considered to represent an 'epochal shift' by Ruggie (1993) and Walters (1995). For less economically developed countries the fashionable term 'globalisation' symbolises the process of integration into the world economy, a process by no means smooth and conflict free. It is a process of restructuring on all fronts: political, economic, social and cultural. The relationship between societies that are undergoing transformations and the global world order is one of dynamic articulation. It is difficult not to agree with Wood (1999) that 'every capitalist economy exists only in relation to others'. Crises that occur in specific nation states are in fact manifestations of the operation of global economic forces. The global structures provide the background within which specific changes in societies take place. In other words, globalisation, which involves transnational processes of the internationalisation of trade, production, technology, finance and social life, acts as the last determinant in the transformation of societies. Specific changes in economic, social and political structures cannot be understood unless the dynamics which shape world-wide transformations are taken into account. In other words, globalisation provides the backdrop against which specific and conjunctural changes can be analysed. In this book the term globalisation will be used with caution in order to avoid some of the pitfalls of interpreting it as an uncontrollable homogenising process operating without much input from any actors.

A brief look at various definitions of globalisation will indicate some of the contradictions generated by the all-encompassing process of globalisation. The definition of globalisation changes according to whether the emphasis is primarily on economic, social or political transformations. For instance, the sceptics like Hirst and Thompson (1999) are critical of the approach that sees globalisation as a world-wide process of integration of national markets. They claim that the less economically developed world was more deeply integrated into the world system in the period of the 'gold standard' than it is today as far as foreign trade and the movement of capital are concerned. In agreement with this view, what Held et al. (1999) call a 'hyperglobalist approach', focuses on politics and power relations between nation states and international business in characterising globalisation. They contend that with the rise of transnational networks of production, trade and finance, nation states have lost their power and authority to control their own economies. The weakening of sovereignty has transformed the state into an entity without much independent power to exert authority over the economy. This declinist view of the state sees the nation state as working on behalf of international business in exerting a market discipline on the domestic economy (Strange 1996). Held et al. (1999) categorise a third approach to globalisation which emphasises social transformation as the defining feature. This approach sees globalisation in terms of time-space compression by arguing that developments in telecommunications and information technology, particularly since the 1970s, have made physical time and space irrelevant. The world has become so small that events even in remote areas can be followed live via satellites, knowledge can be obtained via the Internet, and business can be conducted via e-commerce and e-business. Transformations in the world have generated qualitative changes, which have led to changing concepts of time and space. Cultural, political, economic and technological interactions have converted the world into a 'global village' in which localities, countries, companies, social movements and individuals operate in networks (Castells 1996). Giddens (1990), Harvey (1989) and Robertson (1992) all emphasise the interconnectedness of the world through the process of globalisation, which intensifies world-wide social relations. In the social interpretation of globalisation the new 'network society' has no territorial limits.

For the sake of clarity a distinction can be made between economic, political and social interpretations of globalisation. However, it must be emphasised that all the dimensions of globalisation operate at the same time and reinforce the impact of the others.

GLOBALISATION, HOMOGENISATION AND GLOBAL INEQUALITIES

One other precaution is that fast-expanding interconnectedness and interdependency does not necessarily mean equal participation of people, regions and countries in the process. Hoogvelt (2001:121) challenges Manuel Castells' contention that globalisation brings 'the capacity of the world economy to operate as a unit in real time on a planetary basis'. She highlights the fact that the workings of the world economy in the last few decades have systematically excluded ever more people, segments and regions. She explains this by looking at the history of capitalism and suggests that by the 1970s the expansionary phases of capitalism were over. In her view, throughout its history capitalism has developed mechanisms to overcome its inherent cyclical crisis. The type of capitalism and capital accumulation has determined the nature of these mechanisms. During the colonial (1800–1950) and neo-colonial (1950–70) periods capitalism expanded into peripheral areas in search of economic surplus. In the colonial period, economic surplus was transferred through colonially-imposed international division of labour which thrived on unequal exchange. In the neo-colonial period, the accumulation needs of the centre were largely met through 'developmentalism' and technological rents. Both phases necessitated the expansion of capitalism into the periphery. The evidence for this includes the rising ratio of world trade to output, 'the growth and spread of foreign direct investment through multinational corporation' and the expansion of international capital flows

(Hoogvelt 2001:65–7). From the 1980s onwards, the expansionary phase of capitalism was over. In what may be called the 'incorporatist phase of capitalism' attempts were made to resolve the crisis through debt peonage. In this period some peripheral areas became gradually marginalised as most newly emerging transnational production systems became concentrated in the centres of the world capitalist system.

In its workings in the field of economics, globalisation has been far from having a homogenising effect on the global economy, which depicts immense inequalities in the way in which different nations are integrated into the global economy. In its common use, the term globalisation implies the homogenisation of the globe in terms of economy, culture and politics. Widespread use of American brands all over the world does not necessarily mean homogenisation of cultures as different regions in the world adopt it in different ways and reterritorialise it differently. With the advancements in telecommunications, technology and transportation, the influence of American culture has been felt all over the world, but the complex process of the consumption of American culture has generated a myriad of interactions with local cultures in different regions of the world. This has increased the complexity of local cultures, which are not a direct reflection of American culture.

Likewise, the internationalisation of capital is presented as proof of globalisation as a homogenising factor. However, the internationalisation of capital is nothing new as it has existed since the turn of the nineteenth century. The globalising tendencies of the world economy have accompanied capitalism from its infancy onwards. The prominence of transnational corporations (TNCs) in recent decades has simply speeded up the mobility of capital across borders. Revolutionary technological changes in the twentieth century have allowed capitalism to deal with its inherent crisis in a way that is quite specific to this particular juncture in history. Throughout its history capitalism has managed to develop varying strategies to overcome its historically specific crises.

PERIODIC CRISES AND CAPITALISM

Capitalism is global in nature and national economies are interconnected in this global capitalism. Capitalism develops unevenly on a world scale creating inequalities between nation states. The relationship between the centres of the world economy and peripheral states has been characterised as a dependency relationship (Amin 1980; Chase-Dunn 1989; Frank 1967; Wallerstein 1979; among others). This relationship has been dynamic and changing in conjunction with transformations taking place in the nature of capitalism through its distinctly different stages. Periodic crises, an inherent characteristic of capitalism, force a particular structural arrangement between the core and periphery and this in turn ensures capitalist accumulation globally. Booms and slumps follow each other regularly and each slump necessitates the readjustment of the relationship between the core and periphery. In other words, different phases of capitalist development are characterised by different modes of capital accumulation which necessitate different forms of relationship between the core and periphery.

The regulation school provides one of the best analyses of the differential forms of articulation of the periphery with the centre in different capitalist epochs (Boyer 1988). It postulates that capitalism is able to overcome the crises generated by its internal and inherent contradictions through restructuring and renewal. This view that capitalism's ability to transform itself in response to crises is diametrically opposed to the classical Marxist belief in the self-destruction of capitalism. The regulation school sees the crisis and transformation not as something that is sequential but as simultaneous historical processes (Hoogvelt 2001:65). Crises experienced in individual countries are not isolated cases but deeply rooted in the laws of motion of global economy which bind national economies together. Globalisation is taking place against the background of a long-term stagnation. Crises emerge in capitalism quite periodically 1825, 1836, 1847, 1857 and 1866. In the early years of capitalism, crises emerged and lasted only a few months and brought about recession reflecting falling output, business closures, unemployment and falling wages. However, in advanced industrial capitalism crises are no longer short-lived events but long-term processes with accumulation difficulties. 1893, 1896, the 1930s and the current periodic crises since 1973 are examples which justify the label 'secular system-wide downturn' (Brenner 1998). 1973–74, 1979–81, 1990–91 and the 2001–02 crisis are evidence of how deep and regular the accumulation crises have been. In the last 20 years persistent over-capacity and over-production in world manufacturing have led to a 'long downturn' in capitalist accumulation (Brenner 1998).

In stating that the capitalist crisis is systemic, one does not necessarily mean to eschew the view that crises that have been witnessed throughout the history of capitalism are all the same. The long waves of ups and downs in capitalism have been profoundly different. The good and bad times last roughly about 50 years and each wave 'begins on the basis of a "new capitalist" ' (Weisskopf 1981:13). The aim here is not to provide an explanation of the capitalist crises but merely to point out the fact that crises have been systemic in capitalism in its every phase. Economic crisis in different epochs of capitalism, however, is 'postponed or displaced by imperialistic expansion, the growth of credit money, restructuring of physical production and social relationships between capital and labour, and capital mobility, among other ways, as well as by state fiscal, monetary and other policies' (O'Connor 1989).

For instance, the 1970s marked the emergence of Global Fordism as the dominant mode of capital accumulation, which aimed at overcoming the contradictions of capitalism that had developed since the 1950s in the core. The export of Fordism to peripheral areas where low wages prevailed not only necessitated the restructuring of the relationships between the core and periphery but also contributed to the amelioration of the crisis in the centre. This was significantly different to the mechanisms used to address the capitalist crisis in the post-war period. Economic crisis in the post-war period was overcome by a reconstruction process and a Keynesian state intervention which regulated a balanced relationship between mass production and consumption. The ruins created by war allowed a reconstruction process in the national economies of the advanced centre along Fordist lines. Based on assembly line production and minute division of labour, the Fordist model of accumulation permitted economies of scale. The centre economies experienced phenomenal increases in the production of both producer and consumer goods using flow line technology. On the other hand, Keynesian welfare policies allowed the expansion of internal demand for mass production and relatively stable social and political structures. However, by the mid-1960s the Fordist expansion became unsustainable as the welfare state reached its limits. While the profitability of leading industries declined, it also became evident that working-class wage gains could not be receded. This decline in profitability was largely due to a global decline in demand. For Fordism to maintain capital accumulation, continuous expansion of markets was needed and this was not possible (Hoogvelt 2001:45–50). Global Fordism in the form of the relocation of industrial production units in cheap labour economies emerged as a response to overcome the crisis generated by Fordism. The reloca-tion of industry in order to ensure further accumulation in the core was made possible by technical innovations in production, trans-portation and data processing. Without fragmentation of production, de-skilling of labour, revolutionary developments in containerised shipping, telecommunications and computer applications, the post-Fordist mode of capital accumulation based on the relocation of industry to cheap labour reserve areas in the less economically developed world would not have been possible.

GLOBALISATION AND TNCS

Transnational corporations (TNCs) have been the main actors in the emergence of the so-called New International Division of Labour (NIDL) in which different countries produce only certain parts of a product, rather than carrying out the process of production from scratch to finish. By using their technological and economic superi-ority, the TNCs have been able to organise a flexible specialisation on a global level where they could take advantage of cheap labour and favourable conditions to develop organically integrated circuits of production in different countries. The so-called global era is not anything other than the latest phase of capitalism, and TNCs have come to dominate the world economy. The unprecedented influ-ence of the TNCs on nation states renders it necessary to question the notions of dominance and dependency between the nations in the world economy. TNCs have been rising to pre-eminence in the world economy where nation states are losing their significance as far as capitalist domination and exploitation are concerned. Nation states basically play an intermediary role in the new integration of the world economy dominated by the TNCs who create an interna-tional bourgeoisie and international proletariat in the process. The members of the corporate bourgeoisie operate internationally in pursuing their own interests. They do not see any innate antago-nism between the global interest of the TNCs and the national interest of home countries. The TNCs rely on their class allies in the periphery to gain access to resources and markets rather than rely-ing on the power of their own home states. TNCs' subsidiaries oper-ate globally and continuously look for countries that will offer optimal production and profit locations. Sub-branches of the TNCs that operate in the periphery show impeccable behaviour as far as laws and regulations are concerned. They are instructed to spread the view that TNCs are there to secure the national interest in the periphery. Obviously TNCs move to places where they can find the most suitable conditions for capital accumulation: cheap labour, favourable taxation and other concessions. This in turn contributes to the differentiation of the periphery as some nations manage to industrialise by offering better conditions to the TNCs (Hoogvelt 2001).

GLOBALISATION, INTERNATIONALISATION OF CAPITAL AND THE NATION STATE

The point made by Woods (1999) that the universalisation of capitalism has been accompanied by the universalisation of the nation state is highly relevant here. Globalisation does not mean the disappearance of nation states but increasing interconnectedness of nation states in a hierarchical fashion. Although globalisation erodes the power of the states it does not eliminate their existence. National macro-economic structures are still very important in the globalised world dominated by the market. There is no inverse relationship, as often suggested, between the internationalisation of capital and the weakening of the nation state. Internationalisation of capital enables nation states to take up new roles and in some cases new instruments and powers. The global system of national states represents the universalisation of capitalism which is presided over by a hegemonic superpower (Wood 1999:12). As the Turkish economic crises of post-1980 show, the state has been the instrument of massive and rapid movements of capital across national boundaries. Constant competition, tension and struggles for dominance among national capitalism characterise the contemporary global economy.

The reduction of trade barriers in the 1950s speeded up the process of internationalisation that saw huge increases in the trade volume of goods and services. The 1970s saw the emergence of the NIDL, which was characterised by a rapid movement of investment capital across national borders. The movement of capital internationally was made even easier by the collapse of the Bretton Woods system in the early 1970s. With this, global currency markets were freed of many restrictions. The expansion of global market capitalism received a further boost with the collapse of the Soviet Union and socialism in eastern Europe.

In the internationalised world economy, the power of states to make independent macro-economic decisions has been severely limited. Capital, by virtue of its international mobility, has become the most dominant factor in world market capitalism. All over the world the general tendency has been towards the reduction of state involvement in the economy. As Weisskopf argues:

> the changes in capitalism which have taken place over the last several decades are in many ways the result of deliberate decisions made by the powers-that-be to unfetter the market through greater liberalisation and privatisation and to buttress the emerging global economic system with international institutions that strengthen the capitalist order. (2000:34–35)

However, Weisskopf's contention that in the new international global economy the nation state has lost its importance as an economic unit has to be taken cautiously. He suggests that capitalist enterprises no longer need to rely heavily on national finance, national market or national labour. National economies have periodically become more dependent on the world economy. Capital does not have to please its own national working classes to propel accumulation. This has led to a major shift from national welfare capitalism. It is no longer a priority for capitalist and ruling groups to maintain high employment levels. Therefore the need for an interventionist state has eroded in parallel with the erosion of the power of the nation state and its nationalist ideology of unity (Weisskopf 2000:38). The ability of capital to relocate itself in labour-cheap countries has also been used as a weapon to silence trade union voices in more economically developed countries. In short, in the last few decades global market capitalism has replaced national welfare capitalism as a result of deliberate policy measures to curb the economic role of the national state and to open up national economies to more and more international competition (Weisskopf 2000:40).

These are all fine, as there is no denial that the significance of the state as the only power to rule the economy and policy is being undermined with the increasing integration of states in the world economy. The supremacy of TNCs in the world economy and the internationalisation of capital are reflections of the changes in the nature of capitalism and the nature of the state in order to meet the new exigencies of capitalism. A cosy relationship has developed between strong less economically developed countries and TNCs who have preferred to lend to strong and bureaucratically capable states who in turn have used foreign loans to increase their power over other social classes. In other words, in the epoch of globalisation the state is being structured around a specifically capitalist project. This requires not the existence of isolated individual states but an inter-state system. Globalisation has not changed the capitalistic nature of the state but has assigned it a different role in the inter-state relations in contemporary times. The concept of globalisation or the 'globalising impact' on the nation state in no way refers to the emergence of 'supra-national organisations' or of a 'globalised social system'. It refers to the transformations in the international political economy that ensure a global shift from a state-regulated embedded liberalism to the internationalisation of production and finance. Capitalism has reached a new stage in which the integrity of the national state is eroded. The role of the state has changed with globalisation. The main function of the state now is to reorganise and readjust domestic, economic and social policies to fit the exigency of global capital accumulation. Domestic inequalities and social exclusion have become part and parcel of the new international division of labour steered by globalisation.

THE 1980s AND DEBT PEONAGE

The shift from the Fordist mode of accumulation to the post-Fordist mode meant that the role of the less economically developed world in the global economy shifted from that of providing raw material resources to that of providing cheap labour and production sites to multinational capital. International competition among the core nations for markets and investments and the pressures on less economically developed world governments to create employment for the forever growing urban populations forced core countries to allow a selected number of less economically developed countries to industrialise through the use of western technology. Given the scarcity of capital and technology in less economically developed countries in the so-called 'developmentalist era', the import substituting type of industrialisation was only possible through the purchase of technology and/or through partnership with the TNCs. In either case, borrowing from international banks and granting concessions to TNCs were inevitable. While the established industries remained highly inefficient, the financial burden of obtaining and running such industries led to the accumulation of huge debts in a number of countries, particularly in some Latin American countries.

The debt peonage characterised the majority of the less economically developed countries by the early 1980s as the states had to resort to further borrowing for both the maintenance of inefficient industries and for meeting the public expenditure requirements.

Highly skewed income distribution and rampant poverty in less economically developed countries since the late 1970s have led to market contraction and rendered these economies less attractive for direct foreign investment. Profit maximisation and constant expansion of capital operate globally and penetrate into every share of life in every corner of the globe. The expansion of the capitalist influence into even social institutional and cultural spheres has increased with unprecedented speed in the last few decades. Such an expansion has brought about uneven structures globally, generating marginalisation and impoverishment in some regions and wealth and prosperity in others. Hoogvelt clearly demonstrates that globalisation has brought about the marginalisation and exclusion of an ever-expanding number of people in the world as far as international trade, production and finance are concerned. Globalisation represents an accelerated shrinking of the global map that expels ever more people from the interactive circle of global capitalism (2001: 70). In this accelerated withdrawing of the global capitalism most of the international trade takes place between industrialised nations and the trade with non-industrialised countries has declined considerably since 1953.[1] Another indication of the shrinking nature of the global map and the increasing expansion of the less economically developed world from the interactive circle of global capitalism is the magnitude of the Foreign Direct Investment (FDI). Hoogvelt illustrates that there has been a geographic redirection of FDI from the periphery into the core of the world capitalist system since 1960 (Hoogvelt 2001:78–79).[2] Today the FDI goes to less economically developed countries, not to open new businesses but to obtain the existing businesses in production, commerce and services. Hoogvelt cites that mergers and acquisitions 'have accounted for between a half and two-thirds of world FDI flows in the 1990s' (2001:79–80). Furthermore, international companies use their profits and earnings for re-investment in the less economically developed world rather than bringing in new investment money externally. The expansive phase of capitalism came to an end by 1980, from which time there has been a deepening but not widening of capitalist integration (Hoogvelt 2001:67–93). The concept of 'global financial deepening', borrowed from the UNCTAD's Trade and Development Report of

1990, refers to the process by which the pace of growth of international financial transactions has overtaken those of trade, investment and output.

SPECULATIVE CAPITAL MOVEMENTS

In response to limited outlets in productive investment, dominant capital seeks to find other ways of using huge amounts of surplus capital. The outlet is found in international lending and speculative capital movements. The expansion of credit money into the Third World is used to prevent or postpone threatening general capitalist crises emerging from over-production leading to the drop in the average rate of profits. However, the management of this mass of floating capital requires the elimination of obstacles to the movement of capital and high interest rates. International institutions like the International Monetary Fund (IMF) and the World Bank play a crucial role in ensuring financial openness globally. Despite their international appearances, institutions like the IMF and the World Bank 'are above all agents of specific national capitals, and derive whatever powers of enforcement they have from nation states, both the imperial states that command them and the subordinate states that carry out their orders' (Wood 1999:12). Despite the global influence capital generates, not all capital becomes 'international'. Nationally based capital, nationally based transnational companies, nation states and national economies still continue to characterise the global economy. Governments are forced to liberalise their financial system and introduce floating exchange rates. Local banks in the South and banks in the centre are absolutely vital in the management of the crisis, by pushing speculative finance capital into fragile financial markets in the South and siphoning off the savings from there. While liberalisation of finance accounts and floating exchange rates provide an outlet for the massive amount of idle capital generated by the long-term crisis, it at the same time generates serious volatility in the South through short-term speculative flows. While speculative activities of the finance capital postpone a general crisis of capitalism or pass it into the political sphere and state budget, they at the same time internationalise the crisis through the creation of massive debt in less economically developed countries.

The laws of motion of capitalism operate globally irrespective of national diversities. The analysis of a specific crisis in a specific nation state has to take into consideration both the global processes including international capital flows, currency movements and financial speculation and the international institutions including corporate representatives of capital (such as the IMF and the World Bank) and TNCs. The pressure exercised by the IMF and the US Treasury are responsible for the liberalisation of the financial accounts in many less economically developed countries. This has led to the predominance of short-term financial capital in the financial structure of emerging markets. There is a strong belief that the economic crises in 1997 in East Asia, in 1998–2002 in Latin America (especially in Argentina and Brazil), in Russia in 1998, and in Turkey in 2001–02 are direct consequences of liberalisation of the capital accounts imposed on less economically developed countries (Stiglitz 2000a, 2000b). This imposition did not have a strong economic basis. Speaking at the Spring Meetings of members of the Institute for International Finance, 25–26 April 1999, the former Chief Economist of the World Bank, Joseph Stiglitz, emphasises that 'the drive towards liberalisation of the capital and financial markets without the necessary attention the design and execution of regulation structures appropriate to the circumstances, was based more on ideology than in economic science'. The first half of the 1990s saw enormous increases in the flow of short-term capital into emerging market economies, which in turn experienced some economic growth. Short-term capital was used for imports, credits to the private sector, consumption credits for individuals and for the payments of domestic and external debts.

By definition, short-term capital is speculative, volatile and erratic; it can come and go very rapidly depending on how reliable it sees the financial markets. The reversal of capital inflows generates crises in emerging markets. For instance, in Latin America US$9 billion left the region in 1997 and 1998, precipitating the 1999 Brazilian crisis. Likewise, US$12.1 billion left East Asian countries in 1997 triggering a severe economic crisis (Rodrik 1999:89–90). The fact that money or financial capital as opposed to productive capital has become the dominant form of capital in the age of global capitalism is one of the main reasons behind the fragility of the emerging markets. The deregulation of the financial markets since the 1980s in both the OECD (Organisation for Economic Co-operation and Development) countries and a good number of less economically developed countries has been a vital factor in the fragility created. Governments have intervened to ensure functional mobility of capital as opposed to spatial mobility. Functional mobility refers to the process in which 'monies tied up in productive assets can convert in an instant into pure money form escaping into the cyberspace of electronic circulation' (Hoogvelt 2001:140). Huge profits are made from the circulation of money capital but here capital accumulation is 'disconnected from the social relationship in which money and wealth were previously embedded' (Hoogvelt 2001:140–141). Money capital can easily and quickly move from say Istanbul stock market to another rising stock market without thought being given to the consequences this may have on Turkish companies who are involved in production. Developments in telecommunications and computers have enabled finance capital to search for better investment opportunities and move around the globe continuously.

FLOW OF EQUITY INVESTMENT TO EMERGING MARKETS

Capital flows to less economically developed countries rejuvenated in the 1990s following a lean period in the aftermath of the debt crisis in the 1980s. The nature of capital flows has changed in the last two decades, taking the forms of purchases of shares by institutional and individual investors, investments in various financial instruments and investments in production by TNCs. The massive increase[3] in the flow of equity investment into the emerging markets from 1990 onwards can be explained by a number of factors: the development of stock exchanges in a number of emerging markets; the liberalisation of the financial sector in conjunction with structural adjustment policies; large scale privatisation; institutionalisation of savings in more economically developed countries which led to augmentation of capital in search of higher returns; low rates of real interest in more economically developed countries; the increase in the credit ratings of a number of emerging markets; and the resolution of the debt problems in most Latin American countries by the 1990s (Woodward 2000:156–157).

The herd-like attitude of equity capital can generate ups and downs in stock markets in any country. But the impact of herd-like movement of capital in fragile emerging markets has generated such volatility that it has led to a major economic crisis in many countries: the 1994 Mexican crisis, the 1997–98 Asian crisis, the 1998 Russian crisis and the 2001 Turkish and Argentinian crises.

Equity investment played three distinct roles in the financial crises in Mexico, East Asia and Russia, although their relative importance varied markedly: it helped to inflate speculative bubbles in asset markets; it contributed to the reversal of capital flows which precipitated and intensified the crises; and it was a key factor in the contagion process spreading crises between countries. (Woodward 2000:187)

The question of whether the in-flows and out-flows of equity capital would have caused a crisis without the long-term trends which generate fragility in economies remains to be answered. However, one thing is very clear: the 1990s saw an unprecedented frequency of busts in the world economy. Particularly, the regulation of the crisis in the centres of the world economy had significant repercussions in the rest of the world and particularly in the newly industrialising countries (NICs) and the less economically developed world. The long-lasting Japanese financial crisis since 1990, the Scandinavian crisis of 1991–92, the European Exchange Rate Mechanism crisis of 1992–93, Mexico's financial crisis 1994–95, the Brazilian and Argentinian banking crises of 1994 are a few examples of the crises in the early 1990s. More recently we witnessed the Asian crisis which started in 1997 and still continues, the turbulence in European and American stock markets in October 1998, and the Russian debt crisis and default of 1998. The crises snowballed from 2000–04 and most Latin American economies have been experiencing a huge slump since 1999 (Wade 2001:224). The most recent of all are the current Turkish and Argentinian economic and financial crises which have generated social and political tension leading to the collapse of the Argentinian Government in December 2001.

Financial instability characterises most of the recent crises worldwide. Between 1975 and 1995 more than 87 countries suffered from at least one major currency crisis which had a serious negative impact on the economy as a whole (Wade 2001:195). Concomitantly occurring currency and banking crises usually lead to huge losses in GDP. The fact that major economic crises emerge within a few years of the introduction of financial liberalisation indicates a causal relationship between the two. The Turkish crises of 1994 and 2001 show remarkable similarities to the 1997 East Asian Crisis in that both were due to the fast inflow of capital for four years and then the precipitous flight of both foreign and domestic capital. The Turkish crisis cannot simply be explained in terms of a weak or decomposing state capacity failing to regulate finance and upgrade or co-ordinate the industry (Weiss 1999). There is a need to take into consideration the role played by external factors in generating financial fragility in Turkey, particularly the role played by international capital and the intermediary role of the international finance institutions. Periods of high rates of growth in the Turkish economy since 1980 have been due to inflows of foreign capital. Without foreign capital the economy would have been limited to already meagre domestic savings. Unlike the Asian economies, the credit capacity created by foreign capital inflows was not invested in the real sector to improve productive capacity but was used in financing state expenditures and consumption. In the case of East Asia, the credit was used to increase industrial capacity and purchases in land and stocks. However, the amount of foreign capital entering into the economy surpassed the required levels. Excessive capital led to misinvestments as well as over-capacity in industry. The ensuing crisis of confidence triggered a herd-like attitude in the flight of foreign capital. When the investors attempted to sell their stock shares, at the same time the markets collapsed. The Turkish crisis has been neither due to industrial over-capacity nor to the misinvestments of the funds. It has been due to the fact that capital borrowed on a short-term basis was used to finance public and private consumption thus generating instability and indebtedness. The huge rates of interest, whilst guaranteeing good income for the speculative capital, generated high rates of inflation in the economy as a whole.

THE USA'S ROLE IN THE CURRENT FINANCIAL CRISES

By the late 1960s the Bretton Woods system had started to work against the US interest as some European states and international firms were taking advantage of the over-valued dollar for their speculative activities, so much so that they were exporting capital to the US. The abolition of the Bretton Woods system enabled the US to increase its current account deficit by simply printing and exporting US dollars. In the Bretton Woods system the US dollar was linked to gold and the US could not print dollars at will, as the central banks of other countries asked the US to pay for its deficits in gold. The limitation on the supply of gold in the US prevented the state from printing money to finance its deficits. The line between the US dollar and gold ensured the surplus of the central bank reserve, but meant the deficit of another central bank reserve. Under the Bretton Woods system, the world central bank reserves would grow only slowly. When the Bretton Woods system was abolished in 1971 and the link between the US dollar and gold was severed, it was possible to print dollars and have an increasing current account deficit. Consequently it was also possible to increase central bank reserves at a world level. The resulting surge in world central bank reserves, which ran parallel to persistent US current account deficits, permitted a multiplied expansion of credit (Wade 2001:200–201).

The US saw the changing of the rules of the international payments regime as an absolute necessity for its own economic interest. The delinking of the dollar from gold in international payments allowed the US Treasury to finance current account deficits. Therefore, since the 1970s the US dollar has become a fiduciary currency, and this in turn has allowed the US Treasury to finance its deficits by foreign central inflow through the sale of state bonds. While the change in the international payments regime allowed the US to have continuous deficits, at the same time it caused a surge in world liquidity.

The US considered world-wide financial opening and liberalisation (FOLI) an absolute necessity for its own economic growth and prosperity. In the campaign to ensure a global FOLI, the West as a whole used their own economic and political power of force and persuasion as well as the power of international organisations including the World Bank, the IMF, the OECD and the GATT/WTO. While global FOLI has helped powerful western economies to accumulate wealth and prosperity and relieve their own crises, it at the same time has created serious financial and economic crises in South East Asia, Latin America and Turkey. The push for FOLI has to be understood in terms of the internal transformations of the western economies, particularly those of the US, UK, Germany and France. (The following arguments draw on Wade 2001:216–223.) The financial services industry in the US and the UK grew by leaps and bounds from 1980, so much so that the assets of institutional investors jumped from 59 per cent of the US GDP in 1980 to 126 per cent in 1993. Financialisation of the economy has been the most significant feature of the US and the UK economies in the last two decades. In both countries the share of financial activity in the economy has risen rapidly and institutional investors and security markets (the portfolialisation of savings) have become more important than depository institutions such as banks. Portfolio equity investments represent a significant form of international investments in an increasing number of less economically developed countries. The development of stock markets in the so-called emerging markets has made it possible for non-residents to invest in less economically developed countries through buying shares. Individuals, households and corporate institutions have all become deeply involved in the stock market activities. Specifically, the people who represent the top 20 per cent of income earners have become serious asset holders in stock markets. Furthermore, the change in the pension system which links incomes from pensions to the performance of pension funds in the stock market has made the protection of capital income a serious political issue for governments in the West.

In many less economically developed countries governments issue bonds, treasury bills and other valuable papers to borrow internationally without having recourse to borrowing from banks. The abolition of fixed exchange rate regimes has allowed short-term investments in currency markets and this has become the fastest growing market ever. In recent years short-term speculative currency trade has reached 60 times the value of international trade in goods and services (Hoogvelt 2001:82). Financial openness and computerisation has permitted capital to come in and go out in a flash, in search of relative gains based on ever more minuscule variations in interest and exchange rates between countries. The financialisation of the US economy in particular has made it absolutely vital for US governments to eliminate all the obstacles for free capital mobility. Huge sums of capital in the possession of institutional investors need to be diversified geographically. The US Government has been extremely active since 1980 in promoting market opening and liberalisation. The fact that the US has become politically, militarily and economically the most powerful nation has enabled it to manipulate the decisions of the World Bank, the IMF, the GATT/WTO and the OECD. All these institutions have used all their power to persuade or force the emerging market economies to introduce FOLI. The liberalisation of finance has become the 'last frontier' as most countries have already liberalised their goods markets. The IMF and the World Bank use their lending powers to push the liberalisation of foreign exchange and financial systems. In most of their decisions, the preferences of the US play a significant role (Stiles 1991; Killick 1995). The US pushes FOLI because, according to the US Department of Commerce (2000), the income from US direct investment in finance is as high as the income from direct investment in manufacturing. Recent crises in Mexico, East Asia,

Russia and Turkey have all been created by the speculative activities of financial capital that generates volatility in financial markets.

Massive inflow of volatile capital was due to high interest rate policies designed to defend fixed exchange rates tied to the dollar, as in the case of Brazil, or to a basket of foreign currencies as in the Turkish case. Although the lessons of East Asia, Brazil and Russia were there, Turkey did not make an attempt to learn from them. It was evident that heavy reliance on short-term speculative volatile capital generates fragility in the financial system and any loss of confidence leads to herd-like capital outflows. Dependence of short-term capital also increases the country's vulnerability to external financial problems; the East Asian financial crisis added to fears about the health of the Russian economy and the Russian financial crisis in turn raised fears about the strength of the Brazilian economy. The loss of confidence in the Brazilian economy in 1998 resulted in US$20 billion leaving the country and provoked a deep recession. The Brazilian crisis spread very quickly to other Latin American countries including Bolivia, Ecuador, Uruguay, Argentina, Colombia and Chile. Rescue loans were extended to these countries by multilateral banks in order to save and bail out the big international creditors' investments rather than improving the real sector and standards of living. Without exception, in all rising markets that have experienced recession as a consequence of financial crisis, a huge reduction in state budgets has been speeded up as a panacea. The impact of this compounded with those of lay-offs in industry, public sector services and bankruptcies has added to the enormity of unemployment and social problems. The levels of poverty and extreme poverty, already a companion of neo-liberal SAPs, increased rapidly as a result of increasing inequalities in income distribution.

Mahatir Mohamed blames hot money and fickle international investors for the East Asian financial crisis in 1997. There had been a three-fold increase in net capital inflows in the three years before the crisis. Much of the money had gone to the stock market and real estate rather then to the productive sector (Rodrik 1998:55). The rapid rush out by the short-term speculative capital in the aftermath of the nosedive taken by East Asian currencies which followed the Thai currency relinquishing its peg to the US dollar, led to stock market crashes, widespread company bankruptcies, unemployment and loss of savings by the millions. The IMF moved in with its typical rescue package, which included economic conditions such as huge cuts in government expenditures, introduction of high interest rates and raising taxes. The ensuing economic depression generated massive decreases in production. According to the IMF (1999), the cumulative output losses for the following four years after the crisis were 82 per cent in Indonesia, 27 per cent in Korea, 39 per cent in Malaysia and 57 per cent in Thailand.

This brief elaboration of the nature of the crisis in Turkey indicates the need to situate it in its internal and external contexts. It is clear that the 2001–02 crisis in Turkey was not unique and that a large number of less economically developed countries share similar problems. The ubiquitous nature of the crisis is indicative of common features and general forces that are behind it. The crises experienced in individual countries are reflections of the systemic problems of capitalism. Crises are inherent features of capitalism, and they manifest themselves in a variety of ways in different contexts. The present state of affairs is only symptomatic of a deeper, more enduring crisis arising from the way in which Turkey was incorporated into the international division of labour. The crisis in Turkey is an expression of the international crisis of capital. The crisis and international responses to it have diminished the objective of independent development and self-reliance, which informed the national aspirations of the post-war period. In its place has come control by foreign capital and international finance institutions.

GLOBALISATION AGAIN

In depicting the global financial markets as being irrational, unpredictable and out of control, the globalism discourse simply hides the dialectical relationship between the US Government dollar policy and private actors in international financial markets. Since Nixon's days (1969–74), the US has systematically manipulated international financial markets through various means, including control by the IMF and the World Bank, for its own benefits. Globalist discourse explains US supremacy in the world as an historical accident. By emphasising the fairness of the neutral forces of the market, it simply hides the fact that the US controls the global economy. Globalism as an ideology serves its purpose when people are persuaded about the magical workings of the market. This way there will not be any room for explanations based on US hegemony and bullying. The West uses globalism as an ideology to adjust its economies and societies to the forces of globalisation. Globalism promotes the 'inescapability of the transnationalisation of economic and financial flows' (Hoogvelt 2001:154). Globalist discourse 'serves to obscure the fact the global capitalism is an American political project serving the interest primarily of US capital and the US domestic economy' (Hoogvelt 2001:155). There has been a triple alliance of the western political class, the elites in poor countries and the international finance institutions like the IMF and the World Bank in the shaping of the global economy in an hierarchical fashion, at the top of which the US sits. The intensification of the incorporation into the world economy has forced the political class in the South to abandon national programmes of economic development in favour of international competitiveness and transnational engagement. With global integration, national governments are no longer able to follow nationally based macro-fiscal and monetary policies. There is a strong tendency to move away from expansionary fiscal and redistributive welfare state policies. The preponderance of neo-liberalism, the dominant ideology of globalism, has been instrumental in the restructuring of the state as an active regulating agent of internationalisation. The states have come to play a very crucial role in the newly created multilateral economic order, which is hierarchical and under the dominance of the US. In other words, globalisation has not totally undermined the authority of nation states, it has simply attributed to them a new role in a new phase of capitalism.

Chapter 1 analyses the changing nature of the Turkish State since 1923 and shows that the state is the locus of the struggle to redefine the relationship between society and international capitalism. It highlights the fact that the Republican State has been confronted by simultaneous challenges to promote capital accumulation, sponsor a ruling class and legitimise class rule. Turkey's further integration into the global economy in the 1980s led to the abandonment of populism, nationalism and developmentalism in favour of neo-liberal policies under the guidance of the IMF, the World Bank and the WTO.

Chapter 2 provides a critical analysis of the processes of democratisation in Turkey. Starting from the neo-liberal claim that state intervention is responsible for the failure of development in Turkey and liberal democracy is the key to resolving this impasse, the discussion focuses on the relationship between capitalism, democracy and development. In this way, the chapter attempts to provide answers to a number of questions: Is there a direct relationship between democracy and development? Is the type of democracy advocated by neo-liberalism capable of delivering the expected results? Are the SAPs imposed on less economically developed countries conducive to achieving development and democracy simultaneosly? What are the consequences of the push for liberal democracy in less economically developed countries? Does a multi-party system lead to empowerment of the people? Is equality before law sufficient to create universal liberty? Under economic liberalism, which tends to exacerbate economic inequalities, is it possible for the poor and the marginalised to compete in the political sphere on an equal level with the rich and powerful? Does the reduction of the state's power increase democracy's chances of survival?

Chapter 3 provides an analysis of the long-term crisis and entrenched recession in Turkey and challenges the validity and usefulness of liberalisation as a policy option for overcoming economic and financial difficulties.

Chapter 4 looks at the nature of the agrarian crises in Turkey in recent years and explains this in terms of Turkey's further integration into the global economy. It argues that globalisation has led to the restructuring of agrarian structures and policies away from developmentalism towards a free market economy. Turkish agriculture is gradually falling under the control of multinational corporations, whose priority is not the welfare of the people or national food security. As a result of the restructuring, small farmers are being forced either to abandon agricultural production or to move into the production of high value crops for the global market controlled by transnational companies.

Chapters 5 and 6 address the contradictory tendencies within the process of globalisation and argue that while quite successful in the sphere of economics, globalisation has failed to achieve ethnic and cultural integration. Chapter 5 analyses the growth of political Islam in Turkey and argues that it cannot be explained in terms of identity politics alone. Instead, any analysis should take into account the socio-economic transformations undergone by Turkey and how they relate to contemporary changes in the world economy. The chapter also discusses the rise of the Islamic Welfare Party and its successors in conjunction with the internationalisation of production and the spread of flexible specialisation.

Chapter 6 addresses another dimension of the contradictory tendencies of globalisation by looking at the Kurdish question in Turkey. The chapter considers the tenacity of Kurdish ethnicity in terms of both the forces of globalisation and the power of Turkish nationalism. It argues that globalising forces are operating in Turkey in the context of a long and complex history of conflict and that, by ripening the conditions for demands for cultural and ethnic rights through the imposition of economic and political liberalisation, such forces are exacerbating the existing social instability.

The book concludes in Chapter 7 with an overall evaluation of the themes explored in the previous chapters.

1
The state

INTRODUCTION

This chapter looks specifically at the changing nature of the Turkish State since the establishment of the Turkish Republic in 1923, and in particularly since the 1980s. The underlying idea behind this is that the state is the locus of a struggle to redefine the relationship of a society to international capitalism. The unenviable position of the Turkish State in trying to please different and often competing demands of various classes will be highlighted. The state must inaugurate a process of accumulation which somehow reconciles (or chooses between) the demands of peasants, workers and civil servants, etc. on the one hand, and the realities of foreign capital domination and world economic forces on the other. It will be maintained that in the early days of the Republic, the state was used as an instrument to create a local bourgeoisie under a very strict authoritarian bureaucratic rule. Throughout the history of the Republic, the state has been confronted by the simultaneous need to promote capital accumulation, sponsor a ruling class and legitimise class rule. Until the 1980s, populism, nationalism, developmentalism and foreign aid had enabled the state to carry out its difficult tasks. When there were difficulties of legitimacy, the military came to the rescue. However, further integration of Turkey into the global economy in the 1980s necessitated the abandonment of the primary principles of populism, nationalism and developmentalism. Export oriented industrialisation and export orientation of agriculture meant the main principle that underlined the state policies was to be that of the free market economy. The new industrial elite who came to control the state apparatus in the 1980s had a vested interest in liberalising the economy along the lines imposed by global capitalism and its organisations like the IMF and the WTO. The shift from a nationalist state apparatus to a liberal one has not been smooth under a crisis-ridden economy and society.

STATE INTERVENTION IN TURKEY

The Turkish State emerged from the ashes of the Ottoman Empire, which collapsed in the aftermath of the First World War after a long period of decay under European influence. The newly established Republic (1923) had the mammoth task of reconstructing the economy, which was almost completely ruined as a result of the Empire's integration into the world capitalist system as an open market and supplier of raw materials (Avcıoğlu 1968; Keyder 1981; Yerasimos 1975).

The dominant elements in the mainly agrarian economy inherited by the young Republic were merchants and landlords. As the economy was characterised by the export of agricultural products and the import of manufactured goods ever since the 1838 'free trade treaty', agriculture was the 'primary channel of integration into the world economy' (Keyder 1981). The influence of merchants and landowners on the state is quite evident in the policies followed between the establishment of the Republic in 1923 and the Great Depression of 1930. A large number of measures were taken to commercialise agriculture and increase its productivity. On the other hand, the state attempted to industrialise the country through joint investment with foreign capital as well as through the establishment of State Economic Enterprises in the aftermath of the world depression. Large scale import substituting industrialisation (ISI) type production units were established by the state with a view to complementing private enterprise rather than supplementing it.

The world recession of the 1930s provided an opportunity for the new Republic to follow inward-looking development strategies during what is generally referred as the étatist period (1930–39). The relative freedom from external influence in this period enabled the nationalist Kemalist regime to establish import substituting industries in textiles, sugar, cement, paper, mining, etc. Through the introduction of five-year development plans, the state guided the economic growth in both industry and agriculture with little reliance on external sources (Kepenek and Yentürk 1994:60–79). Through significant internal borrowing and taxation, the state managed not only to establish what was going to be the backbone of the Turkish industry in the coming years but also to develop the infrastructure and transportation facilities. In the étatist period the state's active involvement in capital accumulation and investment in economic enterprises took private interests into very careful consideration. The state entered into economic areas where private enterprise failed or was not strong enough, such as the building of infrastructural establishments, main industrial institutions, electrical power stations, railways and the iron and steel industry. The burden of capital accumulation on internally financed industrialisation was shouldered by the masses. On the other hand the private sector was given every encouragement in their capital accumulation process.

Various class interests were represented in the newly established national assembly and big landlords were still a powerful group within the state. However, due to the state's encouragement and support of private investment between 1923 and the 1950s, the industrial bourgeoisie did increase its strength, though not becoming a dominant force within the state. A significant point to make is that the governments since 1923 have had no intention of eliminating the entrenched interests that had been instrumental during the independence war (1918–22) instead they have followed strategies that help the nascent bourgeoisie to accumulate wealth and capital and take a leading role in industrialisation and development. It must also be emphasised that there was no unified interest among the various sections of the bourgeoisie. The different class interests represented within the state were a significant factor, among others, in the abandonment of a single party system in favour of a pluralistic democratic system in 1950.

The Second World War represents a watershed in the history of the new Republic. During the war years, a new mercantile bourgeoisie emerged through black marketing, profiteering and corruption allowed by the shortages of goods and increasing prices (Kazgan 1999:94). The new bourgeoisie consisting of rich landlords and merchants played a significant role in the opening up of the Turkish economy, which had remained largely closed to external influences since the Great Depression of the 1930s. The landlord and merchant power block that gradually came to control the state hoped that western capital and technology would further intensify their interest and power.

Turkey faced a major dilemma in the aftermath of the Second World War: how to reconcile the aims of nationalistic industrialisation necessitated by the Kemalist principles which had governed the state since the 1920s with the pressures put on the country by the designers of the new world order to integrate with the world economy through the liberalisation of its international trade.

Though very appealing, the adoption of trade liberalisation meant compromising the efforts to reduce the country's dependence on foreign sources of finance. For about four decades after the Second World War Turkey struggled between the opposing choices of trying to keep its relatively independent course of industrial development and further integration into the global economy through liberalisation. Policy-makers found it very difficult to completely relinquish the idea of an 'organically integrated national economy' which was deemed to be a *sine qua non* of an independent economy. However, Turkish policy makers were not in a strong position to pursue the notion of the organically integrated economy; a child of the first Five Year Development Plan of 1933 (Tekeli and İlkin 1982).

The 1950s witnessed the strengthening of Turkey's integration into the world economy. The new government elected in 1950 made every effort to take advantage of the aid bonanza in relation to the reconstruction of Europe. This desire was facilitated by the international conjuncture of the post-war period in which the US attempted to establish its hegemony at the expense of the Soviet Bloc. The fact that the Soviets demanded land from Turkey in the aftermath of the Second World War forced the Turkish State to seek western aid. At any rate, the US wanted Turkey to be part of the New World economic order being created. It was not a coincidence that Turkey was allowed to take advantage of military aid within the framework of the Truman Doctrine and economic aid through the Marshall Plan. Despite the fact that Turkey had not been actively involved in the Second World War, the US did not hesitate to let Turkey benefit from the money allocated for the reconstruction of Europe. In the same vein, Turkey joined the IMF and the World Bank in 1947, the IFC in 1956 and the IDA (International Development Association) in 1960. Other International institutions Turkey joined following the Second World War include the ILO (International Labour Organisation), GATT, OEEC (Organisation for European Economic Co-operation) and OECD.

By joining western institutions, Turkey was gradually moving away from the étatist policies which had marked the period between the world recession and the end of the Second World War. Both internal and external pressures existed to gradually relinquish étatist policies. The desire of the big merchants and landlords to have access to foreign capital could not have been met as long as the state continued to have strong control over the economy. This preference was partly the result of the economic and political expediency that forced the state to follow policies that adjusted the economy to the changing international conditions, and partly due to the influence of the US and the World Bank on the state. The Soviet threat for Turkey's security coupled with the US's desire to contain the expansion and the influence of the Soviets in eastern Europe were quite conveniently in place for Turkey who was suffering from severe balance of payments problems. Turkey's strategic importance for the US was the main factor behind the leniency with which aid was provided to Turkey through bilateral and multilateral channels. However, the US administration would not play into the hands of the Turkish Government by providing funds for industrialisation. Instead both the US and the World Bank insisted that priority should be given to agriculture, in order to take advantage of Turkey's comparative advantage. Furthermore, the US and the World Bank strongly recommended that the role of the state in the economy should be reduced and measures should be taken to lure foreign capital into the country (US State Department 1948; Thornburg et al. 1949; World Bank 1951).[1]

Obviously the recommendations of the US and the World Bank would not have mattered at all if there were not political and economic groups in Turkey who were already against heavy state involvement in the economy and thus were prepared to introduce changes to lead to the liberalisation and privatisation of the economy. From the early 1950s onwards, the Democratic Party Government shelved the industrialisation policies envisaged by the 1946 Five Year Development Plan and introduced a set of policies to pave the way for the liberalisation of the economy and to emphasise agricultural development as the engine of the economy. As a result, Marshall Aid came to Turkey and ensured that Turkey played the role of food and raw materials supplier in the new international division of labour.

In conjunction with western aid and Turkey's participation in liberal organisations like the GATT, some of the principles of the 'integrated national economy' were compromised but not entirely abandoned. Protectionism still continued to be fairly strong until the 1980s in the form of import substitution. The state oscillated between liberalisation and protectionism for about three decades from the late 1940s. Even liberal business people did not see any problem with protectionism as long as it facilitated capital accumulation in the private sector (Sunar 1974). To a large extent it was the

US defence considerations during the cold war that forced the US to be lenient in giving aid to Turkey, in conjunction with the Marshall Plan, and giving Turkey room to continue to follow protectionist industrial policies (Hershlag 1968:150–160). The fact that throughout the 1950s Turkey aimed at obtaining as much foreign financial help as possible without due considerations for a 'sound fiscal policy' was to get the country into trouble with the international finance institutions. The IMF and the World Bank in particular were concerned that Turkey was using foreign funds to avoid adjustments to achieve economic stability (Yalman 1984). In the World Bank's view, the resultant decline in saving rates, chronic budget deficits and over-valued exchange rates were signs of using foreign funds for postponing adjustment rather than facilitating it (World Bank 1985). The resistance of Turkey to implement liberalisation policies to the letter led to the deterioration of relations between the country and the Bretton Woods institutions in the middle of the 1950s, yet these institutions did not have sufficient power at the time to impose their policy preferences on Turkey. The attempts to reconcile the objectives of industrialisation and adjustment in the late 1940s and the 1950s produced incoherent policies as far as reliance on foreign resources and liberalisation were concerned. The prerequisites of the regime's desire to westernise clashed directly with the aim of reducing dependence on foreign economic resources. Therefore the attempts to speed up industrialisation were of an ad hoc nature and justified the label 'planless industrialisation' (Yalman 2001:147).

As the 1950s were a period of expansion of world capitalism, foreign capital came to invest, in co-operation with Turkish capital, in luxury consumer goods. A highly protected and thus profitable internal market contributed to the development of assembly industries in Turkey. In proportion with the rise in importance of the domestic market, the private sector moved into the industrial sector while the state sector concentrated on the production of intermediate commodities as inputs for the private sector (Gülalp 1983:51).

Despite the growing importance of the industrial classes within the state and political parties, the exigencies of the Turkish election system forced governments to follow populist policies, through which the state attempted to please various interests that were in conflict with each other at times. This is very clear in the agricultural pricing policy. Although in the long run the state tried to ensure a transfer of resources from agriculture to industry, short-term political considerations prior to elections resulted in high floor prices for certain crops. In short, the class configuration in Turkey did not allow the state to follow a coherent industrial policy as no single class could control the state on its own. This was also reflected in the composition of the state bureaucracy. The Turkish bureaucracy, particularly in its higher echelons, was not free from the influence of various factions of the dominant classes. With every change in government, high level bureaucrats would be changed thus preventing the formulation of long-term policies.

ECONOMIC POLICIES IN THE 1950s

A string of economic measures introduced in the 1950s included: the devaluation of the Turkish Lira, the slackening of import quotas, the importation of agricultural technology, the encouragement of foreign capital investments, state guarantees for external borrowing by the private sector, permission to foreign companies to search for oil and refine it within Turkey, the establishment of the Turkish Industrial Development Bank to extend cheap foreign currency credits to private investors, the liberalisation of imports by 60 per cent, and attempts to privatise some of the state economic enterprises.

The economic programme of the Democratic Party in the early 1950s was geared to attract foreign capital through a series of measures aimed at opening up the economy. Some of the measures introduced did not seem to work, as investment capital failed to come in to the country in significant amounts. However, the amount of foreign capital in the form of short or long-term credit lending did reach such levels that a financial crisis emerged in 1958 which necessitated a request to the IMF to start a rescue operation (Kazgan 1999:97–108). The stabilisation programme aimed to control inflation and increase exports through monetary measures, price controls and reorganisation of the trade regime. However, the ensuing devaluation did not increase the export earnings, and the availability of short-term trade credits further exacerbated the balance of payments problems.

Western recommendations concerning the priority to be given to agriculture and the minimisation of the state in the economy were not followed in a systematic way, as the state did not hesitate to abandon them when it deemed it necessary. The striking thing about the so-called 'free market economy' policies of the 1950s was their haphazard and *ad hoc* nature. Policies were introduced but were not followed through. Only the external borrowing aspect of the 'free market' programme seemed to be working. The opening-up of the economy became limited to official aid, import credits and other commercial credit, which fuelled imports. In the 1950s, Turkey's integration into the world economy was largely limited to partial liberalisation of the import regime based on short-term borrowing. Increased debt servicing from 1954 onwards started to wipe away a large chunk of the meagre export earnings.

Productive investment by foreign capital remained very limited following the measures taken to attract foreign capital in the 1950s. Although the optimists argued that the TNCs, which came to Turkey through licensing and know-how agreements, helped their Turkish partners to overcome their difficulties in technological, organisational and capital problems, direct foreign investment was restricted only to certain sectors. The incoming capital was mainly directed to joint ventures with Turkish partners. Foreign companies who invested in conjunction with law number 6224 (the 1954 Foreign Capital Incentives Law), in pharmaceutical, electrical, agri-business, transport, consumer durables, petrol and petro-chemicals and banking helped their local partners in technology, capital formation and organisational problems. Well known TNCs like General-Electric, Pfizer, AEG, Sandoz, Pirelli, Unilever, Mobil, BP and Shell went into joint ventures with Turkish partners (Bulutoğlu 1970; Hershlag 1968; Kazgan 1999) but this represented only a small step in terms of the diversification of the economy.

Given that Turkey was not able to diversify its economy to increase export earnings, which had been based on a few primary commodities (cotton, tobacco, hazelnuts, raisins and figs) since the 1920s, a free market economy meant increasing debts. The foreign trade deficit, which stood at US$22.3 million in 1950, shot up to US$193 million in 1952, and by 1958 Turkey's overdue debt was US$256 million (Kazgan 1999:101). The country's inability to service its debt generated a crisis of confidence, which in turn reduced the amount of programme credits necessary for vital development needs. Turkey was forced to accept an IMF stabilisation programme in 1958, which extended a further US$359 million credit as well as postponing the overdue debts of US$420 million.

Although the 'free marketeers' came to power in 1950 they were not powerful enough to ensure a comprehensive liberalisation of the economy. Not only were *étatists* still a powerful force in the parliament, but also the nature of the economy did not lend itself to a wide-ranging liberalisation. To begin with, the economy was agrarian in nature and based on primitive technology. Second, the few state run industrial units in existence were not profitable enough to attract foreign take-over. Furthermore, these establishments were Kemal Atatürk's legacy and no one would dare to completely transform them, as Kemalist ideology was deeply entrenched in Turkish society. In addition, the Government taken over by the Democratic Party in 1950 was not financially sound enough to carry out extensive reforms, which would have disrupted the already troubled economy. Therefore, throughout the 1950s, the Democratic Party oscillated between state intervention and 'free marketism'. Despite attempts to liberalise the economy, state intervention in the economy still remained very strong. For one thing, the state was not able to sell most of the state economic enterprises to the private sector, as it lacked sufficient capital to buy. Furthermore, the private sector had become used to obtaining cheap goods and services from the public sector. The state was also expected to invest heavily in infrastructural development. Consequently, state involvement in economic investments did show a significant increase in the 1950–60 period.

State intervention in price formation, the rate of profits and foreign currency allocation and distribution became a daily event as a consequence of the failures in short-term debt servicing and in securing further external funds. The haphazard nature of state intervention generated a general instability in the economy. The envisaged plans and programmes were quickly shelved and newly introduced ones also suffered the same fate. In this vein, the promise to emphasise agricultural development in congruence with the principle of comparative advantage was soon replaced with policies giving priority to industrialisation. In this period of ups and downs only one thing was constant; the reliance on short-term external borrowing from both official and private sources. The US$1882 billion borrowed between 1950 and 1960 stimulated imports and further added to the balance of payments problems, which had been in the red since 1947 (Kazgan 1999:104).

In the mid 1950s, under pressures from the import-substitution (IS) industrialists and importers, the Menderes Government refrained from devaluing the Turkish Lira but concentrated on other stabilisation measures such as increasing taxes and the control of bank credits. However, all the measures taken to maintain the import requirements of the economy failed abysmally towards the end of the 1950s and the Menderes Government had to adopt an IMF-guided stabilisation package in 1958 (Krueger 1990). The debt crisis of the late 1950s forced Turkey to accept the first austerity programme in August 1958 and consequently US$420 million of Turkey's debt was re-scheduled and US$359 million new credit was extended. The measures introduced to control inflation were not very successful and a stagflation dominated the economy between 1959 and 1961. Likewise, the devaluation of the Lira in August 1958 was not effective enough to increase exports. On the contrary, import expansion due to the decline in world market prices and the availability of further credit imports worsened the balance of payments. Despite all its efforts, the Menderes Government was not able to achieve macro-economic stability throughout the 1950s. The inconsistent policies of the 1950s, which oscillated between state intervention and liberalisation under the auspices of the IMF and led to economic and financial crises, came to a sharp end in 1960 with a military intervention.

THE PLANNED PERIOD 1960–80

The coup signified a shift from a relatively free market oriented approach to a planned economy. The military rule and the civilian rule that followed it emphasised state planning in the economy. The justification behind planning was to enhance the common good by using the scarce resources more rationally (State Planning Organisation 1963).

Despite the claims that planning may be a harbinger of a regime change towards socialism thus threatening the existing order, the plans themselves did not acknowledge any contradiction between the state sector and the private sector. The Turkish bureaucracy which put the plans into action under the auspices of the military saw the two sectors as complementary rather than mutually exclusive and thus antagonistic (Barkey 1990; Öniş 1992a). Three consecutive five-year development plans (1963–67, 1968–72 and 1973–77) brought about a fast and steady economic growth. The Second Five-Year Development Plan (1968–72) eased up the concerns about the regime change with its more market-friendly approach than the First Five-Year Development Plan (1963–67). While it stated its loyalty to private ownership, it declared that state enterprises were to play a significant role in areas where the private sector did not have capabilities. Thus, development plans envisaged a mixed economic framework in which the interest of the private sector was served by the services and production provided by public enterprises (State Planning Organisation 1969). This was evidenced in the Third and Fourth Five-Year Development Plan periods when private investors were provided with all sorts of state incentives in spite of the fact that the private sector was not able to meet the targets set by the plans (Kepenek and Yentürk 1994; TÜSİAD 1980; TOBB 1974). The Turkish bourgeoisie fear of the state power holders as a potential threat to its well-being was intensified by the 1961 Constitution, which provided the legal framework for the working class to unionise. In addition to the bourgeoisie's criticism of planning within the mixed economy, the plans themselves carried internal contradictions in that the main aim of reducing dependence on foreign resources was not compatible with the high rates of envisaged economic growth given the low levels of domestic savings and capital formation. The targets introduced in the plans were obligatory for state enterprises and directive for the private sector investments. In the vanguard of the newly established State Planning Organisation, import-substituting policies characterised the period under consideration. State investment constituted more than 50 per cent of the total investment and controls were introduced to govern the foreign trade and foreign exchange regime. A relative de-linking from the world economy was reflected in the fact that the ratios of exports and imports to the GDP remained 4.5 and 6 per cent respectively. The inward-looking development policies aimed at increasing the levels of profitability in industry and agriculture, while attempts were concentrated on the expansion of the internal market through populist income distribution policies.

The origins of import-substitution policies in Turkey go back as far as the 1930s, but the real impetus came in the 1960s (Berksoy 1982; Boratav 1974). The period between 1930 and 1980 was characterised by increasing involvement of the state in the economy and by almost entirely inward-oriented industrialisation. State intervention was pervasive in the protection of national industries against foreign competition; in the production and provision of certain basic goods and services; and in the provision of legal, bureaucratic and institutional structures to regulate the process of industrialisation, labour relations and income distribution (Erdilek 1986; Gülalp 1980). Measures were taken to ensure the enlargement of the internal market for the sustainability of import-substituting industrialisation (ISI). After the introduction of a pluralist democratic system in 1950, policies to keep the incomes of rural producers and wage earners fairly high had positive consequences for the enlargement of the internal market, which in turn had a positive effect on the development of inward-looking industries. Once ISI took root, the transition from primary import-substitution to secondary import-substitution in the early 1960s was fairly painless, despite some ups and downs (Sönmez 1980). Foreign currency earnings from the export of primary products, external credits and workers' remittances, mainly from Germany, were the most important sources of finance for the easy stage of ISI, and continued to be significant in the early days of the secondary phase of ISI. However, the increasing need for higher technology and inputs necessitated a stable foreign currency income, which could not entirely be met by the export of primary goods and workers remittances from western Europe. As the Turkish capitalists continued to expect resource transfers from public sources to the private sector, rather than relying on their own savings and capital formations, the policy-makers had to approach outside sources including the OECD for funds which were accompanied by some conditions (Bulutoğlu 1967; Öniş and Riedel 1993).

Given that the productivity of Turkish industry was quite low and the industry was not competitive in the world market, the crisis with ISI was inevitable (Arın 1986). In the early days of the planned period, the need to increase foreign currency earnings was simply overlooked. Protection offered to new industries was far from being well planned or organised and included import restrictions, customs duties, quotas and prohibitions. Pampered by such policies, Turkish industrialists were not concerned about technological improvements or cost reducing measures that would increase the competitiveness of the sector. The fixed rate foreign currency policy, which led to the overvaluation of the Turkish Lira, made exports expensive and imports cheap. The state was largely responsible for the unproductive and non-competitive nature of IS industries, as it implemented a protective industrialisation strategy without differentiating between the various sectors of industry.

By the end of the 1970s, the import dependence of industry had reached such serious dimensions that the state could not meet its debt obligations for the money borrowed to continue to pamper the inward-oriented and inefficient industries (Çelebi 1991). Furthermore, the protective measures, which included high tariff walls, import quotas, low interest rates and preferable exchange rates for industrialists, had reached such proportions that industrial interests did not have much incentive to invest in higher technology in order to improve the competitiveness of the industry. However, despite the low productivity of industries, the profitability levels of private industrial establishments were kept high by a large number of so-called 'encouragement measures' offered by the state. Most of the encouragement measures were of a financial and monetary nature. Through overvalued currency and high protective tariff walls, Turkish industry was protected against outside competition. As a result of these measures, a group of rent-seeking Turkish business people went from strength to strength, to such an extent that monopolies in certain areas emerged. Business people were provided with the opportunity to borrow from government sources at rates much lower than the rate of inflation, and thus were able to accumulate capital and wealth at the expense of the Treasury. Furthermore, the private sector was provided with cheap inputs produced by the State Economic Enterprises (SEE) which had been making considerable losses for some time (Boratav and Türkcan 1991). One positive consequence of the state pampering of private capital was the fact that the level of investment in various sectors of the economy showed a considerable increase, though production was largely for the internal market. The impact of western financial institutions on the Turkish economy and politics remained very low in this period. The amount of foreign direct investment remained very low throughout the 1960s and the early 1970s. The fact that the country was able to meet its foreign currency needs from exports, workers' remittances, and private financial sources meant that it was less vulnerable to the imposition of the international finance institutions such as the IMF and the World Bank and other international organisations and treaties like the OECD and the European Common Market (Kazgan 1999:113).

It was during this period that the private sector in industry managed to accumulate capital and develop expertise in an attempt to take a leading role in the economy. Strong state support for industrialisation efforts strengthened the fledgling industrial class who relied heavily on state enterprises for cheap inputs and the expertise developed in such enterprises. Policies like Convertible Turkish Lira Deposits and government protection against foreign exchange risks for short-term borrowings by the private sector were two of the main mechanisms of resource transfer to the private sector. Populist policies aimed at meeting welfare needs generated a stable atmosphere in which the private sector flourished. A relative atmosphere of freedom brought about by the 1961 Constitution helped develop civil society organisations and trade union movements. This overall positive picture gradually started to disappear in the aftermath of the first oil crisis in 1973. Although there was a mild crisis stemming from the balance of payment problems and the difficulties of meeting debt obligations, which necessitated an IMF austerity programme in 1970, Turkey managed to maintain the relative prosperity of the economy.

Despite opposition from the industrial bourgeoisie, the Demirel Government that implemented an IMF requested devaluation policy in 1970 saw this as a necessary evil as it thought this would speed up Turkey's integration into the world economy. The acceptance of the IMF's stabilisation package represented the victory of adjustment over industrialisation. Yet the relationship between governments and the business community was not an easy one as there was no consensus among coalition partners as to the concessions given to business and the implementation of an IMF stabilisation package in the mid 1970s. However, for a short period of time the devaluation policy and the stabilisation package seemed to have done the trick of alleviating the balance of payments problem by speeding up exports and allowing the transfer of workers' remittances. The rate of GDP increase registered 6.7 per cent in 1963–67, 6.6 per cent in 1968–72 and 7 per cent in 1973–76. Both the agricultural and industrial sectors showed positive growth. The rate of industrial growth was as high as 10 per cent on average between 1963 and 1976 (Kazgan 1999:110, Table 3).

Yet the crisis emerged in parallel with a fairly high average rate of economic growth, at 7 per cent per annum. Due to lack of competitiveness in the world market, IS industries could only sustain themselves as long as the state was able to continue to provide cheap input, capital and finances. Although the State Planning Organisation had a large domain of influence between 1960 and 1970, its vision of industrialisation through supporting both the public and private sector prevented it from putting more emphasis on a highly selective group of industries. Therefore it is not surprising that in Turkey the state ran into a huge deficit of balance of payments. The deficiencies of ISI could have been overcome, according to Barkey (1990), if the cleavages within the private sector had not been so severe as to ruin the ability of the state to formulate and implement policies to correct such deficiencies. The conflict and struggle between different factions of the private sector to influence state policies in order to increase their share of the economic rent, prevented the state from following long-term policies to improve Turkey's economic performance. Such conflicting and competing pressures on the state 'led to its ultimate paralysis' (Barkey 1990:110–139 and 149–168). The 'zero sum game' nature of the pursuit of economic rents made it almost impossible to co-operate on a policy which would have had long-term development objectives. Different groups attempted to influence state policies in different directions in order to obtain the lion's share of the rents provided by state interference in the economy. The conflict was reflected in the political-economic stalemate in the relations between the state and the private sector throughout the period from the 1960s to the 1980s.

The problem of foreign currency shortage was exacerbated by the oil crisis and by the world-wide economic recession in the 1970s. The crisis faced by the Turkish economy was evident from the fact that there was a severe drop in overall production, a sharp decline in the rate of economic growth, a slow-down in investment, a debt crisis, and high inflation. The impact of the first oil crisis in 1973–74 was compounded by the US arms embargo, the undeclared western economic embargo as a result of Turkey's intervention in Cyprus and by the cost of this intervention. The balance of payments, already in the red, had gradually become even worse due to the quadrupling of oil prices. The balance of payments was further exacerbated by the fact that industries were run by subsidised petrol and that the over-valued Turkish Lira encouraged imports of capital goods. Despite some increase between 1973 and 1976, export revenues could only meet 37 per cent of the imports. Perhaps one positive impact of negative interest rates, the overvalued Turkish Lira against the US dollar and increased imports was the expansion of the economy by about 9 per cent annually between 1973 and 1976 (Kazgan 1999:110, Table 3).

Petro-dollars accumulated in petroleum producing countries due to high prices in the 1970s had ended up in the US and western banks who were extremely eager to lend to less economically developed countries. Along with countries like Brazil, Argentina and Mexico, Turkey did not hesitate to borrow heavily on a short-term and low interest basis. The rapid economic growth based on short-term borrowing reached its pinnacle in 1979 and then started to decline. The debt burden brought about by short-term borrowing and insufficient export earnings was compounded by the necessity to import foodstuffs, which in turn was triggered by the scarcity of agricultural goods. From 1977 onwards, there were significant signs that a debt crisis was to emerge and in 1978 Turkey defaulted on the interest payment. Fresh funds were obtained from the IMF in 1979 after long and tough negotiations which forced Turkey into accepting the implementation of a string of belt tightening adjustment and austerity measures as well as guaranteeing the payments of both the public and private debts (Kazgan 1999:132–133).

During the negotiations throughout 1977 and 1978, shortages in almost everything, but most importantly in fuel, electricity, cooking oil and gas, contributed to escalating instability in the country. There were several government changes between 1977 and 1979. After several attempts by a few new governments at austerity measures, a comprehensive austerity package was introduced in June 1979 in the wake of an agreement signed with the IMF. Some of Turkey's debt was re-scheduled and some of the short-term debts were converted to long-term debts. Despite some improvements in the balance of payments due to declining imports and increasing workers' remittance, the economy was far from recovering. The rate of inflation soared up from 25 per cent in 1977 to 52.6 per cent in 1978 and 63.9 per cent in 1979. Positive economic growth throughout the 1970s dropped to 0.3 per cent in 1979 (Kazgan 1999:133). External developments and difficulties compounded the chaos in the country. The second oil crisis had a shocking impact on the country, which at the same time experienced a declining terms of trade due to falling prices of agricultural commodities in the world market. Furthermore, the US decision to increase interest rates in the late 1970s worsened the debt burden of the country, which had borrowed with little regard for the floating exchange rates. Under the bottlenecks of the debt crisis and import-substitution the existing industries were operating at around 50 per cent capacity in the 1980s. This was largely due to the expansion and diversification of the economy throughout the 1970s. Cheap credit guaranteed by the state had enabled the private sector to increase the capacity of the manufacturing sector. New holdings reminiscent of the Korean Chaebols had developed rapidly and through joint ventures with TNCs had contributed to the diversification of the economy. The construction sector, the most dynamic sector in the economy for a long time, had made significant strides in gaining large-scale international contracts, specifically in oil-rich Arab countries. Furthermore, the banking sector had expanded significantly, taking advantage of the liberal policies encouraging foreign capital in the 1970s. The fresh funds needed for the operation of all these were not forthcoming as the country had lost its credibility due to the debt crisis. Structural adjustment policies, which would supposedly transform the nature of the economy and ensure its export orientation, were heralded as the solution.

The economic crisis in the late 1970s was paralleled by social and political crises in which armed clashes between extreme right and left in most cities made life extremely difficult for the ordinary citizen. Furthermore, Parliament was not able to function properly due to the uncompromising behaviour of various parties both in power and in opposition. The proliferation of political parties between 1960 and the late 1970s was a direct result of the cleavage of interests between the factions of the private sector. In attempting to please a number of conflicting rent-seeking groups, the state lost its ability to produce coherent long-term policies. There were continuous changes in the government and most of the coalition governments were short-lived due to conflicting interests, not only between coalition partners but also within each of the political parties participating in the coalition. While political parties were at each other's throats for a better share of the economic rent for their own supporters, the country was experiencing a very serious economic and political crisis. The deficit of the balance of payments was increasing rapidly, shortages of many consumer goods were becoming severe and political stability was in real danger as a result of demonstrations and street clashes between the militants of the extreme right and left. In other words, the economic crises of the late 1970s were accompanied by political crises. The two elections since the 1971 military ultimatum could only bring unstable coalition governments who were unable to control the economy and the social tension and street clashes in the country. The crescendo of the social and economic chaos was the 1980 military coup that brought down a Justice Party minority government. With the benefit of hindsight, it is possible to argue that the contradictory policies of trying to invest in industrialisation and trying to ensure the flows of funds to the private sector were the main reasons behind the public deficit and balance of payments problems. A number of observers agree that the demands of industry in general and the private sector in particular for new funds forced the governments to recourse to external borrowing, which meant a great deal of compromise from the development plans' main objective; that of reducing dependency on foreign resources (Celasun and Rodrik 1989; Kepenek and Yentürk 1994; Tekeli and İlkin 1993).

This crisis had serious repercussions on income distribution and industrial relations. Until the end of the 1970s Turkish industrialists were indifferent to the state's populist policies concerning wages and agricultural crop prices (Boratav 1991). In a sense, such policies were a godsend for the protected import-substituting industries, which relied on the expansion of the internal market. However, with the economic crisis and the emergence of an export-oriented accumulation model, industry started to demand regulations and policies which would curb labour costs, open up the economy, ensure its competitiveness in the world market, and establish free market principles. For the import-substituting industrialisation which characterised the 1960s and 1970s, high wages and high agricultural incomes were necessary for the formation of a large internal market.

With the proposed restructuring of the economy towards export-promotion, wages became a high cost of production and thus had to be curbed through state regulations. Such demands also came from the international financial institutions, which claimed that the state's involvement in the economy was largely responsible for the existing crisis which had led to high price rises, production difficulties, balance of payments problems and social and political upheavals.

In the late 1970s, the Turkish bourgeoisie complained that development plans, though useful, lacked sufficient discipline to prevent economic instability and to ensure efficient use of scarce resources. In order to influence industrialisation policies, industrialists organised themselves under the umbrella of the TÜSİAD (The Organisation of the Turkish Industrialists and Businessmen) and the TOBB (the Union of the Chambers of Industry) in 1975. The immediate aim of these two organisations in the late 1970s was to force the state to take the necessary measures to create a vertically integrated industrial structure. In the process they expressed their willingness to obey development plans which would impose the discipline to adopt fiscal and monetary policies to fight economic instability (TÜSİAD 1976, 1977). The envisaged structure of Turkish industry was to combine capital intensive modern industries with labour intensive export-oriented industries. Given the low level of technology in Turkish industry, it was deemed necessary to go into joint ventures with the TNCs. The industrialists demanded a new integration with the world market in which the state would actively promote such transition and provide sectoral planning and other necessary conditions. One thing was clear, in the late 1970s the Turkish industrialists were not completely in favour of Turkey's further integration into the world economy through full liberalisation including trade liberalisation. They wanted the state to provide sufficient protection for industry and find the necessary foreign resources for development at the same time. However, this was not compatible with the conditions set by international lenders and their organisations. The IMF insisted on the implementation of stabilisation measures before lending any furher loans in 1977 and 1978. On the other hand, the European Economic Community (EEC) was insistent on the trade liberalisation stipulated by the Annex Protocol. The Ecevit Government in 1977–78 was caught between the Turkish industrialists who wanted state support for ensuring their entering the world market as strong contenders, and the IMF and the EEC who insisted on liberalisation and structural adjustment. This eventually brought about the downfall of the Ecevit Government who could not please either side. The incoming minority government of Demirel in 1979, though slightly relieved by the two debt resceduling agreements signed by Ecevit's Government, was not able to reduce economic and social problems, nor was it able to reconcile the demands of the industrialists and the international institutions, and it was forced out of office by the army in 1980 (Yalman 2001:172–194).

DEVELOPMENT SINCE 1980

The 1980 coup represents a threshold in the integration of Turkey into the world economy. Under the auspices of the army, Turkish policy-making became an arena in which the IMF and the World Bank had a strong influence. Soon after the coup the Government signed a three-year stand-by agreement in 1980 which could be interpreted as the death of Turkish policy-making and as an infringement on Turkish national sovereignty (Wolff 1987:105). The set of performance criteria for the fiscal and monetary policies imposed simply bypassed the legislative functions of Parliament and centralised the decision-making process. The ironic thing is that the World Bank, which became involved in five Structural

Adjustment Loans (SALs) to Turkey, insisted on the continuation of development planning as a 'medium-term strategy' in order to link the short-term objectives of stabilisation policies with the long-term structural adjustment policies (World Bank 1987:23–24). The Fifth Five-Year Development Plan, which was prepared by the Government with the direct participation of the World Bank, specifically stated that planning was basically a vehicle to establish a free market economy which would emphasise growth with stability.

The sorry state of the economy in the late 1970s forced the Government to emphasise the virtues of the free market economy as suggested by international finance institutions. The stabilisation policies, introduced on 24 January 1980, have been the subject of a long-lasting debate.[2] The essence of the package was to install and strengthen the free market economy. One of the main intentions was to gradually cut back the state by way of privatising the State Economic Enterprises (SEEs) and limiting state expenditure. The integration of the Turkish economy with the world economy was also very high on the agenda. Although the immediate intention of the SAPs was to solve the foreign currency problem and stabilise prices, the long-term desire was to introduce structural transformation measures which would open up the economy and integrate it into the world capitalist economy. Plans and programmes were designed to emphasise a development strategy, which would give priority to export-oriented industrialisation. The policies followed by Turkey since the 1980s reflect a gradual application of the principles of the Washington Consensus which aim to replace a state system with a market system through the opening of the economy, the restructuring of public expenditure priorities, the liberalisation of the financial sector, privatisation, deregulation and the provision of an enabling environment for the private sector.

As a first step in this direction, foreign trade and the foreign exchange system were liberalised at a speed that surprised even the IMF and World Bank officials (Boratav 1991:85). Since 1980, economic policies have continuously encouraged activities which would bolster up exports. To facilitate such policies, other fiscal and monetary measures were also introduced at very high speed. Such policies included the continual devaluation of the Turkish Lira and a flexible exchange rate policy based on daily adjustment. Furthermore, industrialists were supported by policies such as tax rebates and export credits, so that the competitiveness of Turkish products in the world market can be ensured and export business becomes profitable for capitalists. In the pre-1980 period, financial markets were developed in order to speed up the emergence of large scale firms comparable with their foreign counterparts, as even the biggest Turkish firms were quite small compared with large foreign firms. The credit mechanism was the most important tool used in this process (Nas and Okedon 1992).

In order to increase export capacity, domestic demand was restrained through a very tight wages policy and a strictly controlled agricultural prices policy. This started a tendency in which the gains made in wages and agricultural incomes between 1950 and 1980 were gradually eroded. Consequently, income distribution became highly unequal, discriminating against wage earners and the salaried (Arıcanlı and Rodrik 1990). The cutting back of the state on the whole speeded up the process of impoverishment as it meant increased unemployment as a result of privatisation, and ensuing rationalisation and a lower standard of living as a result of the cuts in social welfare provisions.

Another significant change was the continuous manipulation of the rate of interest. Prior to 1980, interest rates were well below the rate of inflation. Since 1980, interest rates have been kept extremely high in the belief that they will reduce internal demand and encourage saving. However, in the absence of proportional wage increases, internal savings have remained very limited, and have been channelled to foreign currency accounts. Additionally, the impact of high interest rates has been very negative on manufacturing industry, as the price of capital borrowings increased to unmanageable proportions. A number of small firms went bankrupt and the tendency towards monopolisation speeded up (Şenses 1994). Some measures were introduced to offset the negative consequences of high interest rates and they included tax exemptions and encouragement premiums offered to business people. The reaction of industry to high interest rates is very interesting. Instead of investing in new technology, which would have improved the competitiveness of industry, the manufacturing sector preferred to invest in order to improve their unused capacity. In the period since 1980, most investments have been made in tourism, housing and small-scale manufacturing industry. Consequently, investments in industries with a capacity to compete in the world market have been extremely limited.

In the decades prior to 1980, the state played a leading role in areas where private capital was not capable of investing large sums, such as steel and iron works and petroleum refineries. Such state investment came to a virtual stop in the 1980s. This disproved the belief that private capital would fill the gap created by the state's retreat. Despite all efforts, private investors kept away from large-scale industrial adventures. Turkish industry, which had been used to negative interest rates, faced a real economic crisis as a result of the high interest rates after the 1980s. Capital fled to the commercial and financial sectors rather than remaining in the productive sector. A consequence of this was that the industrial sector continued to be characterised by weak capital stock, low productivity and low technology.

Despite the facts that Turkish private capital shied away from investing in the productive sector and that the public sector investments in manufacturing were not encouraged by the World Bank, the share of manufacturing in exports showed a steady increase throughout the 1980s and until the mid 1990s (Şenses 1994). This irony that, despite the low level of investment in the manufacturing sector, the share of manufactured goods in total export had shown a significant increase has been taken as evidence of the triumph of the liberal free market economy. Yet the reality had nothing to do with the free marketeers' claim that the restructuring of the economy was realising the targeted export orientation. Increased output was largely the result of the revitalisation of the unused capacity in existing industries rather than due to further industrialisation. The SALs by the World Bank were designed to create a suitable environment for the private sector to take initiatives to restructure the economy to ensure sustained economic growth. In the absence of loans for 'industrial restructuring', the state concentrated its efforts on capitalising on Turkey's newly elevated strategic importance stemming from the events in Iran and Afghanistan in the 1980s. Easily obtained funds enabled the state to implement SAPs without any serious difficulty in the 1980s, but at the same time they contributed to the country's vulnerability to external sources of funds. Public sector investment in industry was not on the agenda throughout the 1980s, as it would have clashed with the IMF conditions.

The interpretation of Turkey's increased exports of manufactured goods as a success of adjustment attracted counter arguments that such increase was due to the reorientation of the pre-1980 IS industries that revitalised the unused capacities created by one foreign exchange crisis. Subsidies and tax rebates for industry as well as real depreciation of the Turkish Lira throughout the 1980s contributed significantly to the competitiveness of the manufacturing industry, not the SAPs. Perhaps one significant contribution of the SAPs was their impact on domestic market reduction emerging from the tight wage policy. A restricted internal market for manufactured goods made more goods available for exports. Given this, it would be mis-leading to talk about the re-structuring of industry in Turkey during the 1980s. The expectation and recommendations of the World Bank's experts that Turkey should follow its comparative advantage by concentrating on the production skill-intensive goods did not materialise (Balassa 1979; World Bank 1988). Since 1980, Turkish manufacturing industry has continued largely to produce for the internal market in establishments that have had substantial help from the state. Investment in manufacturing has been largely aban-doned both by the public and private sectors. At the beginning of the 1980s, the Turkish bourgeoisie abandoned its aim of develop-ment based on integrated industrialisation on account of the reali-sation that the international finance institutions (IFIs) would not support such a policy nor would they give the green light for the much needed foreign loans to run their businesses. Instead of attempting to deepen industrialisation, the Turkish private sector basically attempted to improve the existing industries in order to improve the production of intermediate goods. One plausible explanation for the lack of investment in export industries is that Turkish industry did not have a proper research and development section to ensure its competitiveness in the world market. For this reason Turkish industrialists continuously searched for foreign part-ners to provide them with technology that concurred with the domestic market (Yalman 2001:202). The significant increase in the production of intermediate goods between 1983 and 1988 was accompanied by a parallel increase in imports to support such industries (Celasun 1991). However, on the whole both private and public investment in the manufacturing sector declined significantly (World Bank 1988). The TNCs such as General Electric, Unilever, General Motors, Toyota, etc. operating within the country contin-ued to produce for the internal market rather than the export mar-kets (Yalman 2001:199). While the Turkish capital groups expanded throughout the 1980s, this was not an indication of a new model of accumulation based on the restructuring of industry. Based on interviews carried out with some leading industrialists, Yalman (2001:203) points out that many regret that they failed to become incorporated into the global production organisations of the TNC as manufacturers of components.

HOW SUCCESSFUL WERE THE SAPS IN THE 1980s?

In the early 1980s, the Turkish case was presented by the International Finance Institutions such as the IMF as the shining example of successful SAPs. However, it must be emphasised that the increase in the export of manufactured goods, as explained above, was not the result of a structural transformation of Turkish industry, but a result of continual devaluation, decreasing real wages and encouragement subsidies given to exporting industries.[3] While such measures decreased the cost of production in manufacturing industry and decreased the prices of exported commodities, they also increased the public debt as borrowing financed the subsidies. Despite an increase in the quantity of exports of manufactured goods, no significant change occurred in the nature of products exported. They mostly consisted of textiles, processed food and leather products, glass and metal works. This can hardly be construed as a real technological transformation of the economy. On the other hand, as a result of import liberalisation policies the quantity of imports also rose considerably (Aydın 1997, Tables 3 and 4: 75–76). In addition to luxurious consumer items, large quantities of machinery and technology have been imported since 1980, which indicates an increasingly dependent industry both in terms of technology and inputs. In other words, increased export capacity has been achieved alongside increasing import dependence. In the period since 1980, integration of the Turkish economy into the world capitalist system has been intensified through international trade. Yet, as the declining investments in both publicly and privately owned industries have shown a considerable decline, it is fair to claim that since the early 1980s neo-liberal policies in Turkey have failed to make a positive contribution to industrial development (Öniş 1992:497). In the second half of the 1980s the state emphasised investments in infrastructural development, particularly in the development of the telecommunication systems and highways. It is interesting to note that high cost infrastructural investments have been realised by resorting to internal and external borrowing.

One of the expected results of the SAPs was to get rid of the rent-seeking mentality through the reduction of the state. During the structural adjustment epoch, however, rent-seeking showed a clear ascendance rather than disappearing. A major transformation in the nature of the higher echelons of Turkish bureaucracy was instrumental in the allocation of rents. In the 1980s the political layer of the Turkish state gained the upper hand *vis-à-vis* the bureaucratic layer in decision-making related to the allocation of rents. It seems that the Turkish bureaucracy, which tried very hard to regulate and ensure equality in rent distribution during the ISI phase until 1980, lost its grip on decision making. Since the 1980s, the political layer of the state has been ignoring the detailed regulations prepared by the bureaucracy on issues such as government tenders, import licences and urban land use, and has been operating along the principle of a patron–client relationship in rent distribution (Boratav 1994:166–168). To ensure a clientelistic relationship between the political layer of the state and the business circles, the Motherland Party governments appointed all the top level decision-making bureaucrats from their own ranks and left the traditional bureaucracy in a subordinate position as far as key decisions about the economy were concerned.

Export subsidies replaced import quotas as the dominant form of resource transfer to the private sector from the state (Yeldan 1994). As far as the promotion of a rent mentality and the creation of rents for the private sector, there has not been much change between the interventionist period of 1960–80 and the liberal period starting from 1980. The state was and is actively involved in the creation of rents in a number of ways:

- State Economic Enterprises (SEEs) were run in such a way that the private sector was the main economic beneficiary.
- Salvaging bankrupt banks and industrial firms effectively resulted in the allocation of state funds for the use of such firms.
- State institutions were used for the legitimisation of corruption in official tenders.
- Illegal planning permissions were granted and construction without planning permission were pardoned thus protecting land speculators.
- While the cost of credits were rising, those close to the power holders were being granted preferential credits or their debts were being postponed.
- There were tax rebates for exports leading to the emergence of phoney exports.
- There was privatisation of state enterprises leading to rent creation.

- Tax rebates and funds for the establishment of certain businesses were granted undeservedly. In short, export subsidies, import surcharges, government tenders, fiscal incentives, subsidised credits, building licences, 'salvage operations' for insolvent firms and amnesties for 'economic crimes' are some of the state policies which have led to the enrichment of some business groups (Boratav 1995).

Liberalisation policies and other policies that encouraged speculative activities further fanned the flight of capital to financial and commercial areas where a quick return on investment was possible. The growth of a speculative rent-seeking social class progressed on a par with the weakening of industrial capital. Often it was the same people who moved away from productive activities to rent-seeking activities. The latest example of productive capital's flight to easy rentable activities was related to the state's inability to repay its debts, both internal and external. In recent years, in order to compensate for revenues lost through the privatisation of the SEEs and to meet state expenditure, the state resorted to extensive borrowing from both internal and external sources.[4] Government efforts to meet debt obligations with further internal borrowing created a class of rent-seekers who prefer to sit back and wait for maturity rather than investing in productive activities. This trend brings about a paradoxical situation where a significant decrease in industrial output accompanies a healthy growth in the economy. This was particularly true of the decade prior to the 2001 economic crisis.

In this period, import restrictions on many items were lifted, exchange regulations were changed from a fixed exchange regime to a floating one and foreign currency accounts were legalised. Particularly during the period of military rule, between 1980 and 1983, strict monetarist financial policies were implemented and as a consequence severe reductions in state budgets and public investments were witnessed. In the same vein, the credits given to the SEEs were cut. On the other hand, business groups were favoured in taxation policies as the tax burden was shifted to the waged and salaried classes.

Commensurate with the guidelines set by the IMF and the World Bank, governments in the 1980s became adamant that the state would gradually abandon its role in the economy to move away from the notion of an 'enterprise state'. This was very clear in the

Sixth Development Plan (1990–95) where the state set no targets for the manufacturing sector in order to increase industry's international competitiveness. Instead the plan reiterated the virtues of the 'free market' as the most efficient resource allocation mechanism. The Association of the Turkish Industrialists and Businessmen (TÜSİAD) showed its dissatisfaction with the state's insistence on the free market. Although in the late 1970s and the early 1980s the TÜSİAD lent support to free market ideology and rhetoric this was largely due to the economic expediency of the times rather than an ideological commitment to free marketism. They believed that access to external credits were only possible as long as the IFIs were kept happy, thus they went along with the free marketism. Even during the time when export incentives were offered, TÜSİAD insisted on selective incentives rather than indiscriminate incentives. From the middle of the 1980s, TÜSİAD became quite vociferous in its demands for selective incentives designed to reduce the import dependence of the industry. As Yalman puts it, the position of the industrial bourgeoisie on the role of the state in the economy since the late 1970s has been governed not by ideology but expediency (Yalman 2001:237–240). The same organisation in the late 1970s seemed to be strongly behind free marketism but since the mid 1980s it has been asking the state to act as a developmental state by providing guidance for investment in selective areas in collaboration with international capital. The most important organisation of the Turkish bourgeoisie, the TÜSİAD, has simply been asking for a new system of protection not based on personalised clientelism but on new transparent rules and regulations, regardless of the fact that channelling resources for private capital accumulation may generate macro-economic instability and/or the fiscal crisis of the state.

LIBERALISATION OF FOREIGN TRADE

In the 1984–89 period, although there were attempts to liberalise the trade regime, the actual policies were far from a complete adherence to the spirit of liberalism. Critics argued that not only were the average nominal tariff rates above 40 per cent, but also the introduction of a new system of import levies, which intended to increase Extra Budgetary Funds, tended to distort prices and bias production toward the internal market (Celasun 1990; World Bank 1988). TÜSİAD (1986), the Association of Turkish Industrialists and

Businessmen, complained that multiple exchange rates, import surcharges and export subsidies were used by the Government to favour or punish certain individuals, sectors or firms. In their view the political expediency used by Özal Governments simply represented a return to statist practices which allowed the central authority to have a discretionary power. The interesting thing is that the newly emerging capital groups that had the strong backing of the Özal Governments became active in the domestic market rather than investing in new technologies which would have enhanced international competitiveness. The areas they concentrated on included newly privatised cement, food processing, energy and telecommunications industries.

The international institutions that oversee world trade relations were not very happy with the exports subsidies used by Turkey, claiming that this led to price distortions. Consequently in the late 1980s Turkey gradually reduced export subsidies in accordance with GATT regulations and the IMF demands. One immediate consequence of this was that some exporters left the business and moved into other lucrative activities such as tourism and land speculation. Complete negligence of high technology and diversified export production left the economy reliant upon labour intensive industries such as textiles, steel and iron. Therefore export promotion activities mainly concentrated on efforts to resolve the short-term problems of old import substituting industries to produce exportable goods (Krueger and Aktan 1992:154–167; Öniş 1992b; Şenses 1990).

REPRESSIVE ANTI-TRADE UNION POLICIES

While foreign currency rates, interest rates and prices were liberalised by the new open accumulation model, wages and the working classes were oppressed by the new legislation passed by the military rule and kept intact by the following civilian governments. The so-called 'liberal' economic policies implemented under the auspices of the military between 1981 and 1983 aimed to resolve the 1977–79 economic crisis. The relationship between the bourgeoisie and the working class was far from 'liberal'. The military take-over in September 1980, and the 24 January decisions served to discipline the labour markets through extra-economic coercion. The military regime introduced many institutional changes in consultation with a number of Turkish businessmen's associations like TOBB and TİSK.

The coup in 1980 signifies the authoritarianisation of the Turkish State. The 1982 Constitution, prepared under the guidance of the military, provided the legal framework for a new form of state whose relations with civil society were restructured. The relations between capital and labour were significantly transformed under the newly created politico-legal structures, to the detriment of the working class. Despite the fact that working-class organisations had never been powerful enough to threaten the regime or to become a political party with grassroots organisations, the Turkish bourgeoisie constantly considered DİSK (the Confederation of Revolutionary Workers Unions) and TÜRKİŞ (the Confederation of Turkish Workers) as organisations incompatible with a democratic regime. These organisations' demands for better standards of living and their alliances with left of centre parties were deemed to be indicative of their desire to establish socialism. The military used its iron fist to crush these organisations, particularly DİSK, throughout the 1980s and ensured through the authoritarian 1982 Constitution that the working class would not challenge capital in the foreseeable future. The military regime made it abundantly clear from the beginning that their intention was not to go against the interest of the bourgeoisie and act as an autonomous agent above social classes. Immediately after the coup, the military banned the activities of all associations but asked TÜSİAD to transmit its message that the military junta was going to be loyal to the structural adjustment programme (Yalman 2001:219–220). The military simply smashed the organised working class as well as the intelligentsia on the left of the political spectrum that was considered to have organic ties with the working-class movement. Throughout the 1960s, and particularly in the 1970s, the growing strength of the working class, reflected in their militant demands in collective bargaining, and the support they received from the wider society, increased the worries of the bourgeoisie who were not able to run the economy without running into endless crises. The democratic framework provided by the 1961 Constitution simply tied the hands of the state to put an end to the militancy of the workers, students and disenchanted masses. In a sense, the widespread social tension and street clashes between various factions posed a serious challenge to the hegemony of the bourgeoisie supported by the army. The restructuring of the state with the 1980 military take-over and the authoritarian 1982 Constitution simply put an end to class-based politics (Yalman 2001:220–226).

However, after the return to civilian rule in 1983, the Motherland Party enjoyed the support of the military, especially between 1984 and 1988, which are sometimes called the golden years. The policies followed by the Motherland Party were a combination of a strictly authoritarian approach towards organised labour and a loose populist policy towards the urban poor who lacked a class consciousness and could be recruited to support the bourgeoisie's agenda. Furthermore, the preference for capital in Turkey to move to capital intensive production created further pressure on the working class not to push too much for wage increases. The fact that the Fifth Development Plan, formulated under the auspices of the World Bank, did not prioritise employment creation showed the severity of the situation the working class was in. By the end of the 1980s it had also become clear to workers that the state no longer pretended to be above social classes acting as an arbitrator between employers and workers. One clear indication of this was that the Özal Government forced the state economic enterprises to join TİSK (the Confederation of the Turkish Employers Union) in order to be able to contain the labour movement even better. As the structural adjustment policies negative impact on the working classes started to augment Özal's rhetoric, defending the rights of *orta direk* (literally meaning the medium pole of society; the great majority of the people) it also started to lose its credibility. In its early years, the Özal Government established a variety of clientelistic networks to show the masses that it was serving their interests. Urban squatter areas were particularly targeted through polices including the provision of quasi title deeds to land and property built on state lands, and VAT rebates for wage and salary earners. These policies were introduced not only to hide the cuts in vital services such as health and education but also to indirectly keep the wages low.

In line with the New Right thinking, the new regime emphasised the vigorous virtues of individualism and the necessity of a strong state as a guarantor of economic individualism. In the parlance of the bourgeoisie, the 1980 military regime simply emancipated individuals from 'intermediary, democratic and/or corporatist powers' of organisations like trade unions which supposedly threatened the well-being of the state. Through the media the bourgeoisie and the military started a powerful campaign to discredit the trade union movement as representing the vested interests of 'union lords' creating lawlessness and disorder. In attempts to justify the authoritarian prerogatives of the state, the 1961 Constitution also received its fair share of blame for the social, economic and political chaos of the late 1970s. The 1982 Constitution was designed to curtail most of the democratic rights and freedoms provided by the 1961 Constitution (Özbudun 1991). The ironic thing is that the military was able to obtain the consent of the masses for the new authoritarian regime, which attempted to strengthen the hegemony of the bourgeoisie. The preponderance of lawlessness and economic hardship on the eve of the 1980 coup were sufficient for the people to buy the law and order rhetoric preached daily on state radio and television and in the private media controlled by powerful capital groups. The pre-coup economic and political order was held responsible for the civil strife and disorder as well as the economic crises. Thus liberal-individualists who came to power under the strong support of the army used the rhetoric of 'there is no alternative' borrowed from Thatcherite Britain (Yalman 2001:227). The policies, which they claimed were without alternative, were the policies of structural adjustment which extolled the market. The Turkish bourgeoisie was quite successful in deifying the market ideology and persuading the masses as to the virtues of the market and civil society. The way the market and civil society were presented as autonomous entities with no class connections helped the internalisation of market ideology by the masses and heralded the triumph of the hegemony of the bourgeoisie. By emphasising the futility of class-based politics and appealing to the virtues of individuals, the Turkish bourgeoisie had been following its hegemonic interest without actually being authentically hegemonic (Yalman 2001:231). The regime since the 1980s has not been inclined to allow other social classes to organise themselves into politically autonomous entities, while paying lip service to democracy by concentrating on procedural features such as elections and a multi-party system (Boratav 1993). The way in which trade unions were discredited by military rule and by the labour laws of the post-military regime era is witness to this. In the new market economy, the role of the trade unions was simply reduced to negotiating wages without being in a position to negotiate economic policies with the government (Boratav, Yeldan and Köse 2000). Only pro-government trade unions were allowed to exist throughout the 1980s, as the left wing trade union confederation DİSK was outlawed. The new legislation allowed employers to dismiss workers arbitrarily, replace unionised workers with temporary non-unionised workers and use subcontractors to avoid direct confrontation with workers on issues relating to wages and social security. With the decentralisation of labour unions, and with repressive union laws that increased workers' vulnerability and susceptibility to unemployment, the working class was forced to fight to keep their jobs rather than pushing for higher wages throughout the 1980s.

2
Democracy, development and good governance

The Turkish economy has been experiencing crises regularly since the 1950s. Each new crisis emerges even stronger than the previous one, therefore the 2001–02 economic crisis, which started in February 2001, is much more rigorous than the previous ones. This crisis was multi-dimensional, with the economic dimension being the most significant. Rampant unemployment, poverty and crime, high rates of inflation, large-scale bankruptcies, irrational use of resources, inefficient services, contraction of the productive sector, bad administration of the State Economic Enterprises (SEEs), inflated public employment and a public tendering system conducive to a rent-seeking mentality were some of the indicators of this crisis.

The failure of development in Turkey, particularly since the 1980s, is partly explained by the nature of the state. Explanations revolve around the nature of the state, its interference in the economy and democracy. Given the long history of state intervention in the economy, the advocates of neo-liberalism and SAPs are dissatisfied with the transformations that the Turkish State has been experiencing since its inception in 1923. The debates in Turkey about how and why the state could be held responsible for the failure of development carry many elements of the theoretical expositions of the state in the less economically developed world. The proponents of neo-liberalism in Turkey are in agreement with international finance institutions regarding the idea that liberalism and liberal democracy is the only way to come out of the impasse of development. This contestable statement is the starting point of this chapter. Is there a strong relationship between capitalism, democracy and development? How effective is the export of western style democracy (through the imposition of political conditions or good governance) in bringing about social justice, respect for individual freedoms, human rights and economic development? Is there a direct relationship between democracy and development? Is the type of democracy advocated by neo-liberalism capable of delivering the expected results? Are the SAPs imposed on less economically developed countries conducive to achieving development and democracy at the same time? What are the consequences of the push for liberal democracy in less economically developed countries? Does a multi-party system lead to empowerment of the people? Is equality before law sufficient to generate the utmost liberty for everyone? Is it possible for the poor and the marginal to compete in the political sphere as equals with the rich and the powerful under economic liberalism which tends to exacerbate economic inequalities? Does the reduction of the state increase the chances of survival for democracy?

GOOD GOVERNANCE, DEMOCRACY AND DEVELOPMENT

Since the beginning of the 1990s, official western thinking has been trying to promote democracy as a both desirable and necessary feature of development. Democratisation and respect for human rights have been included in the IMF and World Bank conditions to ensure 'good governance' in less economically developed countries. But the question remains as to whether democratic processes are fully compatible with the economic and social development taking place in less economically developed countries. Is the introduction of elements of democracy necessarily the same as the consolidation of democracy in a given country? The term consolidation refers to the sustainability of democracy without digressions from democratic processes. The question then becomes whether all societies in the less economically developed world have the necessary conditions to sustain democracy.

This chapter will argue that the elements of democracy introduced in less economically developed countries like Turkey in conjunction with political conditionalities based on the notion of 'good governance' are still a long way from achieving democratic consolidation in these countries. In making this argument, I shall first look at what justification the IFIs and western governments provide for their requirement of good governance or the political conditionalities they impose, and what they expect to emerge as a result of adherence to them. The discussion will centre on the effectiveness of procedural democracy in bringing about economic and social justice. Through the analysis of various approaches to democracy and development I shall come to the conclusion that there is no straightforward relationship between the two. I shall maintain that it is the nature of the state that determines whether democracy and development can occur simultaneously. In analysing the nature of the Turkish State I shall be drawing on the extensive literature on the state in less economically developed countries and will suggest that the Republican State in Turkey was a developmentalist state until the 1960s. Following a nationalist agenda, the developmentalist Turkish State emphasised economic growth at the expense of democracy. The last section of the chapter will concentrate on the factors which triggered the process of democratisation and will argue that the limited elements of democracy introduced between 1946 and 1980 were largely in response to threats to national security. Finally I shall analyse the effectiveness of political liberalisation introduced in conjunction with good governance and argue that although there has been an ascendance of civil society, the state has operated in defiance of public demands for participation in decision-making in economic affairs.

Let us start with the concept of good governance which became one of the preconditions of development aid in the 1990s. Although it is not always clear what is meant by good governance the following list is often produced: the implementation of sound economic and social policies which would ensure the establishment of a free market and a greater role for the private sector within it; the need to train government officials to improve administration, rationalise state expenditure and enhance the competence of government; adherence to the principles of transparency and accountability and respect for human rights and the rule of law. One of the first expositions of good governance emerged in the World Bank's report on sub-Saharan Africa in 1989. Other western organisations such as the OECD (1989), the Commission of the European Communities (1991), the UNDP (1991) and western governments such as the British, French, US, etc. also jumped on the bandwagon between 1989 and 1992 (House of Common debates 1990; Hurd 1990; Chalker 1991). The World Bank report on the sub-Sahara (1989) blamed the crisis of governance for Africa's development problems. This has been in tune with the long tradition of the Washington Consensus. Since the advent of the Washington Consensus, the West and its finance institutions, bilateral and multilateral donor organisations have insisted on economic liberalism and liberal democracy as the only way to come out of 'development impasse'. This commitment stems from the conventional explanations that see the emergence of democracy as a result of the popular pressures in less economically developed countries. According to this view, the failure of authoritarian regimes to keep their grandiose promises of achieving high economic growth and raising standards of living led to the loss of their legitimacy, which in turn generated political pressures leading to democratisation in most African countries (Bratton 1994; Clapham 1993; Wiseman 1995). Both multilateral and bilateral donors have been insistent on political conditionality since the 1990s, with the belief that authoritarian regimes who have been the recipients of economic aid will promote democratisation under international pressures in order not to lose their access to economic aid. However, bilateral donors like Britain and the US tend to prefer terms like good governance or democracy, and governance to the term political conditionality, which appears to be too oppressive.

Defining governance as 'the exercise of power to manage a nation's affairs' the World Bank claimed that politics in Africa have been personalised through networks of patronage. The political leaderships have not been accountable for their policies, nor have they refrained from using state coercion arbitrarily to silence any political opposition and civil society organisations. In the Bank's view, in order to overcome the problems of development and achieve sound development there was a need for a fundamental change in the way the public sector was governed. Therefore, from 1990 onwards, democratic politics has been attached to economic conditions as a pre-requisite for lending money for development purposes (Word Bank 1991, 1992). The 'political conditionality' that has become a *sine qua non* of development lending demands wide ranging socio-political changes including democratisation, improvements in human rights and changes in the institutions of the government. The logic behind these conditions is the claim that capitalist democracies with their open markets, competent administrations and liberal-democratic politics not only provide the necessary conditions for economic growth and development but also bring peace and stability (Chalker 1991; Stokke 1995; Short 1997). The proponents of this view see economic and political conditionalities as complementary to each other. While it is expected that economic conditionalities would ensure the entrenchment of the market forces and competition, democratisation and movement towards good governance would level the playing field for the private sector and individual enterprise to act as engines of growth (Chalker 1991:2).

The reduction of the state is at the heart of the economy. The insistence of western governments and institutions to reduce the role of the state in less economically developed countries is deeply rooted in the ascendance of neo-liberalism as an economic and political doctrine in the West. Individual economic and political freedoms constitute the main pillars of neo-liberal theory. Neo-liberals see the state as an institution, responsible for the preservation of peace and order, not as a vehicle of interference in the economy and politics which would constrain the inalienable individual rights and liberties. State intervention in the free play of the market not only restricts freedom of individual choice but also harms the economy by distorting prices (Nozick 1974; Olson 1982; Green 1986). The good governance discourse borrows freely from neo-liberal economic and political theory in arguing that heavy state involvement in the economy inevitably leads to the emergence of rent-seeking and corruption as well as stunting the development of market economies (Laver 1997). Both international finance institutions such as the IMF and the World Bank and western donor governments have adhered very strictly to the principles of the neo-liberal theory, which sees the free market as the *sine qua non* of development. Thus the good governance discourse not only demands changes in the state but also to prioritise the expansion of the market.

The collapse of socialism provided the most suitable conditions for advocating the superiority and inevitability of the market economy, to such an extent that Francis Fukuyama called this the end of history (Fukuyama 1992). Furthermore, the end of the cold war gave the West the freedom to impose conditionalities without fear of losing their less economically developed allies to the enemy camp, communism. Consequently, the creation of western style multi-party democracy, pluralism and market economy have come to sit at the top of the political conditionality agenda, which insists on good governance.

Recent literature on governance and democracy in less economically developed countries treats democracy as something unproblematic and ignores endless debates on the meaning and values of democracy. Both international agencies and governments in less economically developed countries convey an image of it as if there is a world-wide movement of democracy sharing the same goals and aspirations in fighting an oppressive state.

It must be pointed out, however, that the attempts to give prominence to the establishment of a multi-party system and universal
franchise simply ignore the fact that the concept of democracy is
highly controversial and contested. By adopting a minimalist definition of democracy through the adoption of a procedural
approach, the contemporary research on governance and democratisation presents democracy as an unproblematic concept reduced
to an institutional arrangement to ensure a competitive struggle
between various political parties for votes. The victory of a multi-
party system over a one-party regime is presented as the sign of people's empowerment. This raises a number of significant questions. Is
liberal democracy really conducive to the empowerment of the
masses including the workers, peasants, marginals and the poor?
What is meant by liberal democracy and how easy is it to export
liberal democracy to the less economically developed world and
ensure that it brings about social justice, political equality, respect
for human rights and economic development? One of the best definitions of liberal democracy is provided by Schumpeter (1942:271)
who considers a country democratic if 'the most powerful and collective decision-makers are selected through fair, honest and periodic elections in which candidates freely compete for votes and in
which virtually all the adult population is eligible to vote'. It must
be realised that it took almost a century in Britain between 1832
and 1928 to develop its pluralistic democracy and the process
involved protracted struggles between subordinate groups and the
elites. The institutional arrangement which emerged from this
struggle represented a compromise between the radical demands of
the subordinate groups to have popular representation and the
demands of the landed classes and the industrial bourgeoisie to
ensure continuous exclusion of subordinate groups. The struggle,
which still continues, has been the basis of the dominant procedural
view of democracy. What this view evades is that democracy is not
a finished product but is a process of class formation, which still
continues in both more and less economically developed countries.
As long as the struggle for the control and distribution of resources
continues, the process of democratisation will also continue. The
nature of democracy achieved in any particular country will reflect
the nature of this struggle as well. Therefore attempts to export the
western type of procedural democracy to less economically developed
countries through aid and political conditionality are bound to be
of limited nature and are destined to be shaped by the specific class

configurations of the recipient countries. The existence of a multi-party system and regular elections may not always bring about collectively binding decisions. The representatives in the parliament may not be responsive to their electorate, or they may not be accountable to the people. Therefore what is needed is to go beyond the procedural view of democracy and consider the relationship between procedures and institutions with popular control and political equality. The success of democratic transition can be gauged against the extent to which democracy encompasses equality of citizenship, social justice, freedom of rights endorsed in a doctrine of law, and respect for freedom of expression, especially in the media.

The good governance parlance that sees democracy in terms of multi-party elections and political rights virtually leaves aside the questions of socio-economic rights and social justice. At the heart of the liberal democracy deified by the good governance discourse and mainstream literature on democratisation lies electoral competition and multi-party elections. On the other hand, 'democratic theory' is insistent that the concern with democracy and democratisation should move away from the minimalist approach that focuses on equality of rights to an approach that concentrates on the questions of power, equality and degrees of control that all human beings can exercise over their own lives (Allison 1994:10).

This is not to say that neo-liberal political theory is not aware of the socio-economic issues and social justice. People like Diamond, Linz and Lipset (1989), Huntington (1991), Dahl (1956, 1971), and O'Donnel, Schmitter and Whitehead (1986), who have developed the theory of democratic elitism, explain their concern with the procedural approach in terms of scientific objectivity. Dahl in particular insists that democratic theory should be concerned with the description of how a democratic system works rather than with the question of whether such a system is a desirable one. The 'how should it be?' question necessarily enters the realm of the normative, which takes us away from scientific objectivity. The contemporary literature on governance and democratisation seems to have followed the footsteps of early political theorists like Schumpeter, Weber, Lipset and Dahl in ignoring socio-economic criteria and active involvement of subordinate classes in the definition of democracy. People like Karl (1990), Diamond et al. (1989) and Hadenious (1992) maintain that what already exists should provide the basis for our definition of democracy, not what should exist. They claim that in no democracy in the world do we see active involvement of subordinate classes in politics. What characterises the contemporary democracies is 'apathy' on the part of the masses that elect the representatives and hope that the representatives will pursue their interest in Parliament. Masses have the opportunity not to re-elect the same representatives if they are not happy with them. This is how far it goes in democracies; even in practical terms it is impossible for the masses to participate in the decisions taken by governments.

Contemporary democratisation literature informed by the liberal theory tends to dissociate democracy from economic structures and strategies (Diamond, Linz and Lipset 1989). For them democracy is about an equal legal or formal right to vote and campaign to implement reforms, but cannot guarantee that socio-economic equality could be achieved as a result. The questions of social justice and welfare are not the intrinsic features of democracy. The liberal approach to democracy and democratisation treats democracy as a game of uncertainty in which everyone is aware of the rules of the game but not the outcome. By restricting political activity to the question of voting for the representative, democracy separates the political system from the economic system and implicitly accepts that democracy can generate an oligarchy based on the dominance of the rich over the poor (Przeworski 1991, 1992; Beetham 1992). Uneven distribution of wealth, money, resources and education enable the economically powerful to extend their economic power to the political arena through freedom of speech and associations, and influence decision-making for their own interests. When democratic competition takes place against an unequal background, then at least for some interest groups it cannot be a game of uncertainty. Economic inequalities serve to convert democracy into a tool for the maintenance of elite domination. An adherence to a more comprehensive interpretation of the political system, as opposed to the one that sees it confined to local and national government decision-making, will indicate that politics is present in socio-economic relations. Equality before law is only a minimal aspect of liberty. Without economic equality it is impossible to follow a desired course of action, as the material and cultural resources at one's disposal determine one's capacity. Economic liberalism that is supposed to bring about democracy through free and fair elections is far from meeting its promise. Increased competition envisaged by unconstrained market forces inevitably leads to inequalities and increased concentration of wealth and this in turn is likely to restrict the freedom of the poor and the marginal to compete in the political sphere as equals with the powerful and the rich. There are powerful contradictions between democracy and economic liberalism imposed on less economically developed countries by the IFIs. A positive link may be assumed between the reduction of the state and the rise of personal liberty, civil society and democracy, but when the reduction of the state becomes tantamount to the reduction of social welfare, spending on health, education and food subsidies, the conditions for social tension become ripe and in turn this endangers the chances democracy has to survive. Therefore socio-economic rights cannot be easily dismissed as an intrinsic part of democracy, otherwise democracy will be reduced to what the economically powerful elite wants and this would prevent the equitable distribution of resources expected from democratic politics by the poor. The fact that capitalism reduces the capacity of the poor to compete as equals in the political arena and consolidates the bargaining power of the rich *vis-à-vis* the state makes the relationship between democracy and capitalism an ambiguous one. The irony is that, by dismissing the economic democracy advocated by normative theory and promoting democracy and liberalism as one and the same thing, neo-liberalism as the dominant paradigm since the 1980s jeopardises the survival chances of democracy. Obviously the attempt to promote political liberties in less economically developed countries through electoral politics is valuable and necessary, but the disregard for socio-economic rights prevents the poor from exercising their political liberties to secure socio-economic reforms to empower them. The procedural or minimalist approach to democracy is far from achieving democracy's promise of political and judicial equality which may lead to a peaceful transfer of power. The minimalist approach to democracy tends to serve the entrenchment of the status quo by virtue of its tendency to enhance structural inequalities. Democracy for the majority of people can be meaningful only when it provides the necessary platforms to improve standards of living and reduce social tension. The minimalist approach that sees democracy as equal to electoral politics that needs to be accompanied by economic liberalisation and austerity measures is bound to fail to produce such results.

Huntington's (1991) competitive pluralism approach to democracy is only one form of the democratic idea and has no universal validity. In this perspective, democracy is not a form of collective existence but a mode of constituting and controlling public authority, not a way of life but a form of government (Parekh 1993:162).

While acting in the name of the people, elected assemblies actually substitute the will of the representatives for the will of the represented (Hirst 1994:34).

The process of democratisation involves a struggle between subordinate groups and the dominant landed and industrial elites. It is a compromise between radical demands for popular representation and upper class demands for the continued exclusion of subordinate groups. In other words, democratisation is an expression of the process of class formation. The struggle for democratisation is linked to the struggle over resources. This process is in no way a smooth process and can be accelerated or slowed down by a variety of factors, including the impacts of the conditionalities attached to aid-giving by the IFIs.

DEMOCRACY AND DEVELOPMENT

Having clarified that the minimalist approach to democracy is far from satisfactory as far as liberties and equalities are concerned, it is time to return to the second assumption of neo-liberalism: that democratisation and good governance will generate economic growth and development. In spite of long-term concerns over the relationship between democracy and development, the subject is still contestable. Even the concerted efforts of western governments, international organisations and neo-liberal theorists to push the idea that democracy is the best political system for economic development have not been sufficient to silence the opposite views. However, what their new tide of global democratic change discourse has done is to turn the old debate on the relationship between democracy and development on its head. In the controversy in the 1960s and 1970s, modernisation theorists and Marxists/neo-Marxists believed that democracy was an outcome of capitalist industrialisation. People like Lipset (1960), Apter (1965) and Eisenstadt (1966) gave primacy to economic development and saw democracy as a political system that emerged with industrial capitalism. They believed that liberal democratic politics was nurtured by the socio-economic transformations such as structural differentiation, rationalisation, bureaucratisation, individualism, urbanisation and secularism engendered by industrial capitalism. Similarly, Marxist and neo-Marxist tradition, while not directly concentrating on the question of democracy, saw liberal democracy as a limited form of democracy which could only emerge with industrial capitalism.

The downfall of the state socialist systems in eastern Europe seems to have strengthened the widely held belief that capitalism and democracy are identical or at least almost inseparable. At the root of this argument is the contention that the free market constitutes the material base for democracy, and democracy in turn is the political form of capitalism. Although on first impression there seems to be a frequent association between capitalist development and democracy, nevertheless, history witnesses the development of capitalism under non-democratic authoritarian regimes, such as South Korea, Taiwan, Brazil, Chile and Nazi Germany (Rueschemeyer *et al.* 1992:1–2).

There are three possible conclusions regarding the relationship between democracy and development: either the two are friends, enemies or strangers. The conflict models assert that if both objectives are simultaneously pursued they will weaken the chances for success in both spheres. Lipset, among others, claims that countries must reach a certain level of socio-economic development prior to democratisation, as poor nations cannot afford democracy because open political contests are too diverse. In the 1970s, the conflict perspective argued that the very nature of democracy would hinder the economic and social development of a state, while a more authoritarian state would be better able to promote such goals. On first impressions, the experiences of the East Asian NICs between the mid 1960s and late 1980s underpins the conflict model, weighing the argument that authoritarian regimes have more space to implement radical reforms. The South Korean case is clearly another example, where Park and his successor Chun kept labour power subservient to the state by banning unions. Rapid economic development took place under a repressive government. Taking into consideration the experiences of the bureaucratic authoritarian regime in Brazil since 1964, the East Asian NICs and South Korea, the conflict perspective suggested that a less economically developed country could not have democracy and development at the same time and thus faced the cruel dilemma of choosing between democracy and development (Bhagwati 1995:50). As Sirowy and Inkeles (1990:128) point out, in the 1970s democracy was perceived to be a luxury that less economically developed countries could ill afford.

At the other end of the spectrum, compatibility models claim that democracy is a seed that can grow in any soil and poor nations cannot afford not to have democracy (Beetham and Boyle 1995:125; Diamond 1993:61). In this perspective, democracy is conducive to economic and social development and actually promotes it. Democracy and development are, it is argued, inherently linked and are complementary ideals, whereas authoritarianism only hinders the progress of development by corruption and personalised government. This is the general consensus of western governments, manifest in the content of aid conditionality. The compatibility perspective has taken precedence since the early 1980s with the emergence of a new orthodoxy by much of the West, heads of state and international agencies. In British and US official documents it is clearly stated that plural democracy and good governance are conditions for economic aid. It is also reiterated that only within a democratic environment will a state be able to achieve equitable and sustainable development. This coercion toward Hegelian teleological ends, as advocated in Fukuyama's work *The End of History* (1992) is frankly disturbing, given that the empirical evidence does not indicate a positive correlation between democracy and development.

Regarding the third position that sees no direct relationship between capitalism (or development) and democracy, I will concentrate on two very important works on the issue, Rueschemeyer *et al.* (1992) and Leftwich (2000). Rueschemeyer *et al.* (1992) take issue with the view that capitalism or the free market economy provides the best conditions for the rise and development of democracy. For them, democracy is a question of power and power relations among classes and class coalitions. The emergence, stability and maintenance of democracy are determined by class relations, and by 'the structure, strength and autonomy of the state'. Three vital factors have a strong influence on the process of democratisation that can be defined as a process of increasing political equality: 1. the balance of power between classes and class coalitions; 2. the nature of the state and its interrelations with civil society, and 3. 'The impact of transnational power relations on both the balance of power and on state-society relations' (Rueschemeyer *et al.* 1992:5).

The rise and persistence of democracy cannot be explained by the simple correlation of the occurrences of the two. The overall structural correspondence of the capitalism and democracy thesis is refuted by the meticulous analysis of Rueschemeyer *et al.* (1992). Basing their arguments on studies of advanced capitalist countries in Latin America, Central America and the Caribbean, they arrive at a conclusion which does not support the claim that there is an overall structural correspondence of capitalism and democracy which mutually reinforce each other. Their conclusion also represents a challenge to the contention, shared by classic liberal and Marxist-Leninist theories, that the bourgeoisie is the main agent of democracy. Rueschemeyer *et al.* (1992) maintain that it is the contradictions of capitalism that provide the basis for the emergence and development of democracy, not the capitalist market or capitalists. It is the class transformations brought about by capitalism which provide the most suitable conditions for the struggle for political equality. The weakening of the landed upper class and the strengthening of the working and middle classes simply trigger the process of democratisation.

Looking at the behavioural patterns of various classes historically, Rueschemeyer *et al.* argue that the 'working class was the most consistently pro-democratic force' (Rueschemeyer *et al.* 1992:8). Compared with the rural subordinate classes, the working class 'was more insulted from the hegemony of dominant classes' and better equipped to demand more political inclusion. On the other hand, the landed upper classes saw democratisation as a threat to their control over the cheap labour supply. Similarly, the bourgeoisie saw the political inclusion of the lower classes as a threat to its class interest, while on the whole it supported constitutional and democratic government. The extent to which both the bourgeoisie and the landed classes support democracy is determined by the extent of their perceived threat from popular pressures. They would not hesitate to oppose or even undermine democracy if the threat were seen to be strong. Rueschemeyer *et al.* (1992) found that the middle classes supported democracy and democratisation when it suited their interests. They tended to give full support for democracy under the conditions where they formed alliances with a sizeable and powerful working class against intransigent dominant classes, and withdrew their support for democracy when they felt threatened by popular pressures under democracy and lent support to authoritarian regimes.

In addition to the balance of power between classes, the relative strength of the state and civil society could be a determining factor in the process of democratisation. Rueschemeyer *et al.* define civil society as 'the totality of social institutions and associations, both formal and informal, that are not strictly production related or governmental or familial in character' (Rueschemeyer *et al.* 1992:6). Where the state is relatively autonomous and strong relative to civil society, as has been the case in Latin America, then democratic development could be slowed down or stunted. They also high-lighted the fact that economic dependence has a negative impact on the process of democratisation, as in Latin America and the Caribbean. The transnational structures of power shape the class structures in dependent countries, which either reinforces the position of large landowners in agro-export economies or keeps the working class small and weak in an industrial sector that depends on imported technology. Furthermore, the support given to oppressive regimes and direct intervention in the domestic affairs of less economically developed countries by dominant powers in the global economy enhances the state's power relative to civil society.

Lastly, Rueschemeyer *et al.* emphasise the role of strong political parties in both the installation and consolidation of democracy. While strong political parties are necessary for the emergence of democracy, the very existence of these parties also brings about strong reactions from dominant classes to curtail the threat to their interests from subordinate classes. Consolidated democratic systems are entrenched when there are two or more powerful political parties and when at least one of them allows the dominant classes to have direct access to the state (Rueschemeyer *et al.* 1992:9).

Three clusters of power play a vital role in the development or demise of democracy in the process of capitalist development. The class power, state power and transnational structures of power interact in varying ways and in varying sequences to determine political developments (Rueschemeyer *et al.* 1992:269). The existence of a powerful organised working class is a key factor in the growth of full democracy almost everywhere. In agreeing with Barrington Moore, Rueschemeyer *et al.* see large landlords as a hindrance to the establishment of democracy, as the landlords strive hard to influence the state to maintain cheap labour through the subordination of the peasantry. They also illustrate that the bourgeoisie and their political parties rarely attempt to introduce full democracy. Depending on circumstances the bourgeoisie would form alliances with other classes and strive for the introduction of a parliamentary system, the development of a civil society and the inclusion of the middle classes. However, the bourgeoisie's support for full democracy is often circumscribed by the growth of a strong working class. They give the examples of Germany, Sweden and Denmark, where the bourgeoisie supported early liberal reforms but strongly opposed a full parliamentary government when there was the possibility that socialists could gain entrance to Parliament (Rueschemeyer *et al.*

1992:270). The posture of the middle class is also very significant in the process of democratisation in any given country. The middle classes' role in democratisation has been ambiguous due to its heterogeneity and its shifting alliances with other classes. It is possible to see the middle classes supporting non-democratic projects aimed at establishing the hegemony of the dominant classes. It is also possible to find the middle classes siding with the working classes for more democratic and civil rights.

The development of capitalism undermines the power of landlords and strengthens the working class. With capitalism, agriculture becomes commercialised, rural–urban migration speeds up, urbanisation expands and factories provide industrial work for the working class. Subordinate classes that end up in cities come in close contact with each other and establish organisations to defend their interests. Technological transformations brought about by capitalism enable better nation-wide transportation and communications, which speed up the development of civil society. 'Capitalism creates democratic pressures in spite of capitalists not because of them' (Rueschemeyer et al. 1992:271).

Although capitalist development and democracy are linked to each other through changes in the balance of class power, Rueschemeyer et al. (1992) argue that the level of democratic development cannot simply be inferred from the level of capitalist development. 'The interrelations between dominant classes and the state' are also very significant in the establishment and consolidation of democracy. Furthermore the timing and nature of the country's integration into the world economy have significant repercussions for democracy as they affect 'the structure of the economy and the class structure' (Rueschemeyer et al. 1992:272).

Class alliances are shaped to a significant extent by the interactions between social classes, the state and transnational structures. Once the state is able to establish a monopoly on organised force, there will be constant attempts by dominant classes to penetrate the state and use its consolidated power to repress demands from subordinate classes. The extent to which the coercive state apparatus can be used as an anti-democratic force would depend on a large number of factors, including the relative strength of the classes, the extent of divisions within the dominant classes and the nature of the external influences (Rueschemeyer et al. 1992:255–256). In Latin America, the relatively autonomous state used coercion or direct military intervention to restrict contesting among elites and/or between elites and wider groups, stifled the organisational potential of the subordinate classes and/or excluded the already organised subordinate classes.

The chances of democracy are also affected by transnational power relations such as 'war, the structural effect of economic dependence, and economically and geo-politically conditioned intervention of foreign powers' (Rueschemeyer *et al.* 1992:277). The aid given by dominant countries in pursuance of their economic and geopolitical interests helps the state apparatus to assume a high degree of autonomy. Notably, the possibility of socialism or leftist regimes in less economically developed countries was seen as a threat by dominant countries who supported anti-leftist, authoritarian and military regimes in less economically developed countries, who in turn suppressed organisations of the subordinate classes.

It could be concluded from the foregoing that the work of Rueschemeyer *et al.* (1992) clearly shows that the relationship between development and democracy is very complicated and requires a careful analysis rather than simply looking at the correlation of the occurrences of the two. A similarly careful analysis is provided by Adrian Leftwich (2000), who takes a sceptical position on the relationship between development and democracy and argues that it is the character, aims and ability of the state that make a difference in economic development, not the regime type itself. To justify his position, Leftwich clearly shows that between 1965 and 1990 high growth rates in terms of GNP per capita could be observed under both democratic (Singapore 6.5 per cent, Botswana 8.4 per cent and Mauritius 3.2 per cent) and non-democratic (South Korea 7.1 per cent, Taiwan 7 per cent, China 5.8 per cent) regimes. Furthermore, negative growth was experienced under both democratic and non-democratic regimes, notably Jamaica −1.3 per cent, Venezuela −1 per cent, and Senegal −0.6 per cent among democratic regimes, and Zaire −2.2 per cent, Zambia −1.9 per cent, Libya −3.0 per cent and Nigeria −0.1 per cent among non-democratic regimes. Logically, the evidence undermines the credibility of both schools of thought as it suggests that there is no relationship between economic development and regime type (Leftwich 1993:614).

Leftwich asks two significant questions about the relationship between democracy, good governance and economic development (Leftwich 2000:108). First, whether or not democratic politics is a necessary or sufficient condition for good governance. Second, even if the answer to the first question is a positive one, whether or not the existing conditions in less economically developed countries are sufficient to consolidate and sustain democracy and thus 'to protect and promote the practices of good governance' (Leftwich 2000:108). He argues that unless the state is developmental, economic development will not take place. He defines the developmental state as:

> a transitional form of modern state which has emerged in late developing societies, from the nineteenth century to the present. It is a state whose political bureaucratic elites have generally achieved relative autonomy from socio-political forces in the society and have used this in order to promote a programme of rapid economic growth with more or less rigour and ruthlessness. (Leftwich 2000:167)

Developmental states can be democratic or non-democratic. For both democracy and development to take place in less economically developed countries, the state has to be democratic and developmental at the same time. By looking at the experiences of a number of developmental states in the less economically developed world, Leftwich clearly demonstrates that there is no direct relationship between good governance and an effective public capacity for promoting and managing development. Likewise, democratic politics is neither a necessary nor a sufficient condition for development defined in terms of economic growth. To present good governance as a part of a wider conception of democratic governance does not make a positive contribution to our understanding of development problems but has been instrumental in creating a conceptual confusion. Despite no clear relationship between democracy, development and good governance, western governments and aid institutions have been insistent on good governance and democracy as preconditions for loans. At the heart of good governance lies institution building and capacity building. Yet the West does not recognise the fact that in less economically developed countries the nature of the politics is vital for instituting and sustaining good governance. Without taking politics into consideration, changes introduced in institutions may not yield the expected results. Without fundamental changes in the structure of the state, well-established corruption or crony-ism will not simply disappear through the introduction of a particular form of democracy (Leftwich 2000:124).

One of the reasons behind the insistence of the West on political conditionality has to be sought in their belief that incompetent and corrupt governments in less economically developed countries were responsible for proper implementation of the SAPs which were supposedly to bring economic growth and prosperity. No doubt one can challenge this contention by pointing out that complete implementation of the SAPs necessitated strong states by virtue of the fact that strict adherence to SAPs generates social tension. Devaluations, drastic public-expenditure cuts, strict wage policies and reductions in subsidies all had a devastating impact on the poor in a number of less economically developed countries including Egypt, Ghana, Peru, Turkey and Zambia. To keep disenchanted masses under control, most of these countries used military force. Therefore it is ironic that western governments and aid agencies since 1990 are pushing for the reduction of the state. This irony stems from the West's technocratic approach to development, which seeks solutions through managerial and administrative changes without considering the nature of the state or the politics of development (Leftwich 2000:109–112).

The fact that neo-liberalism operates with limited definitions of democracy and development is at the heart of the problem. It equates democracy with elections, civil liberties and the right to organise, and development with economic growth. As such, it is impossible to categorically claim that democracy necessarily impedes or promotes development, as the examples above clearly show that it can be accompanied by positive and negative economic growth. For this reason, there is a need to move beyond futile discussions based on the procedural definition of democracy and to consider how democracy can be an effective mechanism to increase the material well-being in society. This in turn will require looking at how democratic the strategies are that are used to promote economic growth. To what extent do existing development policies allow people 'to participate in decisions about and effectively exercise political power over their economic lives?' (MacEwan 1999:2). Instead of limiting the argument to 'liberal democracy' and 'economic growth' there is a need to concentrate on policies that deliver the benefits of development to the population generally, thereby enhancing their power. MacEwan (1999) calls this a democratic strategy which is capable of increasing economic growth and improving the basic standard of living of the great majority of people by ensuring equitable distribution of income, preserving and repairing the physical environment, maintaining and strengthening social community, and promoting broad participation in decision-making about political, social and economic affairs. This democratic strategy is fundamentally different to the SAPs imposed on less economically developed countries in that it prioritises democratisation of economic affairs with the belief that once they are organised democratically, democracy and development can be achieved together. On the other hand, the SAPs imposed on less economically developed countries in conjunction with the Washington Consensus are far from achieving either development or democracy. They simply prevent the implementation of democratic development programmes by leaving things to the market at the expense of the social regulation of private economic activity. This prevents people from exercising political control over their own economic affairs and solving their own economic problems. For instance, neo-liberalism would not allow the state to implement policies to help small-scale food producers through subsidies and import controls, as this would be considered a direct interference with the market. Likewise, neo-liberalism would not allow workers to have powerful unions to follow strategies for better wages, health and safety conditions in the workplace. With its emphasis on the reduction of the state, neo-liberalism would not allow the state to create employment in the public sector, to invest in education, health, environmental protection or to give priority to equitable income distribution programmes (MacEwan 1999:148–155).

By following neo-liberal policies, the great majority of governments in less economically developed countries simply avoid the implementation of programmes that would meet the basic material needs of the majority. Neo-liberal policies not only serve the interests of powerful elites but also create economic hardships for the masses and political instability for governments. The fact that neo-liberal hardship programmes cannot be implemented without a repressive state makes a mockery of the idea of the minimal state and democracy as an accompaniment of economic growth strategies. Democracy and development are treated in isolation from each other. In neo-liberalism, democracy is confined to the sphere of politics and limited to procedural democracy. On the other hand, economic development is equated with economic growth with no consideration of the nature of this growth. Whether or not the organisation of material life is 'democratic' is not an issue in this view. But there is the expectation that democracy will be an outcome of economic development. The separation of democracy and development by neo-liberalism is deliberate in that only in this way is it possible to avoid giving priority to meeting the basic needs and environmental protection. Political participation and popular control of social processes are not on the agenda, as they would have strong implications on the way economic change is organised. The ways SAPs are implemented are undemocratic, as the decisions are controlled by the Bretton Woods institutions, which act on behalf of advanced capitalist societies. Therefore it is difficult to see how democracy will emerge from such an undemocratic process which does not allow political participation of the masses. It is not sufficient to assume that the existence of a multi-party system, universal suffrage and elections will ensure democracy and popular participation. As long as huge income gaps exist in societies, economically powerful groups will always dominate political affairs. As in India and Turkey, local politics and local institutions can be dominated by local elites, who in turn will use them for political patronage, which will be in contradiction with the spirit of democracy.

The drastic refashioning of the state in less economically developed countries by international pressures virtually kills the developmental nature of the state. In its new form, the state is virtually reduced to a night watch guard rather than being an active force in economic development. The enforced reforms – which reduce the size of bureaucracy and transform its position in the state, curtail the regulatory role of the state over the economy, liberalise finances and international trade, privatise state enterprises, and reduce social services – undermine the power and autonomy of the state. The state can no longer maintain its relative autonomy and follow nationalistic policies. Furthermore, the externally driven macro-economic policies in trade and tariffs, exchange rates, fiscal and financial management are not conducive to national capital accumulation. Taken together with externally imposed austerity measures on social welfare spending, macro-economic policies are far from ensuring economic growth, equity and social welfare which cannot be traded off with, but are mutually reinforcing with economic development. The fact that externally directed macro-economic policies are not receptive to local needs and priorities means their influence on democracy is a negative one. The promotion of both abstract democratic rights and procedural democracy, that do not provide a platform for people to influence economic decisions that affect their lives directly, are far from the principles of democracy. The restructuring of the economy under external influences has led to unmanageable debt problems in less economically developed countries. In countries like Turkey, the debt service payments far exceed state revenue and fresh loans are needed to run the economy. The inability of the state to meet the demands of the masses for better standards of living endangers the prospects for democracy.

The type of democracy advocated by international agencies and business classes in less economically developed countries leads to an increase in the autonomy of capital in relation to the political elite as well as the society as a whole (Robinson 1996). This happens because economic liberalisation reforms reduce state control over the behaviour of firms and industrial enterprises. As the companies become more and more independent, their demands for further economic reforms to liberalise the market also increase. Liberalisation further enhances the autonomous capacity of enterprises and the autonomy of capital in relation to the dominant political elite. Economic liberalisation leads to diffusion of power within the state and changes the nature of the state from a developmental one to a regulatory one.

When this happens in a state, the language of bureaucratic authoritarianism becomes less relevant while the language of democracy lends itself to the shift from coercive to regulatory state. The declining power of centralised state agencies allows an increased amount of plurality within the state, allowing the formerly excluded capitalist elite to exercise an increasing amount of political influence. This can be seen in a shift of governance from exclusionary to inclusionary corporatist policies. Under these conditions, democratisation can be seen as reflecting a conflict within the state where societal actors are co-opted in the pursuit of the objectives of some actors (Jayasuriya 1999:125). It seems that the deified democratisation is not about the broadening of state–society linkages but rather about the diffusion of power within the state. The expansion of electoral politics has enabled businesses to invest in politics by financing individual candidates or, in certain cases, running for election. Liberalisation in East Asia concerns the political management of elite differences rather than the assertion of autonomous interests in civil society. The predominant role of state power in economic development has meant that major political cleavages are not between labour and capital but between the dominant political elite and capital. Political restructuring can allow groups of businesses to come under increased public scrutiny, allowing public officials greater leverage to discipline errant companies. Democratisation allows public officials to set state autonomy in the safer and more secure area of electoral legitimacy as well as in new coalitions that include significant sections of the new middle class.

THE PREDOMINANCE OF THE STATE

One conclusion to be drawn from the foregoing analysis is the crucial role of the state in understanding the processes of development and democracy. Both Rueschemeyer *et al.* (1992) and Leftwich (1993, 1996, 2000) agree how crucial the role of the state is in the nature of development in any given society. The nature and level of economic growth and the level of social development, reflected in human and social indicators such as life expectancy, literacy and child health, are strongly determined by politics and the nature of the state. Economic and social development emerge from the ways in which resources are used, organised, mobilised and distributed. The fact that societies are not homogeneous and that the use of resources reflects the diversity of interests, values and ideas, means conflicts, disagreements and antagonisms are bound to emerge among the holders of varying interests. Winners and losers will emerge from many configurations of the use of capital, land and human resources. The processes of conflict, co-operation and negotiations in the mobilisation of resources belong to the domain of politics. Development is an outcome of both economic and political struggles. The ways in which resources are used determine the levels of economic, social and human development. The state plays a crucial role in the way resources are mobilised and used in production and distribution. Without the state's managerial and co-ordinating functions there would be chaos, as many economic agents would want to steer development towards their own interests. The state, as the only capable agent on a national level, acts as a 'co-ordinating intelligence' and guides the direction of development (Weiss and Hobson 1995:2). The state can use its power and authority in a variety of ways. It can either completely own and control its economies, as is the case with Soviet type states; or it can use its power, authority and capacity to manage or govern the market, as with developmental states; or it can use its power to promote cronyism, clientelism, corruption and incompetence, as is the case with non-developmental states such as Haiti under the Duvaliers or the Philippines under President Marcos (Leftwich 2000:7–8).

One of the common contentions of the growing literature on the state in the less economically developed world since the 1980s is that such countries are not comparable to western states as far as their institutions and their role in social and economic transformation are concerned. The works of people like Evans, Rueschemeyer and Skocpol (1985), Kohli (1991), Sandbrook (1992) and Evans (1995) agree on one thing: that the enormous variations of states in the less economically developed world did have serious implications for the course of their development. Therefore concepts borrowed from the analysis of western capitalism cannot be sufficient to provide an adequate explanation of the state in less economically developed countries. What is needed is an understanding of the social forces that shape the state and are shaped by it. This in turn will give high premium to more detailed empirical analysis, while not completely ignoring the relevance of the theory.

Although capitalism has been taking roots in less economically developed countries for some time, the nature of capitalism is different to western capitalism. What may be called dependent capitalism in the less economically developed world has been an outcome of a complicated process of integration of these countries into the world economy in which both external influences in the form of colonialism and neo-colonialism and internal class formations have been vital. The nature and the role of the state in the process of development in the less economically developed world are reflective of both the way they have been integrated into the world economy and the internal class struggle. Consequently, the theories of the state developed to analyse capitalist states in the West may not be suitable for the analysis of the state and its role in the process of development in the less economically developed world.

Although Marx and Weber's theories of the state may not be applied wholesale to the less economically developed world, at least some elements of them have been used to construct theories of the state for the analysis of less economically developed countries. Two main conceptions of the state can be identified in the writings of Marx. In both the *Communist Manifesto* (Marx and Engels

1888/1958c) and the *Preface to a Contribution to the Critique of Political Economy* (Marx 1859/1958b) Marx portrays the state and its institutions as the committee of the bourgeoisie in capitalist society. In this instrumentalist view of the state, the dominant class in capitalist society uses the coercive institutions of the state against the subordinate classes, especially the proletariat, to enhance its own class interest. The conceptualisation of the state as the agent of the bourgeoisie may be true of advanced capitalist societies, but runs into difficulties when it is applied wholesale to oppressive states in less economically developed countries where dominant classes may not be characterised as the bourgeoisie.

The *Eighteenth Brumaire of Louis Bonaparte* (Marx 1852/1958a) presents the state as having a relative autonomy from the narrow interests of the bourgeoisie. However, although the state bureaucracy does have a relative autonomy *vis-à-vis* the bourgeoisie, its actions within the state are constrained by the imperatives of capitalism. This view of the state has found a large number of supporters among the contemporary Marxists, such as Nicos Poulantzas (1973), who have attempted to move away from a simplistic and vulgarised conception of the state. In this conception, the state is seen as acting to smooth away the conflicts and contradictions of capitalism and ensure socio-economic cohesion. Leftwich's (2000:75) observation that Marx's second conception 'is essentially a conception of a modernising state, one which is active, pervasive and disciplining in the promotion of capitalist development' seems to be quite pertinent to the understanding of some of the developmental states in the less economically developed world. Marx saw the modern state as part and parcel of capitalist development. The lack of, or limited development of, industrialisation and modern capitalism in the less economically developed world led some analysts to analyse the nature of the state by taking their historical specificity into consideration.

What exists in most less economically developed countries may be characterised as dependent and distorted capitalism, which lacks the basic features of either what Marx calls a capitalist state or what Weber describes as modern or rational state. Despite the fact that most states in the less economically developed world saw development as the main goal, only a very few managed to industrialise in the post-war period. One explanation finds the nature of the state in these societies to be responsible for this state of affairs. The theory of the post-colonial state or over-developed state developed by John Saul (1974) and Hamza Alavi (1972) looked at the legacy of colonialism in institutional and power structures in less economically developed countries. In their views, the post-colonial states found in less economically developed countries did not emerge as the result of the internal dynamism and class configurations of these societies. Their origins lay not in the indigenous societies but in the metropolitan societies to which they were subordinated during colonial times. The post-colonial state was a product of the colonial state, which reflected the interests of the metropolitan power. Therefore it is not pertinent to attempt to apply classical Marxist theory of the state to these societies. The post-colonial state to a large extent exists to extend and facilitate the interest of the metropolitan commercial interest. The classes that control the state have not emerged from the internal politics or internal struggles over the indigenous economic resources. Most institutions and procedures in place in post-colonial societies have been imposed by the metropolitan interests and are not reflective of economic imperatives of the indigenous society. In fact they are the continuation of the structures that were set up during colonial times. As the institutions and the rules and regulations reflected the prerogatives of the metropolitan power, they had no political and economic base in the colonial society. As such, the state and the superstructure are over-developed as they represent the prerogatives of the metropolitan power. The over-developed state structures, which were inherited at independence, were controlled by a bureaucratic-military apparatus which organised production, distribution and commerce on behalf of the metropolitan power at the expense of indigenous classes. Independence saw the strengthening of the power of the over-developed military-bureaucratic state which neither represented the interest of a single class nor was autonomous. It mediated between the interests of the metropolitan bourgeoisie, indigenous bourgeoisie and the landed class. For instance, in Pakistan, Alavi argued, after independence the state did not act as an agent of capitalist transformation and development but as the guarantor of a certain political structure and economic context within which the conflicting interests of the dominant classes would be reconciled. Through the control of a large number of public agencies, parastatal authorities and politics, the state in Pakistan regularly intervened in the democratic processes to prevent any policy that would threaten the main interests of these three groups. This relatively autonomous state in post-colonial societies such as India and countries in Africa differed significantly from both the conceptions of the state developed by Marx and Weber, as it neither represented a single class interest nor displayed features of modern or patrimonial states. For both Alavi and Saul, the lack of capitalist development in post-colonial societies needs to be situated in the organisational, bureaucratic and military legacy of colonialism. It is this legacy that has shaped the political forces that came to control the state in postcolonial societies. Despite intermittent appearances of democracy, the military and bureaucracy dominate the local politics in a relatively autonomous fashion to mediate between the interests of a substantial land-owning class, a small but powerful bourgeoisie and the metropolitan bourgeoisie. A national development project is not on the agenda, as the pursuance of these contradictory interests would not allow a coherent programme.

A bureaucratic state apparatus becomes relatively autonomous in places where high civil and military office holders neither emerge from the ranks of the dominant landed, commercial or industrial classes nor forge close relations with them immediately after coming to power (Trimberger 1978). Leftwich argues that this is the key to the success of developmental states in bringing about economic growth within a short period. By referring to Johnson's work (1981, 1982, 1995, 1999) on developmental states in Japan and East Asia, he distinguishes developmental states from the Soviet-type command economies and liberal democratic and social democratic states. The state in developmental economies has close connections with the private sector and operates within the market. While the state is heavily involved in planning and in directing the activities of the private sector, it is far from simply either just regulating the economy or using the resources for the enhancement of the state enterprises. The developmental state in Japan, for instance, has been setting substantive social and economic goals for the private sector without completely overtaking them. The power, continuity and autonomy of their elite bureaucracy also distinguish developmental states from other states. By drawing on a large number of case studies and making use of the work of people like Burmeister (1986), Castells (1992), Wade (1990), Woo-Cumings (1999a, 1999b) and Pempel (1999), Leftwich (2000) maintains in all developmental states, state bureaucracies have used the ideology of nationalism to mobilise the masses behind efforts to become both militarily powerful in order to be able to withstand any external threat, and economically strong in order to close the gap with the West. The major components of Leftwich's model of developmental states, developed from a study of diverse concrete forms, include:

> a determined developmental elite; relative autonomy of the developmental state; a powerful, competent and insulated economic bureaucracy; a weak and subordinated civil society; the capacity of effective management of private economic interests; and an uneasy mix of repression, poor human rights, legitimacy and performance. (Leftwich 2000:160)

It seems that some features of both the post-colonial state and the developmental state fit into the history of the state in Turkey, particularly in the 1930–60 period.

THE TURKISH STATE

Although some features of the post-colonial state or over-developed state may be useful in the characterisation of the Turkish State between 1923 and 1950, it cannot be applied wholesale. For instance, the military bureaucratic authority that ruled the new Republic since its inception in 1923 was at pains to state that its role was to ensure that no class would override the interest of others. This was done at a rhetorical level through the denial of class conflict. Throughout the 1920s and 1930s Kemal Atatürk, the founder of the Republic, reiterated over and over again in his speeches that the Turkish society was not characterised by social classes with different interests, but by a division of labour among the members of different profession groups, therefore indicating that the state was above socio-economic classes (Kuruç 1963:15; Tezel 1994:144). However, most analysts are of the opinion that this relatively autonomous state was guided by a nationalistic development strategy which saw western style industrialisation and modernisation as the ideal type to be imitated. Yet there was the realisation that there was no indigenous bourgeoisie to play the leading role in such a modernisation project. Following the downfall of the Ottoman state and its replacement with the Republic, the civilianised military bureaucracy who controlled the new state simply eliminated the comprador commercial bourgeoisie of Christian and Jewish origin (Keyder 1987; Tezel 1994). The Kemalist revolution that followed the war of independence was also a cultural revolution which intended to get rid of the Christian influences. The fact that the non-Muslim commercial bourgeoisie's close ties with the West during the last 60 years of the Ottoman Empire had given them clear advantages, had generated strong resentment among Muslim merchants. Thus the Republic's determination to get rid of the collaborators of the West, particularly the merchants of Greek origin who had welcomed the Greek invasion of Anatolia in the wake of the First World War, was very much welcomed by the indigenous merchants who had felt discriminated against by the Ottoman state, which had granted free trade privileges to the West and their local agencies.

Unlike the post-colonial states in Africa and over-developed state in Asia, the state in Turkey between 1923 and 1950 had a clear nationalistic development strategy that favoured the promotion of a Turkish bourgeoisie. However, the civilianised military bureaucracy in this period needed to appear autonomous of class interests in order not to lose the support of powerful landlords and religious and tribal leaders who played a vital role in mobilising support for the independence movement headed by Atatürk. In its reconciliatory role, the military bureaucratic state provided the necessary conditions for the commercial bourgeoisie to enrich itself. In turn, the commercial bourgeoisie did not challenge the authoritarian nature of the bureaucratic state for at least three decades following the establishment of the Republic. The political class in Turkey between 1923 and 1950 resembled the militaristic bureaucratic class of the over-developed state as far as authoritarian rule was concerned, but differed from it in the fact that the political class in Turkey did have a clear nationalistic development project which aimed to create an indigenous bourgeoisie to lead the development of a western style capitalism in the future. During the period in which the bourgeoisie was maturing, the state took a leading role in promoting capitalist development in the vanguard of the civilianised bureaucracy. For capitalist development there needs to be not only a capitalist class with the ability and interest to invest and transform the productive basis, but also legal and institutional structures in place to provide the conditions for capital accumulation. Capital accumulation and the transformation of the productive forces that are necessary for the development of capitalism may take a long time. Transformations of the legal, cultural and organisational structures necessary for the development of capitalism would take even longer if they were left to evolve naturally. The civilianised military bureaucracy simply speeded up legal, cultural and organisational transformations to allow a faster development of capitalism. Within a short period of time, a large number of substantial reforms were passed under the authoritarian rule of the Kemalist civilianised bureaucracy. Any opposition to the reforms, which ranged from the abolition of Islamic rule, replacement of the Arabic scripts with the Latin alphabet, introduction of a civil and penal code derived from European codes and introduction of a dress code, was punished severely. The legal and institutional framework put into operation within a short period of time generated a discrepancy between the economic base of society and the superstructure. This feature of the Turkish bureaucratic state is quite reminiscent of the over-developed state conceptualised by Hamza Alavi in the context of Pakistan, but with a significant difference. The Republican state emerged as a result of a national struggle against both the decadent and crumbling Ottoman state and the occupying allied forces; thus it was not under any obligation to serve the interest of a colonial bourgeoisie, as in the case of Pakistan and the post-colonial states in Africa. Although between 1923 and 1929, due to the expulsion of the Christian bourgeoisie, foreign capital in the Turkish economy became more and more involved in export-oriented commercial agriculture and industry, this resulted in a serious crisis in parallel with the Great Depression (Keyder 1987:93). Therefore state bureaucracy decided to put into operation its nationalistic economic policies named *étatism*.

In order to pursue its nationalistic development strategy and create an indigenous bourgeoisie, the bureaucracy had to operate autonomously of social classes in the short term. Here again there seems to be a resemblance to the post-colonial state, in the sense that the state would not allow class politics to take root, at least in the first few decades of the Republic. Any movement that was considered to be divisionist or conceived to be a potential threat to the secular basis of the state would attract the wrath of the state. For instance, many religious sects were banned and their members were persecuted; likewise a number of ethnically based Kurdish rebellions were harshly suppressed in the early decades of the Republic.

The attempts of the civilianised military bureaucracy to follow a modernisation project to promote capitalism and industrialism and to eliminate any obstacles in the way, through harsh authoritarian measures, have led some Turkish social scientists to characterise the state in terms of a strong state tradition running through from Ottoman times to contemporary times (Heper 1985, 1992). The economic and political crises that have regularly hit the country since the middle of the 1950s, and particularly the 2001–02 crisis which had been augmenting since 1994, have all been attributed to the ever present dirigiste state (Akat 1994; Heper 1985, 1992; Rodrik 1991b). The fact that the global preponderance of the New Right thinking has led to strong demands for a moving away from state interference in the economy towards an understanding of the state that leaves almost everything to the self-regulatory market, has made the proponents of this approach in Turkey quite vociferous since the 1980s.

This disenchantment with the state since 1980 is founded upon the belief that the main characteristic of the Ottoman state, the centre–periphery dichotomy still prevails and retards the development of fully fledged capitalism and a civil society. The concepts of centre and periphery were developed by Şerif Mardin (1973) to highlight the main nature of the state in the Ottoman Empire, the predecessor of the modern Turkish Republic. Mardin used the centre–periphery dichotomy to suggest that the main lines of social cleavage in the Ottoman Empire were between the state bureaucracy and the people, not between social classes. The Ottoman state was qualitatively different from the feudal state in the West and the Islamic state, in that the state bureaucracy was mainly concerned with the maintenance of the existing hierarchy in order to ensure social peace and order. As such, the Ottoman state was unique in its lack of interest in taking a main role in the regulation of the economy. The bureaucracy was mainly interested in perpetuating its status and political interest.

The essence of centre–periphery explanation resurfaces on a regular basis in the analysis of the relationship between the state and economy in the history of the Turkish Republic. The irony is that in its original use the 'state tradition' approach emphasises the non-involvement of state bureaucracy in the national economy, keeping itself away from mercantile and productive activities (Mardin 1980, 1990; Islamoğlu-Inan 1994). Yet some analysts of various periods in the economic history of Turkey see state involvement in economic affairs as an attempt by the bureaucratic elite to protect and enhance their own interests (Ahmad 1981; Barkey 1990; Heper 1977; Keyder 1987; Saybaşılı 1992). Keyder in particular elevates the bureaucracy to the state of a class who attempts to transform the existing socio-economic system in order to maintain its privileged position. Most particularly, the *étatist* period (1930–39) has been the subject of a controversy between the proponents of state tradition and their critics, such as Boratav, who see the period as one in which interest groups gradually started to make their way in to control the state. Boratav (1993) among others maintains that the world economic crisis in the 1930s provided not only an opportunity for the state to weaken its link with the centre, but also allowed the nascent bourgeoisie to use state protection to strengthen its economic position in exercising control over the use of resources. In both interpretations of the period, the state and society are portrayed as having a confrontational relationship in the tradition of 'centre–periphery cleavage' (Yalman 2001, 2002).

The existence of state interference in the economy is not a sufficient basis from which to argue that there has been a state tradition in Turkey that is only interested in the reproduction of a state class. All class societies have state interference in the economy. The proponents of the 'state tradition' invoke this concept to highlight the fact that the state does not represent the interest of any social class, but the interests of the state bureaucracy or a political class who control the state. This implicit refutation of Marxism's contention that the state is an instrument of the bourgeoisie is unaware of the conceptual difficulties it faces. This amorphous notion of the state class has no analytical value in that it tells us nothing about the nature of economic and productive relations in which the state is enmeshed in different periods. Nor does it tell us about the transformations that the state itself has gone through since the Ottoman times. Conceptualised only in terms of its interventionist and oppressive features, the state has no analytical value as all states are interventionist and use physical force. In order to understand the specificity of the state, there needs to be an assessment of its class character. However, it must be made clear that, the fact that the state in capitalist societies appears to be relatively autonomous of social classes generates a problem. In order to overcome this apparent anomaly that stands in the way of characterising the state as an institution of class, one needs to decipher the mediations through which the state serves the interests of dominant classes (Clarke 1991). In class societies, the institutional forms of the state are separated from the dominant classes. 'The mediations between class and state have to be developed in every form of class society, for in every class society the state is institutionally separated from and "external" to, the exploiting class' (Clarke 1991:185). In all class societies, conflicting interests continuously struggle to influence the state to gain the upper hand. The state decisions that are taken at any particular moment in history reflect not the general interest of the dominant classes but a particular solution to conflicting interests at that particular junction.

This is what should be done when looking at the state during different periods in Turkish history since the beginning of the twentieth century. It is very difficult to accept the view that the establishment of the Turkish Republic in the aftermath of the First World War did not represent a complete overthrow of the Ottoman state structure. The state tradition school view of Turkey sees a strong continuity between the Ottoman state and the Republican state as far as the unchecked political power enjoyed by state bureaucracy is concerned. However, what they ignore is that the Ottoman state was basically a predatory state. The state bureaucracy plundered without any regard for the welfare of the citizens. The ways in which resources were wasted without providing many 'collective goods' by the state during the Ottoman times, justifies the label of predatory state conceptualised by Evans (1995). On the other hand, state bureaucracy in the early Republic during the period 1923–50 was interested in modernising the society through industrialisation, supported by a nationalistic ideology. Although the state took a leading role in the process of industrialisation it had close connections with the private sector. With no powerful propertied class to control the state, the bureaucracy enjoyed a supreme position *vis-à-vis* the people it ruled. While the Ottoman state would not allow any propertied class to be powerful enough to challenge the power of the Sultan and the state bureaucracy, the new Republic also eliminated whatever mercantile interest had managed to flourish among the non-Muslim populace, who had been protected from the whims of the Ottoman state by the free trade treaty of 1838 signed with Britain. The beneficiaries of the distribution of the properties of the non-Muslim merchant bourgeoisie not only became the supporters of the state but also constituted the basis of the nascent bourgeoisie in the new state. Due to its lack of power, the nascent bourgeoisie remained dependent on the state who in turn, while remaining relatively autonomous, mobilised its resources to strengthen the bourgeois class in the long run. The state assumed a leading role in the co-ordination of economic activities in order to facilitate private capital accumulation in the future. It cannot be denied that policies followed during the *étatist* period neither actively supported competitive freedom of the citizens nor attempted to instigate a *laissez-faire* economy. However, the policies followed clearly indicated that the state was supportive of private capital accumulation in the long run, and had taken a leading role in the development of the productive forces. This was largely due to the fact that in a war-torn economy trying to flourish on the ashes of the economically bankrupt Ottoman Empire, there was no business class strong enough to carry out large-scale productive and infrastructural investments. *Étatism* played a strong role in efficient resource allocation during the severe world recession of the 1930s, and under the ramshackle conditions inherited from the Ottomans. The state in this period was quite responsive to the business community, while it did not allow the working class to get organised. The fact that the ruling classes were repressive during the early decades of the Republic does not necessarily mean that the centre–periphery tradition of the Ottoman state was maintained to ensure the supremacy of the bureaucracy. The new Republican state took a strong and repressive position in the first few decades of its existence as the result of the weak and fragile nature of the bourgeoisie. During the period since 1923, the transformations brought about in the areas of civil, commercial, family, inheritance and criminal law aimed to prepare the ground-work for the formation of a capitalist economy and society. Extensive reforms in education, religious institutions, property rela-tions and the status of women all contributed to the conditions conducive to a bourgeois society.

The state capitalism from the 1930s onwards not only represented a shift from the mercantile mode of accumulation to a productive mode of capital accumulation, but was also instrumental in the establishment of state economic enterprises in industries such as sugar, textiles, cement, food, etc. State propelled industrialisation took place, in co-operation with the dominant classes who contin-ued their economic activities in commerce, banking, insurance, transportation and agriculture. The activities of the state and the economically dominant classes were complementary rather than conflicting. However, the process of generating a bourgeois class who could assume a leading role in the process of industrialisation was very slow, and therefore the economy between the beginning of the Great Depression and the end of the Second World War remained under the complete control of the state that regulated capital accumulation.

The emergence of a political elite in Turkey and its accession to power after the Second World War and throughout the 1950s was mainly the result of a combination of the aspirations of the nascent bourgeoisie to become a part of the power block and the exigencies of the new global order which saw the supremacy of the US. The 1950 general elections were very significant, not only for bringing to an end the power of the Republican People's Party, which has been accused by the 'state tradition' school of following oppressive policies to ensure the supremacy of the state bureaucracy, but also by representing the end of one-party rule. The statist paradigm saw this as the victory of the periphery over the bureaucratic centre (Mardin 1978). Keyder (1987) explains this in terms of the increased ability of the bourgeoisie to challenge the bureaucracy for control of the state and to put an end to the autonomy of the state. While taking an anti-elitist stand, the sections of the bourgeoisie that came to power in the 1950 elections prevented other elements of the periphery (i.e. workers, peasants, etc.) from having their own autonomous organisations. Instead, they established patron–client relations with the rest of the society through populist policies mobilising state resources.

Yalman (2001) represents the instrumentalist view of the state in arguing that there had been continuity between the *étatist* and anti-statist hegemonic project as they both deprived the dominated classes from establishing their own economic and political organisations. What the multi-party politics brought was the opportunity for political representatives of the bourgeoisie to have a foot in the government and to introduce policies to liberalise the economy and politics. While the attempt to adopt economic liberalism and parliamentary democracy led to the rise of a new political elite in the political sphere, it proved to be unworkable in the economic sphere as the economy was not strong enough to maintain liberalism. The return to state-led economic development in the period after the 1960 military coup indicated that the state class was still the dominant force in the economy, while the bourgeoisie were still in the process of developing under the guidance of the state. In the planned period, which began in 1960, technocrats and state elites spearheaded an import substitution mode of capital accumulation. The relationship between the business class, the state elite and the political elite was not an easy one during that period. While the state never abandoned its principle of facilitating the development of the bourgeoisie, the allocation of resources did generate tensions between various factions of the bourgeoisie, the state elite and the political elite. However, the strict framework brought by the 1960 military coup placed the state class in the driving seat and enabled them to intervene and direct the process of capital accumulation. Again, the restrictive legal framework of the 1960 coup ensured the subordination of the political class to the state elite. Although some factions of the bourgeoisie did complain from time to time about the way the state elite intervened in the economy, on the whole the bourgeoisie were quite happy with the support they received from the state. They gave their approval to the 1961 Constitution, which provided a legal framework to allow the establishment of workers' organisations, collective bargaining and the right to strike. The 1961 Constitution aimed to establish the bourgeoisie as a hegemonic class by ensuring social justice to alleviate the rising social tension in society. However, some sections of the bourgeoisie considered the working-class organisations and the holders of the state power as a threat to their well-being. The emergence of powerful working-class organisations such as DISK (the Confederation of Revolutionary Labour Unions), and their demands for higher wages supported by large-scale strikes, heightened the fears of the bourgeoisie about the future of the regime.

By the end of the 1970s, the sorry state of the economy and the heightened social tension, that was manifested in the form of street clashes by various political factions, were sufficient for the bourgeoisie to insist that the democratic regime and the liberal-democratic state were in danger, and that DISK and similar organisations on the left were largely responsible for it. By the 1980s, two processes became so prominent as to determine the course of future economic development and politics in Turkey: the crisis of the import substitution mode of accumulation, and the confidence of the bourgeoisie as a class strong enough to establish its hegemony within the state and society. After the Great Depression, the world's economic and political environment allowed the Turkish state class to follow nationalistic developmentalist policies. The lack of any powerful propertied class to challenge the power of, and authority of, the state class also allowed the state class to have a relatively free hand to pursue nationalistic developmentalist policies aimed at generating a local bourgeoisie. By the end of the 1970s, it seemed that a capitalist business class was in place to run the economy. Given the dependent nature of the ISI, the emerging bourgeoisie in the country was far from a 'national bourgeoisie' in the sense that it would operate independently of the influences of international capital. The Turkish bourgeoisie was no different from other peripheral bourgeoisies in terms of the control of technology, capital accumulation and international trade. The Turkish bourgeoisie's ascendance had been dependent upon being heavily reliant on the state for privileges, and upon the TNCs for technology and know-how. While the Turkish bourgeoisie owed its existence to a large extent to the state, at the same time, until the end of the 1970s, it had been quite wary of the fact that the state and state policies might seriously endanger its interests. The rapid process of globalisation changed the situation quite significantly. The further integration of Turkey into the global economy increased the internationalisation of the Turkish bourgeoisie; this in turn alleviated some of its fear of the state.

Through joint-stock companies, international trade and investment, the Turkish bourgeoisie have been linked to similar capitalists all over the world, therefore they tend not to identify their interest with the nation state. The victory of neo-liberalism as a world ideology since the 1980s has forced the states in less economically developed countries to stand back and to be less interfering in the economy. This, in turn, has given the bourgeoisie in these countries a new lease of life in challenging the power of state elites.

This is what has been happening in Turkey since the 1980s, when the bourgeoisie has been trying to establish its economic and political hegemony.[1] The 1980 military coup and the civilian rule that followed it under the tutelage of the army, was part and parcel of the bourgeoisie's attempt to strengthen its hegemony rather than the continuation of the 'state tradition'. The army acted on behalf of the dominant classes in order to pave the way for the restructuring of the state, which would ensure the functioning of the economy in such a way as to speed up Turkey's integration into the capitalist global economy. Economic and political crises became endemic in Turkey after the 1950 elections, as a result of the inability of any single faction within the power block to have sufficient weight to control the economy and the state on its own. It must be pointed out that the fact that (in order to speed up the development of a capitalist democracy) the dominated classes were allowed to organise themselves by the 1961 Constitution was not welcomed by some sections of the power block. While some saw this as a vehicle to ensure social justice and equity that would bring stability to the country and thus provide conditions for improved economic performance, others within the power block became wary of the fact that rising working-class consciousness may pose a threat to the regime. The 1971 military intervention aimed to establish mechanisms to keep working-class militancy under control and to warn the power block to put their own houses in order. Yet by 1980 neither aims seemed to have been achieved. The bourgeoisie and the military were not able to stop the political and economic crises. The 1980 military intervention came with the rhetoric of law and order but the real intention was to put an end to the class-based politics (Yalman 2002:40–41). The virtues of individualism and market economy were praised and trade unionism was portrayed as representing the vested interest of union leaders. It was not too difficult to obtain the consent of the masses for an authoritarian state as the lawlessness of the late 1970s had made life simply unbearable for the man in the street. Yet both the military and the civilian governments that followed it were at pains to promote the idea of how 'individual liberties' were harmed by the previous order. On the economic front, liberalisation and further integration into the world economy were heralded as saviours (Yalman 2002). The two pillars of the new order, namely authoritarian individualism and a free market economy, were invoked to ensure the hegemony of the Turkish bourgeoisie. This necessitated new forms of state intervention in the economy.

One conclusion to be drawn from the foregoing analysis is that development or a lack of it emerges from economic and political struggles. The state plays a vital role in the ways resources are used and conflicts are resolved among many interests in any given country. The many trajectories of the use of state power and authority bring many forms of management of resources and co-ordination of economic activities. It is these varied uses of state power and authority than enable analysts to label states as capitalist, developmental, predatory, post-colonial, etc.

The ability of the state elites and state institutions to keep relatively free from the influences of particular interests has led social scientists to call the state in some less economically developed societies 'relatively autonomous states'. Often the relatively autonomous bureaucratic class derives its strength from its long tradition, its role in a revolutionary take-over and its reliance on external sources of finance. The actions of the relatively autonomous state in overriding specific interests are to a certain extent governed by its close ties with both non-state and other state actors. In other words, the developmental objectives defined by the state reflect the collective interest, or the national interest. This embeddedness in society prevents the relatively autonomous state from being completely arbitrary in setting the agenda of development (Evans 1995). The support of the army in Turkey, either through direct intervention or through the National Security Council, has been the main source of power for the relatively autonomous state in Turkey. For instance, following the 1960 military take-over, the State Planning Organisation masterminded the planned economic development under the auspices of the military. The State Planning Organisation (SPO) consisted of competent, career-based bureaucrats who had the authority to direct, shape and manage both economic and social development. The SPO played a similar economic role to the Economic Planning Board in Korea and the Economic Development Board in Singapore. However, insufficient internal and external funds have been a major factor behind the relative failure of the SPO to achieve similar results to those achieved by its counterparts in South Korea and Singapore.

Following Leftwich and Rueschemeyer *et al.*, I argued that the state in the Turkish Republic was a developmental one between 1930 and the 1950s and the integration of the Turkish economy into the global economy gradually eroded this feature and has brought about periodic crises since the middle of the 1950s. The Kemalist state since the 1930s has been determined to westernise the country in order to catch up with the West economically, socially and institutionally. The Kemalist bureaucratic elite, the founders of the Republic, were nationalist, idealist and uncorrupt. Though small in numbers, the leading elite were seriously committed to economic growth and social transformation. The higher echelons of the state bureaucracy consisted of nationalistic people of both military and civilian origin. Most of the civilianised bureaucracy had been heroes of the war of independence, which was fought against foreign invaders and their local collaborators. The army and the civilianised bureaucracy saw themselves as the guardians of the nation, a long-term tradition which still continues today; therefore they remained vigilant in the early years of the Republic in the pursuance of the goals of development. Corruption gradually seeped into the system, as one of the mottoes of the new regime was to support private capital accumulation in the long run. The introduction of the multi-party democracy allowed patron–client relations to ripen under the conditions where the role of the state in economic life became intensified. As in many developmental states such as Thailand and Indonesia, developmentalism in Turkey was gradually accompanied by a mixture of centralisation, technocratic economic management, coercion and corruption. By the 1990s, corruption got out of hand as political parties in power used state resources to reward supporters and corporations in the name of supporting economic development and growth. The 2001 economic crises and the events following have demonstrated the pervasive nature of corruption in the use of state resources and in the distribution of economic privileges. The parliamentary commissions set up in June 2003, in conjunction with efforts to join the EU revealed widespread corruption involving ex-Members of Parliament and a number of prominent businessmen. For instance, in June 2003, in order to investigate the corruption in the energy sector, several workplaces belonging to Genç Party leader Cem Uzan's family were placed under police control during the investigation.

The relatively autonomous state that emerged in the aftermath of the Great Depression and intermittently consolidated its power until the early 1970s, started to decline from the 1980s onwards as far as the power of the bureaucracy was concerned. With the rise of liberalisation and democratisation, political elites have been gradually pushing the bureaucratic elites to the back stage. The increasing integration of Turkey into the global economy, and the rising influence of international capital and their local collaborators, have eroded the power, authority and the relative autonomy of the state. It could easily be argued that the power, authority and capacity of the developmental state in Turkey declined in direct proportion to the rise of both national and foreign capital. In the early years of the Republic, the state was able to determine the role that the private capital could play in the economy. The erosion of this powerful influence of the state was slow, but from the second half of the 1970s it speeded up and in the 1990s it reached its peak when the state was forced to liberalise its foreign trade and financial accounts. However, this has been the more or less inevitable outcome of the deliberate state policies, as the Turkish Republican State from its inception committed itself to the development of western style capitalism. In the absence of a strong bourgeoisie, the state itself became the main agent of development, establishing small and big industrial enterprises while also encouraging the development of a private sector. State capitalist development was built on the principle of a mixed economy in which state enterprises and private enterprises would complement each other. This way it was possible for the state not only to arrange direct deals with foreign capital but also to provide help to private capital to accumulate through direct or joint investments with foreign companies.

DEMOCRACY IN TURKEY

What does all this mean for the development of democracy and democratisation in Turkey? This section specifically concentrates on this question. The Turkish developmental state had to be undemocratic considering the circumstances in which it emerged. The mammoth task of instituting a new republic by dismantling the Sultanate, separating religion and the state, abolishing the sacred Sharia law and replacing it with laws borrowed from the West, introducing a dress code totally alien to the society, replacing the sacred Arabic script with the Latin one, introducing nationalism as a guiding ideology in place of the 'millet' ideology of the Ottoman Empire, attracted the wrath of many internal and external groups. Therefore, until 1946 an authoritarian one-party system headed by a 'national chief' prevailed in the country. No opposition to the principles of Kemalism, which included nationalism, secularism, *étatism*, revolutionism and populism, was tolerated. The introduction of a multi-party system in 1946 represented a watershed in the political life of the country. There are two main explanations for the reasons behind the transition from a single party authoritarian regime to a multi-party democracy: one sees it in terms of the exigencies of international politics, and the second finds class transformation due to the class structure behind it.

Yılmaz (1997) represents the first view, that the introduction of multi-party system was the beginning of a periodic upsurge to democratise the country in reaction to external events. Yılmaz (1997) highlights very clearly that the dismantling of the one-party regime and the initial transition to a multi-party regime in the 1940s was a state-led change of regime which was introduced in response to the international context rather than changes fuelled by internal social forces and class struggles. He makes use of Dahl's work (1971) to account for the effects of international factors on authoritarian breakdown and democratic development. Dahl maintained that a government will tolerate opposition only when the expected cost of toleration is less than the expected cost of suppression. Yılmaz (1997) quite convincingly explores the expected external benefits of democratisation in Turkey, which included the enhancement of the state's general international prestige, countering the criticisms of international human rights organisations, obtaining trade concessions and economic aid from the democratic states and qualifying for membership in international organisations like NATO and the EU (1997:4–5).

The Turkish State had been a one-party authoritarian state since its inception in 1923. Turkey's reluctance to participate in the Second World War on the side of the allies, and her close relations with Germany since the First World War had alienated western powers. The country's relative isolation was compounded by Soviet demands to form a special relationship with her to allow the Soviets to participate in the defence of the Turkish Straits. The Kemalist ruling block saw any rapprochement with the Soviet Union as a threat to its own political survival. In order to prevent the Soviet-backed groups from gaining ascendancy to threaten the control of the state, the civilianised Kemalist leadership (ex military officers of the independence war as opposed to civilian Kemalists) opted to repress them while trying to become a part of the West. However, the single party regime's reliance on a 'National Chief' and anti-democratic rules realised in the forms of press censorship, discrimination against minorities and the like, did not square with the spirit of Roosevelt's Atlantic Declaration of 1941. Freedom of speech, freedom of conscience, freedom from poverty and freedom from fear were the main pillars of the declaration. The authoritarian regime in Turkey felt that unless Turkey showed the US and its western allies that she was serious about the basic tenets of democracy and was a staunch enemy of communism she could not run away from the Soviet threat. The prerogatives of realpolitik of the time forced the state to introduce a limited and controlled democratic reform to influence US policy towards Turkey. With the directives of the 'National Chief', İsmet İnönü, government representatives made special efforts in international venues to declare that the Turkish State was beginning to institutionalise reforms to lead to full democracy (Yılmaz 1997:7–9). This was seen as a green light by civilian Kemalist leaders to attempt to strengthen their position within the Republican People's Party (RPP). The manifesto of four prominent civilian Kemalist Leaders (Celal Bayar, Refik Koraltan, Fuat Köprülü, and Adnan Menderes) in 1945, demanding the supremacy of the Constitution, the national assembly and individual rights, was met by a surprising suggestion from President İnönü that there was a need for the establishment of an opposition party. This was welcomed by the 'gang of four', who soon formed the Democratic Party (DP) rather than continuing to control the Republican People's Party from within. As far as the principles of the new party were concerned, they did not differ much from those of the RPP's six principles. However, the main emphasis was on populism, nationalism and republicanism at the expense of the other three principles, statism, secularism and revolutionism. The civilian Kemalist leaders of the newly formed DP hoped to form an alliance with dissatisfied bureaucrats, discontented young army officers and the liberal intelligentsia. But the civilianised Kemalist leadership prevented the formation of such a coalition by organising mob attacks on liberal intellectuals, their newspapers and properties. But, knowing that further oppression of the opposition might have a negative influence on US–Turkish relations, the Government undertook a series of liberalisation policies concerning freedom of the press and freedom of association in 1946. The fact that the US gave strong signals that it did not appreciate the Soviet plans towards Turkey and would welcome closer ties with Turkey was a proof that the civilianised Kemalist leaders had made the right calculations. The Truman Doctrine's stipulations that US aid to Turkey was conditional upon democratisation in the country further encouraged the civilianised Kemalist leadership to gradually abandon their policies of oscillating between democratisation and the oppression of the opposition in 1946–47. After long negotiations, the US Congress was eventually persuaded to approve military aid to Turkey, despite some strong opposition to it. Turkey's strong desire to be included in the Marshall economic aid acted as a further catalyst to continue with liberalisation and democratisation. Furthermore, the establishment of NATO without Turkey further increased the external cost of the internal oppression of the opposition. Consequently, the civilianised Kemalist leadership of the Government allowed the 1950 elections to take place without any attempt to rig them, as had been the case in the 1946 elections. The DP won an overwhelming majority in the elections, largely due to the Government not being able to understand how people's feelings had developed over decades of hardship since the First World War. The leadership were convinced that they could capitalise on their status as the heroes of the independence war of 1918–22. The generations after this war expected rapid improvements in their standard of living but the young Republic was not capable of delivering welfare benefits to masses due to a large number of factors, including the world recession of the 1930s and the war economy of 1939–45. The heavy-handedness of the Kemalist regime to implement comprehensive reforms in every sphere of life, including the abolition of the Caliphate, the closures of religious orders and the replacement of Arabic scripts with Latin script, had also alienated the state from some sections of the society. Consequently, the DP who promised to move away from state oppression and provide better living standards won a landslide victory in the 1950 elections (Yılmaz 1997).

The second interpretation that class forces were largely behind the transition to the multi-party system is represented by Keyder (1987), Boratav (1994) and Yalman (2002). Although external influences played a determining role in the introduction of democratic rules and institutions, one cannot simply ignore the societal basis of this transformation. A number of social groups had been disenchanted with the bureaucratic state since the 1920s. The commercial bourgeoisie that had managed to accumulate capital and wealth during the war was particularly interested in becoming a part of the state apparatus hitherto controlled by a Kemalist bureaucracy. Their discontent with the state was exacerbated by the introduction of a wealth tax introduced during the Second World War. Similarly, landlords felt threatened by the 1945 Land Reform Bill, which envisaged the confiscation of land from landlords and its distribution to the landless. Consequently mercantile and landed interests were quick to take advantage of the relatively relaxed atmosphere generated by the international conditions that forced the Government to initiate democratisation from above. The merchant–landlord alliance skilfully exploited the discontent of impoverished rural and urban masses, as well as the members of religious orders who felt socially excluded by the secular state. In election rallies, accusations of bureaucratic mismanagement and corruption were used to mobilise the support of the socially excluded (Keyder 1987). The emerging government after the 1950 elections was in no way a complete eradication of Kemalist bureaucracy from the state. This was largely because the merchant-landlord class was not powerful enough to get rid of a military-bureaucratic state tradition. It is difficult to disagree with Yılmaz (1997) and Boratav (1994) that the Turkish bourgeoisie and landlords did not have the organisational and ideological capacity to establish their own hegemony at the expense of the state bureaucracy. The DP leadership that came into power in 1950 included civilian Kemalists, as opposed to the civilianised leaders, as well as landlords and merchants. What emerged from the elections was a 'delegative democracy', not a representative democracy. The change of government was not as a result of the representatives of the bourgeoisie, merchants or peasants pushing their way into the state through the support of a social base, but as a consequence of a split within the Kemalist ruling block. The civilian Kemalist block sought the support of masses and the backing of merchants and landlords to control the state. Thus, they became the 'surrogate' representatives of some social classes who delegated their will to the party leaders in return for certain gains. In a nutshell, political power was transferred from civilianised Kemalist leadership to civilian Kemalist leadership as the result of the democratisation process promoted by the state in conjunction with the international interest of the country. Civilianised Kemalist leadership reluctantly agreed to allow civilian Kemalist leadership to control the state, as the external cost of repression would have been high (Yılmaz 1997:30–33).

Democracy is a continuous process of struggle for the control and distribution of resources. Being able to use the system to get into Parliament, the dominant classes have been striving to control the state and state bureaucracy has been trying to mediate between the interests of conflicting classes. The institutional arrangements of multi-party democracy in Turkey did not just stem from the class struggle between the dominant and subordinate classes, but was initially introduced from above in conjunction with security issues, international politics and economics. This meant that the process of democratisation involved a struggle, largely between the state elite, the political elite and the economic elite, until the 1970s and the role of the dominated classes in this process remained insignificant. The representatives in Parliament were not very responsive to the electorate, nor did they feel accountable. The masses were not given an opportunity to participate in the decision-making process. With the gradual incorporation of Turkey into the global system, the rising bourgeoisie managed to penetrate the state and demanded more plurality within the state. Therefore, from the 1970s onwards, a gradual shift from an exclusionary governance to an inclusionary corporatist governance started to take place.

LIBERALISATION AND DEMOCRATISATION SINCE 1980

Since 1980, the liberalisation attempts have brought some changes towards further democratisation, but the situation still remains limited as far as the consolidation of democracy is concerned. Liberalisation has aimed at the management of the different interests of political, economic and state elites, rather than promoting the expansion of civil society in Turkey. The attitude of the political class throughout the 1980s and 1990s has been quite paradoxical in that, while it has preached the virtues of liberalism and a free market economy, it has also been using state power and state resources to strengthen its dominance. Populist policies of generous public sector salary adjustments, employment creation in the public sector and subsidising agricultural production on the eve of elections have been widely used by governments in office. Instead of introducing more efficient and effective taxation to increase state revenues, the political class has used internal borrowing to meet public sector expenditures. In other words, the state has used public resources as instruments of legitimisation throughout the 1980s and 1990s instead of concentrating on democratisation (Cizre-Sakallıoğlu and Yeldan 2000:498–499).

Perhaps one significant outcome of the wave of liberalisation in Turkey has been the ascendance of 'civil society' organisations. However, the existence of a civil society does not guarantee the responsiveness of the state. The state has simply ignored the grievances expressed by civil society. 'Turkey's political class does not just resist, ignore or fail to resolve the explosive social-political problems. Rather it often operates "in defiance" of widespread public demands' (Cizre-Sakallıoğlu and Yeldan 2000:494). Political irregularities have become an everyday event, and human rights violation, public corruption, violence and crime have been rampant and the state has not taken into consideration the public demands to tackle them effectively. The gradual restructuring of Turkish political life, in tandem with economic liberalisation, has enabled the political class to isolate itself from the rest of society. Under the authoritarian conditions created by the 1980 military intervention, the working-class movement was severely undermined and its ties with political organisations were cut off. The marginalisation of the trade unions has continued until now in order to allow the repressive wage policies of the neo-liberal economic project to be implemented. The heightened possibilities of unemployment and competition for jobs in the formal sector tended to pacify the working class as a force for putting pressure on the state. Furthermore, the deepening of divisions within society enabled the state to ignore the differing demands from the public. The multiplication of political parties due to the multi-party system, coupled with the state's efforts to prevent the working class from having a political representation through organic links with political parties, has resulted in a situation where the political parties lost their social bases.

Political parties became indistinguishable as far as their party programmes were concerned. Parties became organisations controlled by their leaders, who were interested in promoting their own political advancement. The issue in Turkish politics has become the issue of who is going to administer a more or less fixed set of policies congruent with the neo-liberal project.

The influence of the military in Turkish politics has been ubiquitous, even at times when there has been a democratically elected government. The military sees itself as the protector of the Republic against any interest. The regularity with which the military intervenes in politics is a testimony to its power. The military claims to have inherited the right to protect the nation from the founding father of the Republic, Mustafa Kemal Atatürk. It does not hesitate to take severe action, which may not square with the constitution or democracy, against threats to national security which may emerge in the forms of communism, Islamic fundamentalism or ethnic secessionism. The structural transformations and constitutional changes instituted by the military rule following the 1980 coup have strongly weakened parliamentary democracy. In the ensuing limited democracy, only the political parties that were considered to be fit by the military were allowed to participate in the elections. Since the 1980s, the banning of individuals and party leaders from politics and the closure of political parties, have become a common practice on the part of the military (or the constitutional court in congruence with the military's wishes). Politics has not been able to function smoothly within the institutional structures established under the close observation of the military since 1980. Under such circumstances political parties are not able to formulate programmes and policies in response to the demands of their electorate. This in turn further strengthens the military's position in Turkish politics, as time and again the military intervenes in the political processes, using the justification that the political system has failed to defend the secular pillars of Atatürk's Republic (Cizre-Sakallıoğlu and Yeldan 2000:495–497).

The last intervention in 1997, popularly named the '28 February Process' by the Turkish media, came up with a reasoning that the revival of Islamic fundamentalism was due to the absence of an effective government. On this occasion, the army did not directly take over but gave a very powerful message to the existing government who felt the need to resign. The military's interventionist tactics range from direct assumption of power, as in the 1960 and 1980 coups, to issuing ultimata to governments, as in 1971 and 1997, or to advising governments on politics, in conjunction with national security issues, through the meetings of the National Security Council which emerged as a creation of the post-1980 Constitution. The military has been careful not to damage its image by not clinging to political power openly. Within a few years of toppling governments, it returned to its barracks in favour of civilian governments following the 1960 and 1980 coups. However, on both occasions, and in the 1971 and 1997 ultimata, the military not only made it very clear to civilian governments that they had to operate within the political terms set by it, but also introduced vital structural reforms to establish its supremacy. The salience of the political regime is succinctly summarised by Cizre-Sakallıoğlu and Yeldan (2000:497):

> There are ... both pluralist and monistic features articulated by the regime: civil society has some latitude but no real strength; the Parliament contains oppositional forces but has no real authority; the Judiciary operates with some independence at times but is by and large politically controlled ... The ability of civilians to control the military is weak, but the polity is not a military regime.

Furthermore, the political parties, the most important institutions of parliamentary democracy who are supposed to represent people through democratic elections are not democratic within themselves. They are not strongly rooted in society and their development in recent decades has lagged far behind civil society (Özbudun 2000:150). The leadership of the political parties is highly personalised and oligopolistic, and the leaders do not feel accountable to their supporters. Key political decisions are made alone or with a few favoured colleagues, by party leaders without much consultation with others, even without the Parliament when in power. Strong party discipline and the docility of party members is required from the Members of Parliament as nomination of parliamentary candidates remains under the monopoly of the leader. Therefore it is not surprising that the European Union uses the lack of democracy and democratic consolidation as a vital factor in delaying Turkey's accession into the Union.

Turkey is an interesting case as far as the emergence and the consolidation of democracy are concerned. Since the establishment of the multi-party system (1946), the country has experienced 13 free and competitive elections and three military interventions, followed by the restoration of the parliamentary system. Yet Turkey has not been able to convince the European Union that democratic institutions and practices are in place in the country. Turkey is the only candidate that has been told it must meet the Copenhagen Criteria prior to the start of accession talks. The Copenhagen Criteria insist that candidate countries must have 'institutional stability as a guarantee of democratic order and the rule of law, and for ensuring respect for human rights, as well as respect for an the protection of minorities' (Van Westering 2000:96).

The EU-Turkey Association's decision on 6 March 1995 to establish a customs union between the EU and Turkey was approved by the European Parliament on 1 January 1996. The Government's initiative to introduce a number of reforms after this date, in the move towards democratisation was no more than cosmetic. Although the extension of political rights to civil and professional associations through constitutional amendments was something positive, the reforms on freedom of speech, minority rights, freedom of conscience and the anti-terror law were extremely limited and superficial. The state's concern was not so much to strengthen democracy as to meet the political conditions imposed by the 1993 Copenhagen Criteria in conjunction with Turkey's accession in the EU. The EU had demanded that Turkey, as any other candidate, should meet the criteria designed by the European Council in 1993. The Copenhagen Criteria stipulate that new members should have institutional arrangements to guarantee democracy. Members should strictly obey the rule of law, respect human rights and protect minorities. Structures should be in place to enable countries to ensure the primacy of the free market economy, as well as an adherence to the political, economic and monetary aims of the EU. The half-hearted attempts at democratisation in the 1990s, and since the year 2000, have been in congruence with the state tradition in Turkey since the Second World War to introduce elements of democracy in response to the exigencies of international politics and economics (Yılmaz 1997).

As far as social and economic justice, political equality and respect for human rights are concerned, the Turkish democracy has a long way to go, and the trajectory of liberal democracy Turkey has been following with the strong support of the international finance institutions and western governments since 1980 seems to be incapable of bringing about the desired changes.

3
Cyclical crises since 1980

A sudden economic crisis hit Turkey hard in February 2001 after a row between the President, Ahmet Necdet Sezer, and the Prime Minister, Bülent Ecevit at a National Security Council meeting. Soon after the conflict was announced the Istanbul stock market crashed. The IMKB (Istanbul Stock Exchange) national 100 index dropped by more than 30 per cent in just two days. The Government immediately decided to drop exchange rate controls in favour of allowing the Turkish Lira to float, which effectively meant the devaluation of the Turkish Lira. Currency markets witnessed chaos and interest rates soared up to 7000 per cent on the inter-bank money market within a few days. About US$10 billion left the country very quickly in this chaos. Panicking banks bought US$7.6 billion in the market in order not to face shortage of liquidity in the dollarised Turkish market. The fears that the IMF may not release the requested $7.7 billion emergency aid and that some public banks would fail to meet their debt redemption were reduced to a certain extent by the IMF's declaration that it would help Turkey to overcome the crisis. However the IMF's declaration was conditional, its condition being that Turkey should speed up privatisation of the energy and telecommunication sectors and should reform the banking sector.

Any serious student of contemporary Turkey is well aware of the fact that such a crisis, which led to a drop of about 100 per cent in the value of Turkish currency and caused the collapse of the currency markets, cannot be reduced to one simple reason; the political row between the President and the Prime Minister. Investors are sure to have been scared away by the row, but the argument between state officials was basically a triggering factor rather than the root cause. Beyond this simple reasoning some serious attempts to explain the crisis have been made by various circles, but the explanations provided by the IFIs and neo-liberal academics are far from satisfactory. As usual, the Turkish Government, its crony capitalism and corporate misguidance were blamed. There was no acceptance of the fact that long-term policies which sought to establish the hegemony of the so-called 'free market' economy may have been responsible. Nor was there any recognition that IFIs such as the IMF and the World Bank may have played a significant role in the crisis in Turkey. Along with other IFIs the IMF and the World Bank have pressed hard to consolidate and extend the liberalisation process by ensuring that the conditions for the liberalisation of international capital movements are established, by securing the liberalisation of access to financial services (banking and insurance), and by making sure that the Multilateral Agreement on Investment is open to everybody. Trade liberalisation may have had some modest benefits for Turkey, but current and capital market liberalisation have had a devastating impact on productivity, growth and income distribution.

Since 1950 Turkey has experienced a number of serious crises. The frequency of crises in Turkey has increased since the 1977–78 crisis. The most significant of all are, first, the 1980–81 economic crisis in the aftermath of the 1980 political crisis which brought about a military coup. This was followed by the 1983 bankers' crisis, then came the 1988 stock market and currency crisis, the 1994 economic crisis, the 1998 textile crisis, and the November 2000 and February 2001 crises.

The main causes of these recent problems are rooted in the policies that were implemented to overcome the crises of the 1970s. Since the 1980s new attempts have been made to establish a neo-liberal economy through the privatisation of most economic activities. This has meant the abandonment of Keynesian policies and the introduction of a new taxation system that has been favourable to capital through its reduction of taxes paid by the business community. The neo-liberal policies implemented since the 1980s have eroded the 'social state' in Turkey. Starved of public income, the state has resorted to both internal and external borrowing. This has coincided with the fact that over-abundant financial capital in advanced industrial countries has been in search of new investment outlets. International finance capital has been interested in short-term lending with guaranteed high returns.

Since the 1980s, finance capital has become independent of investment capital. Finance capital is distinct from productive capital in that it circulates in pure money form without being tied up in productive assets. Developments in telecommunications and computers have enabled finance capital to search for better investment opportunities and move on them in no time at all. It exists for its own interest rather than existing as a supporter of investments. This is indicative of a new mode of capital accumulation in which the dominant power becomes the power of money-holders and lenders. The new mode of accumulation is not production-centred. One of the most significant features of global capitalism is the fact that capital movement has overtaken commodity movements. Today the predominant feature of the world economy is no longer production and commerce but financial speculation (Braudel 1982; Arrighi 1995; Hoogvelt 2001).

Since the 1980s finance capital has been searching for new sources of capital accumulation and moving into the stock markets in the so-called 'emerging markets'. In this way the integration of less economically developed countries into the capitalist global economy is being further intensified. This, in turn, further exposes less economically developed countries to structural crises faced by capitalism. Additionally, the inflow of finance capital into fragile economies in less economically developed countries generates conditions for crises in the short term. First it leads to overvaluation of the local currency, thus making imports attractive and exports unattractive. Consequently deficits emerge in current accounts. Second, when foreign finance capital senses any problems in the economy it leaves the country rapidly, making devaluation of the local currency inevitable. The impact of these two processes on the already fragile economic structures and the infant banking sector can be devastating and a crisis can become unavoidable. This is what has been happening in Turkey in recent years. The Turkish economy has become extremely vulnerable to the movements of international finance capital due to the liberalisation of the economy. The 2001–02 crisis in Turkey was largely due to the structural weaknesses of the economy and Turkey's further integration into the global economy through liberalisation.

At the root of this crisis lies the very fact that the new mode of capital accumulation based on financial activities was no longer sustainable. The state is at the epicentre of the new mode of accumulation. Internal and external borrowing to sustain this have reached such levels that more than half of the consolidated budget expenditures are allocated to the payment on interest and the principal.

In Turkey public financing is at the centre of the financial markets. Taxation constitutes only a minor part of public financing. With a very small tax base the state is only able to tax small-income earners (mostly salaried and wage earners) while the high-income earning classes mostly escape from paying income tax. The way in which the Turkish financial markets operate helps the state transfer resources to high-income earners. Public financial needs play a significant role in this form of income distribution. State bonds, shares and other valuable papers are sold to the banks and to the public through the banks in order to raise money domestically. High interest rates paid for the state bonds also attract short-term foreign financial capital. Particularly since 1990, foreign financial capital has been actively encouraged by the state and the Turkish financial circles to bring in short-term capital. The long-term effect of this has been the fact that the state has lost its grip on the economy. With the enactment of decree number 32 in 1989, capital movement has become completely liberalised and thus the Turkish Central Bank has lost its capacity to use foreign currency and interest rates as policy measures independent of each other. With this decree the national financial market has come under the control of the short-term speculative foreign capital movement (Yeldan 2001a).

It is not surprising that Turkey has been facing a serious economic crisis since February 2001. Three-quarters of the IMF members, whether more or less economically developed, have experienced financial crises since 1980. Irma Adelman (1999) summarises the salient features of financial crises in this period. One common feature of all post-1980 financial crises has been the fact that foreign capital inflows (FCI) preceded the crisis. Consequently economies experienced periods of economic growth and increases in investments. Furthermore, in all cases significant appreciation of the domestic currency followed FCI. The economies flourished in tandem with big budget deficits and cheap money policies which led to high levels of inflation. As a result of currency appreciation the current account deficits widened and the economies lost their competitiveness.

At some point, foreign lenders get worried about sustainability of the twin deficits and, fearing a devaluation, curtail lending and start withdrawing capital. This triggers a sharp devaluation. Futile currency stabilisation efforts reduce foreign reserves to perilously low levels. This accelerates capital flight and leads to precipitous decline in exchange rates. A severe domestic credit crunch ensues as banks and corporations scramble to repay foreign debts with much more expensive dollars. They sell off domestic assets to generate liquidity, and stock and real estate markets crash. Eventually, the country is forced to approach the IMF (Adelman 1999:1).

The IMF conditionalities, which include reducing budget deficits, raising domestic interest rates, curtailing wages and social spending and closing insolvent banks, lead to the escalation of social and political unrest. However, 'eventually, the country's international credibility is restored and the crisis transformed into a severe and prolonged recession' (Adelman 1999:1). It seems that foreign currency inflow has been crucial in the financial crises experienced by a large number of countries since the 1980s. It must be emphasised that foreign finance capital flows into the 'emerging markets' only when certain structural transformations have been in place. The Bretton Woods institutions have been extremely instrumental in these transformations that liberalise less economically developed countries. Most international finance institutions seek to achieve three things in their attempts to consolidate and extend the liberalisation process to all countries: to establish the conditions for liberalisation of international capital movements; to ensure the liberalisation of access to financial services (banking and insurance); and finally to ensure that the Multilateral Agreement on Investment (MAI) is open to everybody including non OECD members. Such transformations increase the fragility of less economically developed countries *vis-à-vis* the finance capital (Buğra 2001).

Despite the primacy of the structural conditions in the 2001–02 crisis, the IFIs and their local supporters have been insisting on 'mismanagement' of the state and on conditions specific to Turkey. Factors such as an undisciplined financial sector, weaknesses in the banking sector, economic and political corruption, populist state policies, political instability and misguided investment policies have been blamed. Similar accusations have been made for the Asian crisis of the late 1990s.[1] Obviously one cannot deny the existence of such factors in Turkey, but to reduce the crisis to these factors alone and to ignore the role played by the movement of international finance capital is not acceptable. For one thing the IMF has changed its position on the question of overvalued local currencies. Throughout the 1960s and 1970s it insisted that less economically developed countries should devalue their currencies and adopt a realistic currency policy. Ever since 1973 countries have been forced to adopt flexible exchange rates instead of fixed ones and implement open capital market policies instead of closed 'short-term capital markets and regulated foreign investment flows'

(Adelman 1999:1). Yet the same IMF in the 2000s gives the green light to currency policies which leads to the overvaluation of local currencies. This is largely because in less economically developed countries the IMF prefers to have stable currency policies instead of realistic currency policies in order to facilitate free movement of financial capital (Buğra 2001:47–49). As a result of the US and IMF pressures, less economically developed countries have not been able to follow coherent policies that would take lessons from the experiences of other countries. Consequently, governments have lost their economic autonomy to implement their traditional policy instruments unilaterally, and this has created the right conditions for financial crisis (Adelman 1999).

RAPID LOSS OF ECONOMIC AUTONOMY

In Chapter 2 I argued that the state played a crucial role in the process of industrialisation in Turkey. The difficulties encountered by the import-substituting industries and the state's overall inability to run a crisis-free economy speeded up Turkey's further integration into the global economy. The country's loss of economic autonomy occurred in parallel with its integration into the global economy through development policies that emphasised liberalisation, outward orientation and export-oriented industrialisation.

In order to overcome a severe foreign currency shortage which had existed since the early 1970s and reached its peak in 1977–79, Turkey introduced export-oriented industrialisation in 1980. This was part and parcel of the SAPs introduced in 1980 under the directives of the IMF and the World Bank. The need for structural adjustment has surfaced periodically in Turkey since the Second World War. However, the stabilisation programme launched on 24 January 1980 was so comprehensive that international finance circles and Turkish political and business circles have interpreted it as a turning point. The new strategy envisaged a new mode of integration into the world economy, in that the 1980 policies distinguish themselves from the previous ones by becoming a development strategy rather than merely being limited to the standard stabilisation packages (World Bank 1988). Export-oriented development based on the principle of comparative advantage and market-oriented resource allocation were the main pillars of the new strategy (Krueger and Turan 1993:356).

High hopes were placed on the new market-oriented strategy to initiate high rates of accumulation, efficient resource allocation and productivity increases. It was expected that the new emphasis on output recovery would overcome the output-reducing difficulties posed by the pre-1980 stabilisation policies. What was envisaged in the second half of the 1980s was a programme of 'structural adjustment with growth' which would enable the country to expand its production and thus its debt servicing ability. As such Turkey could become a model for other indebted countries in Africa and Latin America (Celasun 1991; Derviş and Petri 1987; Rodrik 1990b; World Bank 1988).

In the following years the export of manufactured goods did show a considerable increase while exports from other sectors of the economy, though improving, were not very significant. However, it is vital to note that increased exports in the manufacturing sector were not accompanied by a serious attempt to increase the productive capacity of the sector. The increases in production and investment lagged behind the increases in exports in the manufacturing sector. Exports were increased in the 1980s by making more effective use of the existing productive capacity in the manufacturing sector.[2] Increased exports were achieved by reducing export prices through devaluations and by shrinking the internal market through a strict wage policy throughout the 1980s (Boratav *et al.* 1994; Boratav *et al.* 2000; Yentürk 2001:3).

On the other hand, the prices of imports increased significantly as a combined effect of devaluation, export subsidies and other incentives given to the export sector in order to reduce export prices. This has seriously impeded investments in the manufacturing industry as the industry had been dependent on the imports of semi-finished and capital goods. The most significant beneficiaries of these policies have been a few firms engaged in international commerce but not interested in investments in the productive sector. The label of 'export-oriented industrialisation' used to characterise the 1980–88 period is in fact a misnomer as the policies in this vein have not led to capital accumulation and investments in the productive sector. Increased exports were mainly due to a regulated foreign exchange system and control on capital inflows. Furthermore the suppression of wages through severe labour control policies was used as a policy option to limit internal demand.[3] The structures established under the regime of export promotion and commodity trade liberalisation were not sustainable, first because they discouraged savings and investments. Second, this coincided with huge tax evasions and increasing costs of export subsidisation which in turn generated disequilibrium in the macro-economy. Public expenditure soared as a result of fiscal obligations of the state and the state's debt servicing. Export revenues and international borrowing constituted the two main sources of deficit financing between 1980 and 1988. However, increased foreign borrowing led to difficulties in debt servicing and increased tension in the economy. Despite the fact that neo-liberal policies were followed to the letter, the results were not positive.

In the 1980s Turkish policy-makers' main concern to ensure the country's credit-worthiness in the international finance markets, as the main aim of structural adjustment policies fitted quite well with the main capital groups' aim to maintain and reproduce the import-substituting industrial structure (Yalman 2001:205). Creditworthiness was considered as a *sine qua non* to ensure the continuous availability of external funds for import-dependent industries. For a variety of reasons, including the initial increases in exports and rescheduling of its earlier debts, Turkey was able to maintain an uninterrupted debt service and thus its creditworthiness until the late 1980s. The World Bank praised Turkey for having a successful adjustment, compared with Latin American countries, by being able to meet its debt requirements in the 1980s (World Bank 1990:122–124). The World Bank and the Organisation of Turkish Industrialists and Businessmen (TÜSİAD) shared the optimism that as long as the economy kept growing and the current account deficit was financed on a sustainable basis debt would not be a problem. To facilitate this, the Government partially lifted capital controls in 1984 and actively encouraged the private sector in general and commercial banks in particular to take advantage of the differential interest rates by borrowing abroad. Capital groups and municipalities were allowed to borrow externally with a fixed exchange. This raised concerns for the Bretton Woods institutions that Turkey should not confuse economic liberalisation with the relaxation of controls on the growth of foreign debt and borrowings (World Bank 1990). The policies that followed in the 1980s were mainly geared to finding new mechanisms of transferring wealth to the private sector while ensuring that the public sector carried the weight. Higher exchange rates were not only instrumental in ensuring an inflow of foreign exchange but also led to considering foreign exchange as an asset.

Commercial banks and individuals rushed to keep their cash in foreign currency and this led to the dollarisation of the economy. The financial liberalisation allowed a section of the Turkish bourgeoisie to become key agents in the money markets through their banking activities. Given the problems of the low level of technology in industry and the dependence on the state for fresh funds, some capital groups moved some of their capital to speculative money markets in co-operation with international finance capital. The banking system expansion between 1982 and 1988 was largely due to savings in foreign exchange. Yet the international finance community started to raise serious concerns about the country's ability to keep borrowing and paying debts without any serious structural change to ensure foreign currency earnings. The Central Bank was in real trouble as it was responsible for meeting debt obligations. It attempted to introduce measures, such as raising interest rates, to reverse the currency substitution in order to finance current account deficits from internal sources. From the mid 1980s onwards, domestic borrowing gained significant momentum in order to contain external borrowing. The substitution of domestic debt for foreign debt through high interest rates or government securities, which were both well above the spiralling inflation rate, had a detrimental impact on the productive sector. Turkish industrialists simply refrained from investing in the productive sector and became heavily involved in speculative capital for two reasons: one, the cost of borrowing became very expensive thus there was no incentive to invest in the productive sector; and two, investments in state bonds guaranteed high and quick returns. For these reasons many capital groups established their own banks to take advantage of this lucrative monetisation of state deficits. In other words, the state's attempt to resolve its fiscal crisis with monetarist policies helped the financial sector to strengthen its position within the economy. It is ironic that the state introduced further liberalisation in 1989 in the form of complete capital account liberalisation in order to alleviate its balance of payments problems. This was done in response to the demands of the Bretton Woods institutions. Accordingly the Turkish Lira was made fully convertible in foreign exchange markets and through the continuation of high interest rates foreign capital was attracted. This reliance on portfolio investment to fuel economic growth simply increased the economy's fragility by making it susceptible to the whims of the international financial markets (Ekinci 1996; Yeldan 2001a). By the end of the

1980s the optimism shared by the World Bank and TÜSİAD faded away as fresh signs of fiscal and financial crises became more prominent. The economy still suffered from macro-economic instabilities. It was realised that the goals of 'adjustment with growth' were not achieved. 'Stagflation' characterised the economy and the debt stocks and debt servicing soared to such an extent that the state was forced to search for new loans to meet the country's needs (Akat 1994; Anand *et al.* 1990; Boratav 1990; Rodrik 1990a, 1991a).

FINANCIAL LIBERALISATION AND THE 1994 CRISIS

Many analysts, including Boratav *et al.* (2000), Öniş and Aysan (2000), Ekinci (1998), Yalman (2001) and Yentürk (2001), believe that the year 1989 represents a turning point in the recent history of the Turkish economy as the policies introduced in this year have had major and lasting impacts, culminating in the 21 February 2001 crisis. Decree number 32 passed by the Government in 1989 ensured a complete liberalisation of capital account in Turkey. The purpose of the 1980 stabilisation-cum-structural programme was to shift the economy from being inward-looking to being outward-looking. Throughout the 1980s the economy was gradually liberalised under the close control of the IMF and the World Bank. The measures introduced to reform the capital account in 1989 represent the summit of the liberalisation process. The capital account regime was even freer than its counterparts in advanced industrial societies. Despite the fact that Turkey had been following the recommendations of the 'Washington Consensus' the Turkish economy did not become a relatively crisis-free economy. The reform policies followed in conjunction with the spirit of the 'Washington Consensus' included policies which aimed to achieve macro-economic stability through the control of inflation and the reduction of fiscal deficits; liberalisation of trade and capital account and liberalisation of domestic product and factor markets through privatisation and deregulation.

One of the first policies introduced to overcome the 'stagflation' in the late 1980s was complete deregulation of foreign capital transactions and the convertibility of the Turkish Lira. Thus was the so-called 'financial revolution' and was aimed at establishing a more efficient and flexible system whereby savings and investments would be promoted. However, the results were disheartening: speculative foreign capital flows encouraged by high interest rates caused havoc in the domestic asset markets which culminated in the collapse of the financial system and the emergence of a severe economic crisis in 1994. The inflow of speculative money led to the appreciation of the Turkish currency against other currencies, thus making exports more expensive and imports relatively cheap. Consequently, production and export of manufactured goods in Turkey slowed down between 1989 and 1994. The fact that interest rates were kept very high in the post-1989 period contributed significantly to the drop in investments in the manufacturing sector as a whole.[4] Within a short period of time the negative consequences of the financial liberalisation became quite evident. The trade deficits increased from 3.5 per cent of GNP in 1985–88 to 6 per cent in 1990–93. Fiscal balances also deteriorated significantly in the post-1989 period. Public sector borrowing requirements rose from an average of 4.5 per cent of GDP during 1981–88 to 8.6 per cent in the period between 1989 and 1997 (Boratav *et al.* 2000:6, 24).

There have been two important sources of public sector borrowing since 1989: international financial markets and internal borrowing by the state. With the liberalisation of the financial markets in 1989 the Turkish economy was opened up to global financial competition. Through its borrowing policy the state has actively encouraged short-term speculative financial activities as most of its borrowings were of a short-term nature. Consequently speculative finance has avoided lending to the productive sector; instead it has preferred to invest in state bonds which could guarantee high returns in a short period. Furthermore, a considerable portion of the capital accumulated in the productive sector moved to speculative activities and invested in highly profitable state bonds. In 1995 a study produced by the Istanbul Chamber of Industrialists (ISO 1995) demonstrated very clearly that a significant proportion of the profits in the productive sector originated from activities outside production.

Unlike the 1980–88 period, the appreciation of the Turkish Lira after 1989 did not have the effect of increasing investment demand. The concomitant existence of short-term capital inflows and high interest rates had the impact of depressing investment in the productive sector. The principal aim of Turkish financial liberalisation has been the growth of the financial sector for its own sake, rather than being used as a vehicle to speed up the growth of production and investment in the real sector. The mistakes of the pre-1994 crisis were repeated throughout the late 1990s, culminating in the November 2000 and February 2001 financial collapses and the ensuing economic recession. Furthermore, Turkey did not make use of the policy of sterilisation in order to prevent inflationist pressures generated by the inflow of speculative finance. Instead, the incoming speculative money was used for the expansion of public expenditure through the state bonds. This provided the state with funds which led to complacency about any serious attempt to increase the public income.

Populist policies in the few years preceding the 1994 crisis were largely responsible for the crisis. The government since 1989 have been very keen to take advantage of the inflows of foreign capital to help in overcoming their internal fiscal problems and speeding up the rate of growth. This has pushed them into a trap: as the incoming capital is of a short-term nature and tends to move out immediately if high interest rates are not retained, they then leave governments in even greater need of outside finances. The growing imbalances generated by increasing foreign debts in turn led to a crisis of confidence which prevented finance capital from coming to the country. Structural and institutional weaknesses in Turkey encouraged short-term financial capital to seek speculative gains and quick profits. However, once the country's debt reached unsustainable levels and the prospects of high interest rates receded, the short-term capital fled the country in a flash.

A combination of populist high wage policies, the contraction of investments in the productive sector, the rise of a rentier type of accumulation fired by the speculative capital movement, and an economic growth based on short-term borrowing generated suitable conditions for the 1994 financial crisis. In the absence of sufficient investment in the productive sector, increased demand was met through imports. This in turn worsened the balance of payments which was already alarmingly negative. The vicious circle of a growth model based on extensive borrowing, high interest rates and a distorted foreign currency regime was inevitably going to lead to a severe crisis. Yet for political expediency this growth model was preferred to the ones which could have emphasised investment in the productive sector and taxation which would have increased state revenues (Yentürk 2001).

Although the 1991 coalition government of the True Path Party (DYP) and the Social Democratic People's Party (SHP) was in theory committed to carry out a comprehensive stabilisation programme to address the problem of macro-economic insatiability, the parties' concerns to please their respective electorates constrained them. Prior to coming to power both parties had promised populist distribution policies to raise the incomes of the working class and the farming community alike. Policy-makers welcomed the opportunity to allow short-term capital inflows to ensure economic growth and populist distributional policies. Within three years (1990–93) the amount of incoming capital increased from US$4.03 billion to US$8.96 billion and short-term capital constituted a significant part of this. The state used the short-term capital inflows through its domestic borrowing mechanisms to meet its growing public expenditure. It seemed that for at least three years everybody was a winner, except the state. Through the budget, different groups were allowed to take advantage of the incoming capital. Farmers were given relatively high support prices, workers were granted wage increases, industrialists were allowed to pay low taxes and low input prices, but the lion's share was taken by the financial sector (Öniş 1996:9–10). In the absence of an adequate tax base the state used domestic borrowing with guaranteed high interest rates to meet its budgetary needs. Both the financial sector and the industrial sector lent heavily to the state through the purchase of treasury bonds. Burdened with the payments of huge wage and salary bills, interests on domestic and foreign borrowing and transfer payments, the state budgets were not in a position to allocate funds for investment. In other words, short-term political expediency had forced the Government to follow policies which would have negative consequences for long-term development.

By 1993 the economy was in serious difficulty. First there was not sufficient income generation for the increasing budgetary expenditures. Second, the deficit in the balance of payments reached such serious levels that the two major credit rating institutions, Standard and Poor's and Moody's, reduced Turkey's credit ratings which in turn led to a loss of confidence in the eyes of investors. Large sums of short-term capital fled the country in 1994. According to Central Bank figures, the short-term capital movement dropped from US$3 billion in 1993 to US$5 billion in 1994. This further exacerbated the balance of payment crisis and thus the Government decided to implement a major stabilisation programme in 1994 known as the '5th April decisions'.

The explanation preferred by the Bretton Woods institutions and the neo-liberals in Turkey that the 1994 crisis was mainly due to government mismanagement is highly technocratic. They insisted that if the Government had been able to increase its revenues through privatisation and more efficient taxation and had managed to control public expenditure the crisis would not have occurred. This technocratic approach has to be challenged. Given the power bases of a weak coalition government it would not have been possible to prevent the crisis (Öniş 1996:12–13). The existence of a large number of political parties and the reality that the line between being or not being in power was so fragile led governments to use the opportunity while in power to expand their chances of re-election. Therefore they tended to use any opportunity that might strengthen their power base within a short period of time. '[The] underlying policy mismanagement and failure to achieve fiscal equilibrium is a severe case of distributional crisis which a comparatively weak coalition government elected on a populist platform, by its nature, could not effectively counteract or deal with' (Öniş 1996:12).

The 1994 stabilisation policies had different meanings for different classes. The labouring classes lost the income gains made in the late 1980s and early 1990s. Their share in total factor incomes dropped from 36.8 per cent in 1992 to 26.5 per cent in 1994 (Öniş 1996:14, Table 4). This was largely due to a decline in output and employment which in turn had serious implications for the working-classes' bargaining power.

Although some elements in the business community were affected negatively by the stabilisation programme which led to the contraction of production, a significant section of the business community was able to protect itself from the negative influences of the crisis. Declining domestic markets provided an opportunity for some to export and recoup their losses this way. The most significant protection mechanism used was getting involved in rentier activities. The great majority of big firms shifted their efforts to the financial sector at the expense of production. The fact that the state was issuing highly lucrative bonds in its efforts to raise funds for budgetary expenditures enabled the firms to invest in the rentier activities. Consequently, according to a survey carried out by the Istanbul Chamber of Industry, the share of non-operational profits in the total profits of Turkey's 500 largest industrial establishments increased from 33.3 per cent in 1990 to 54.6 per cent in 1994 (ISO 1995:70). In other words, while firms were able to protect themselves from the crisis and ensure profits through rentier activities, their contribution to the real economy declined.

The stabilisation package following the '5th April decisions' and the devaluation of the Turkish Lira in the aftermath of the 1994 crisis produced some positive results in the next two years. The deficit in public spending was reduced due to increased taxation and more careful spending. Exports showed a slight increase due to the devaluation of the Turkish Lira. However, these relative improvements came to a halt in 1996 when Turkey witnessed a rapid inflow of speculative capital, dollarisation of the economy and the appreciation of the Lira. Consequently, imports increased without a comparable increase in exports leading to a worsened balance of payment deficit. In order to meet public spending demands the state used public borrowing from internal and external sources offering dangerously high interest rates. Net gains from interest on the US dollar jumped from 17 per cent in 1993 to 46.8 per cent in 1995 (Yentürk 2001:7). The fluctuating rate of growth in the five years following the 1994 crisis was a significant sign of instability. It is interesting to note that the measures introduced in conjunction to the '5th April decisions' were far from solving the crises' underlying structural problems.

DISINFLATION PROGRAMMES AND THE 2000–01 CRISIS

The 1990s were characterised by mini cycles of growth–crisis–stabilisation. Yet policies which ensured mini growth and stabilisation were not capable of reducing high inflation rates that sailed above the 100 per cent mark in the second half of the 1990s. Furthermore, increased public borrowing requirements led to unmanageable debt servicing (Yeldan 2001a; Boratav and Yeldan 2001; Konukman, Aydin and Oyan 2000; Türel 1999). However, the Government foresaw the coming of the crisis and attempted to introduce measures to prevent it. After a series of failed attempts to control inflation, the Government presented two consecutive letters of intent to the IMF in April 1998 and December 1999. Although the IMF promised no money in response to these letters, Turkey granted the IMF the authority to inspect the economy at three-month intervals. The 1999 disinflation programme aimed to prevent a possible crisis rather than combat an existing one. The aim was to reduce price inflation to a single digit number by the end of 2002 by following an austerity programme which would cut down public expenditure. The programme chose policy instruments that were based on exchange rate monetary controls. It envisaged an exchange rate programme which would control daily depreciation of the exchange rate according to pre-set targets. Accordingly the Central Bank 'committed itself to a policy of no sterilisation, whereby changes in the monetary base would directly reflect changes in the net foreign assets of its balance sheet' (Yeldan 2001b:2). In addition to fiscal and monetary measures the programme foresaw structural reforms which aimed at establishing and maintaining stability in the economy. Those structural reforms included privatisation and changes for the social security system, agriculture, privatisation and the banking sector. The ambitious nature of this programme was evident in the fact that it attempted to resolve structural problems, which had evolved over many years, within a short timespan. Most of its aims were in fact so unrealistic that in the first year of the programme's implementation very little had been achieved.

In the implementation of the monetary policies the Central Bank was assigned the status of a *semi-currency board* which meant its liquidity generation was limited to its net foreign asset position (Yeldan 2001a:167–168; 2001b:3). The expectation was that, once a *nominal anchor* of a currency basket was established and the rate of the currency depreciation was accorded to the basket and controlled, it would be possible to reduce the rate of inflation. Therefore an exchange rate basket consisting of 1US\$ + 0.77 Euro was established and a daily depreciation rate was decided. The exchange rate based disinflation programme was introduced without devaluating the overvalued Turkish Lira. The plan was to allow only a 20 per cent cumulative exchange rate depreciation by the end of 2000. This meant the elimination of exchange rate risk which further encouraged the FCI and this in turn contributed to the appreciation of the domestic currency. External borrowing reached unmanageable levels registering a huge increase from the 1988 levels. Foreign debt increased from US\$96.89 billion in 1988 to US\$103.34 billion in 1999 and US\$117.84 billion in 2000 (State Institute of Statistics <www.gov.tr>). As in many other countries with FCI, the rate of growth in GDP increased from −4.7 per cent in 1999 to 7.2 per cent in 2000. This significant growth was due to the FCI which not only ensured the expansion of domestic liquidity but also financed the current account deficit. The huge difference between the growth rates in exports and imports is a testimony to this. Between 1999 and 2000, imports jumped from US\$39.7 billion to US\$54 billion, registering a colossal 35.9 per cent increase, while exports increased from US\$29.3 billion to US\$31.6 billion showing a 7.9 per cent growth.

On the other hand, the second important element of the disinflation programme, lower interest rates, did not lead to savings and investments in the productive sector as envisaged. The programme was too optimistic in its expectation that relatively low interest rates would have an immediate investment impact on the productive sector. The productive sector had been starved of investment possibilities for a long time and had shifted its focus to rentier activities in the financial sector. It was neither in a position to shift its funds to investments in the crisis-prone economy nor did it have any inclination to do so. One consequence of the drop in interest rates and the appreciation of the Turkish currency was an explosion in the import of consumer goods. Through consumer credit schemes demand increased and pushed the price increases above exchange rate prices. In turn the Turkish Lira appreciated further, leading to further imbalances in the import–export ratio. The exchange rate based disinflation policy may have succeeded if it had been complemented by measures to ensure production internally. However, this was not the case in Turkey as the policies designed to encourage production were far from realistic (Yentürk 2001:8–10).

The 2000 disinflation programme was fairly comprehensive and aimed to balance the economy through a number of rapid structural reforms in public institutions, banking, agriculture, social security and the budget. However, a close reading of the letter of intent would reveal that there was no indication of how these comprehensive structural reforms were to be implemented. Boratav goes as far as saying that there was no call for the 1999 standby agreement as there was no excessive demand, no budget deficit and no need for urgent external financial help. In 1999 there was no excessive demand as the rate of economic growth was −6.1 per cent (Boratav 2001:105). The balance of payment deficit in the same year was less than 1 per cent of the national income, and the high rate of inflation had been chronic but it was not leading to hyperinflation or a crisis. In Boratav's opinion, the November 2000 and February 2001 crises emerged as a consequence of the deflationist policies imposed by the IMF. The whole programme was based on the manipulation of foreign currency rates: nominal rates were decided to be much lower than the past inflation rates. The sustainability of such a programme was dependent upon the existence of strong foreign currency reserves. As such reserves were lacking, the Government used external borrowing as a last resort and by the end of the year the problem of an excessive balance of payments emerged. Realising the nature of the problem an exodus of capital took place and the ensuing liquidity shortages put a significant constraint on the currency reserves. The IFIs reluctance to renew Turkey's short-term credit put further pressure on the liquidity crisis (Boratav 2001:106). Boratav simply blames the Government's eagerness to volunteer for an uncalled for standby agreement and to implement an inappropriate policy based on the manipulation of currency prices.

Although in broad agreement with Boratav, Yeldan (2001a, 2001b) shows that the 2000 disinflation programmes were modestly successful in maintaining exchange rate targets, monetary controls and fiscal targets.[5] Therefore the argument that blames the Government for failing to meet these targets is unsustainable. The underlying cause of the Turkish currency crisis of 21 February 2001 has to be found in the extreme fragility of the financial system (Yeldan 2001b:10–12). Although weak regulation of the banking sector, increased corruption and large fiscal deficits did contribute to the crisis situation, the real culprit was 'the external fragility generated by the unregulated in- and out-flows of financial capital which were excessively mobile, excessively volatile, and subject to herd psychology' (Yeldan 2001b:10). The ratio of short-term foreign debt to the Central Bank's international reserves is usually considered the most significant indicator of external fragility. Considering the financial crisis in a number of East Asian countries in 1997 it is calculated that the threshold for fragility is 60 per cent. Yeldan finds it alarming that since the liberalisation of the capital account in 1989 the Turkish financial system had been operating constantly within the danger zone as the indicator had not fallen below 100 per cent. The 2000 disinflation programme allowed huge inflows of speculative capital which led the fragility index to increase to its highest level, 145 per cent, since the eve of the 1994 financial crisis. The FCI was bolstered by a policy of high interest rates which was not sustainable. When the crisis hit, the short-term 'hot money' fled the country in a rush. A series of macro-economic adjustment measures including huge devaluation, curtailment of the aggregate internal demand and high interest rates were introduced to ameliorate the situation but the damage was already done. 'The programme, by dismantling all tolls of stabilisation and monetary control of the Central Bank, has left the economy defenceless against a speculative run and "sudden stop" ' (Yeldan 2001b:13). The piecemeal solutions implemented served only to postpone the day of reckoning and the crisis returned in 2001 with a vengeance.

It became evident that the stabilisation and disinflation programme of the year 2000 was not sufficient to overcome the structural problems which underlay the 2001 crisis.

REPERCUSSIONS OF THE 2001 CRISIS

The GNP plunged to US$148.2 billion in 2001 from US$202 billion following the two crises in 2000–01, then the GNP figure showed signs of improvement at the end of 2002 when it reached US$179.9 billion. Consequently the per capita income also showed a sharp decrease from US$2986 in 2000 to US$2160 in 2001, then increased to US$2580 by the end of 2002. Contrary to the IMF's prediction, the contraction in the economy in 2001 was 9 per cent not 3 per cent. The negative growth was accompanied by a decline in production and international competitiveness, increased bankruptcies, rising unemployment, rising debt service and the need for further borrowing from outside. The three-year programme initiated by the IMF in 1999 necessitated US$3.6 billion in credits but the total credit requirement of the recovery programme shot up to US$24.9 billion to be extended by the IMF (US$18.1 billion) and the World Bank (US$6.8 billion).

Internal debt stocks and interests have also been severely influenced by the two crises. Increasing interest rates and reduced repayment periods exacerbated the burden of public finances. The domestic debt stock showed a considerable increase in connection with the attempts to save several banks. The sale of state bonds and treasury bills contributed to the domestic debt which increased from 36.4 quadrillion Turkish Lira in 2000 to 122.2 quadrillion Turkish Lira in 2001 and to 170 quadrillion Turkish Lira by the end of 2002. The ratio of the domestic debt to GNP increased from 29 per cent in 2000 to 89.2 per cent in 2001, but reduced to 54.8 per cent by the end of 2002. Interest payments on domestic debts registered a 101 per cent increase in 2001 and jumped from 20.4 quadrillion Turkish Lira in 2000 to 41.1 quadrillion Turkish Lira in 2001 and to 52.1 quadrillion Turkish Lira by the end of 2002. The interest expenditure of domestic debts represented 18.8 per cent of GNP, 85 per cent of all the tax revenues and 56 per cent of the consolidated budget expenditure in 2002. On the other hand the total public investments were only equal to 5.7 per cent of the expenditure on interest paid by the state (State Treasury at 2001).

By the end of 2000 the average rate of interest had dropped to 38 per cent while the average repayment period was 410 days. In the aftermath of the November 2000 and February 2001 crises the average rate of interest shot up to 105 per cent while the average repayment period dropped to 144 days. Due to extra borrowing to streamline the banking system and increasing interest rates, the additional domestic debt burden amounted to US$45 billion in 2001. The total additional financial burden engendered by the two crises amounted to US$127 billion, consisting of the losses in the national income (US$57 billion), additional external borrowing (US$25 billion) and additional internal borrowing (US$45 billion). This represented 88 per cent of GNP (US$145 billion) in 2001 (Sönmez 2002).

Industrial establishments simply stopped investing in new technology and equipment. This not only meant the loss of competitiveness in the world market but also a significant decline in the manufacturing industry. The year 2001 witnessed differential decline in various sectors of the manufacturing industry. The contraction in the first months of 2001 was 7.5 per cent on average. The sector worst hit by the decline was the transportation industry with a 39 per cent contraction. Capacity use also shrunk from 76.3 per cent in October 2000 to 64 per cent in June 2001. Business closures were paralleled by rising unemployment. According to the State Institute of Statistics in the first half of 2001 more than 800,000 people lost their jobs: 239,000 in manufacturing industry; 312,000 in construction industry and 287,000 in commerce and services.

Only people with liquid assets come out as winners from the crises. In the first year of the crisis, interest payments from the Treasury for domestic debt reached 52 per cent of the total budgetary income. It is interesting to note that rentiers were paid 40.5 quadrillion Turkish Lira in interest while 7.2 million agricultural producers (35 per cent of the population) were given less than 1 quadrillion in agricultural subsidies. Interest paid on domestic borrowing is equal to 22 per cent of the national income. The Turkish economy relied on internal borrowing throughout the 1990s but never in the history of the Republic had internal debt reached such unsustainable proportions. Domestic borrowing represented 21.2 per cent of the national income in 1996 when the rentier economy reached its pinnacle. The increase in domestic borrowing in 2001 reached unprecedented levels, shooting up from 36.4 quadrillion

Turkish Lira in 2000 to 106 quadrillion Turkish Lira at the end of 2002.

Civil servants were one of the worst hit groups of people by the crisis and state policies. In 2000 salary increases in the public sector remained 15.5 per cent behind inflation. Despite almost monthly salary increases, by the end of 2001 civil servants' incomes had decreased by 4 per cent in real terms, representing a total income loss for public servants of 15 per cent. Similarly, public sector workers' real income loss in 2001 was estimated to be 11 per cent. The income loss for minimum wage earners above the age of 15 was about 13 per cent in 2001. Real income depreciation for pensioners and widows in 2001 ranged from 0.2 per cent to 3.5 per cent depending on their social security system. These real income losses were also reflected in the decline in the share of the waged in the national income. The share of the wage earners (who constituted 49 per cent of the total population) in the national income declined from 30.7 per cent in 1999 to 28.7 per cent in 2000 and this trend continued in 2001.

THE TRANSITION TO A STRONGER TURKISH ECONOMY PROGRAMME OF 2001

The transition to a stronger Turkish economy (STE) programme was introduced in May 2001 to overcome the severe crisis which had surfaced in February 2001. The fact that such a programme has been developed is tantamount to recognising that previous policies were incapable of ensuring a stable, sustainable economy. The two consecutive crises in November 2000 and February 2001 were the culmination of an unsuccessful exchange rate based disinflation programme introduced at the beginning of 2000. The STE document admits this failure by stating that 'the aims of the new programme are to eliminate speedily the crisis of confidence and instability that emerged as a result of floating exchange rate, and simultaneously to create a framework for restructuring the public administration and economy in a way which will prevent the re-emergence of this situation' (State Treasury 2001:13).

A close look at the programme reveals that it aimed to radically reform the economy, society and state–society relations. Comprehensive changes include reforming the banking system, the financial system (to ensure transparency in financial administration) the agricultural system of subsidies, the social security system, abandoning the exchange rate based monetary policy in favour of a floating exchange rate system, and speeding up the process of privatisation. These aims are congruent with the main aims of the letter of intent entitled 'Structural Policies for a Stronger Economy' presented to the IMF on 3 May 2000. It also reflects the spirit of decree number 32 of 1989 which ensured the complete liberalisation of the financial sector. This in turn had the effect of preventing investments in the productive sector through the inflow of short-term speculative foreign capital which preferred to be active in foreign currency markets. The STE sets out to eliminate the structures that led to 'the development of an unsustainable debt dynamic'. It admits that policies implemented throughout the 1990s 'created a vicious circle of debt and interest payments, pushing Turkey into an ever more difficult financial position' (State Treasury 2001:3).

The new economic programme, which is to be completed by the end of 2004, has been supported by the IMF which has already pledged US$16.2 billion for it. It envisages a recovery of the national income to pre-crisis 2000 levels. In other words the heavy damage caused by the economic crisis in one year is to be mended in three years.

By the end of 2003, first impressions suggest that this was achieved, as the GNP figures at 1987 constant prices increased from 119 trillion Turkish Lira in 2000 to 123 trillion Turkish Lira in 2003 (State Treasury 2004 at <www.hazine.gov.tr>). However, when population growth is taken into consideration, such a meagre increase in gross figures will become negative in per capita GNP. Again at 1987 constant prices, the per capita income of 1,741,000 Turkish Lira in 2003 is less than the per capita GNP in 2000 (1,766,000 Turkish Lira).

The STE went beyond its economic growth target of 3 per cent in 2002 and achieved 7.8 per cent in that year and 5.8 per cent in 2003. Furthermore, the programme has made positive progress towards the target of reducing the rate of inflation to 12 per cent and the rate of real interest on state bonds to 20.5 per cent by the end of 2004. 2003 witnessed a significant drop in the rate of inflation in consumer prices from an average of 51.2 per cent in 2002 to 27.4 per cent in 2003. In parallel to the deceleration of price inflation, the annual compounded rate of interest in state bonds was reduced from 62.7 per cent in 2002 to 29.4 per cent in 2003. Likewise, exports increased by 11 and 16 per cent in 2002 and 2003 respectively. However, the STE has failed to achieve its target of reducing the rate of growth in imports from 34.7 per cent in 2001 to 6 per cent in 2003. The increase in imports has sailed upwards much faster than the export earnings of 15.7 per cent in 2002 and 27.1 per cent in 2003, further exacerbating the balance of payments problems. The current account balance has increased from −US$1.5 billion in 2002 to −US$6.8 billion in 2003 (State Treasury 2004 at <www.hazine.gov.tr>). The programme has also failed to achieve its target of reducing the ratio of domestic debt stock to GNP to 45.2 per cent as it stood at 48.3 per cent in 2003.

In the programme the emphasis has been put on the contraction of internal demand through a very restricted wage policy. In the absence of policies to improve productive capacity in the economy, draconian wage policies are far from being sustainable in the long run. The short-term nature of measures to increase exports and decrease imports is both the strength and the weakness of the programme. It has been able to achieve some success in the short term at the expense of social tension, but it is doomed to fail in the long run as there is virtually no investment policy in the programme which would make the economy internationally competitive. Furthermore, in order to be able to sustain high rates of economic growth and low rates of imports concomitantly, as envisaged by the programme, one needs a powerful economic base. As in the 1960s and 1970s, when the Turkish economy registered high rates of growth, imports increased at a even faster rate than the economic growth in 2002 and 2003. Yentürk's prediction (2001:10–11) that the expected 5–6 per cent overall economic growth was not compatible with the target of reducing the growth of imports to 6.9 per cent by the end of 2003 has proved to be correct as imports grew by 27.1 per cent in 2003.

International finance institutions, the Turkish media and the JDP Government have interpreted the positive rates of growth as the end of the crisis and signs of the success of neo-liberal policies. The JDP Government has been praised for its crisis management based on free marketism and good governance. However, there is a failure on the part of the IFIs, the media and the Government to question the sources of this positive growth, its sustainability and socio-economic consequences. In fact, as shown by Bağımsız Sosyal Bilimciler (2004), Yeldan (2004) and Sönmez (2004), conjectural developments in the international currency markets and inflows of short-term international capital were largely responsible for the economic growth in 2002 and 2003. While price levels increased by

70 per cent in cumulative terms in 2002 and 2003, the value of the Turkish Lira against other currencies remained more or less the same in nominal terms and the Lira continued to appreciate at the expense of current account deficits. Economic growth targets were achieved largely through external and internal borrowing rather than investment in the productive sector of the economy. The total public debt increased from US$131.2 billion in 2001 to US$209.6 billion in 2003, consisting of US$139 billion domestic debt and US$70 billion foreign debt (State Treasury 2004 at <www.treasury.gov.tr>).

The sustainability of economic growth based on debt management, borrowing, devaluation and exchange rate is questionable. With these new policies, the STE expects that the envisaged structural changes will achieve increased economic efficiency, thus facilitating sustainable growth with current resources. With better public finance balances the state will be able to allocate more resources to welfare services such as education, health and social security which will in turn have a long-term impact on total factor productivity. Increased revenues will be used in raising living standards, improving income distribution, reducing poverty and eliminating regional inequalities (State Treasury 2001:34–35). A precondition for these long-term development objectives is to ensure macro-economic balances in the short term. The changes in the banking sector occupy a central role in the attempts to break the debt dynamic. Therefore, reforms in the fiscal and money markets need to be given the highest priority.

It is clear that the STE aims to maintain policies that emphasise the influx of short-term speculative capital which brought about the crisis in the first place.[6] It does not seem to be offering anything better than the 2000 disinflation programme which ended with a disastrous outflow of short-term speculative capital in February 2001. The state had no policy to control the composition of imports in the years following the 1989 financial liberalisation nor did it have a policy of encouraging the import of capital goods. The short-term speculative capital, therefore, avoided entering investments in areas which would have enhanced foreign currency earning capacity. The STE simply does not address the problem of uncontrolled imports, but it hopes that the demand for imports will be reduced as a consequence of the contraction of internal demand and reduced rates of growth. In other words, hopes are pinned on the reduction of national income. The STE ignores the associated problems of unemployment, reduced welfare and long-term development. Furthermore, the STE expects an increase in exports within a short period of time. As there is nothing in the programme about how to improve the production capacity of the productive sector, hopes are based on exchange rate and wage policies. It has been possible to increase the international competitiveness of the economy through favourable exchange rates and low wage policies, but these policies are ineffective in the long run, as in recent decades strategic marketing, investments in technology, and the direction of international capital, rather than differences in foreign exchange rates, have proved to be the determinants of international trade. It must also be stressed that strict wage policies will lead to political instability which will in turn generate problems for sustained economic growth. In conjunction with this there are serious reservations about debt servicing; it seems that given the unrealistic expectations concerning imports and exports the only way to keep up with huge debt servicing is to resort to further borrowing. This will bring Turkey back to where it started; the vicious circle of indebtedness, crisis and growth based on further borrowing.

The real cause of the crisis is not the public deficits but the fiscal policies of the state that transfer resources to capital. The fact that the financing of the public deficits has been carried out by the banking sector is a direct consequence of the dominance of monetarism since 1980. In this monetarist period the state has gradually restricted its role in the economy to the planning of public services and has relinquished the financial decisions about them to the speculative banking sector. The uncontrolled short-term borrowing by the banking sector was used to finance public services via the medium of Treasury bills and state bonds, which ensured high rates of real interest for the financial sector (BSBIG 2001:13).

The STE indicates that the income of the blue-collar workers in the public sector showed a 6 per cent increase on average between 1991 and 2000, while the improvements in the income of white-collar workers in the public sector showed only a 0.6 per cent average increase in the same period. Therefore, the STE declares that it aims to eliminate the income disparity among public sector employees. In other words, the STE is trying to emphasise the existence of a clash of interests among public employees and in so doing it is attempting to obtain social and political support for its repressive wage policies by dividing any possible opposition. However, the Independent Social Scientists Group (BSBIG) shows clearly that the figures produced by the STE do not reflect the reality and could in fact be contradicted by figures provided by the state's own Central Bank (BSBIG 2001:19–20). According to the Central Bank's annual report for 2003, real wages dropped by 30 per cent in the crisis year of 1994, then between 1994 and 1998 real wages were continuously depressed. Only in 1999 and 2000 was an improvement registered in real wages and even this was only an 11 per cent increase on 1994 levels when real wages had dropped by 30 per cent. In other words, in 2000, wage earners had not even recovered the losses they encountered as a result of the 1994 crisis. The contraction of real wages has continued throughout 2001, 2002 and 2003. Table 3.1 below shows that between 2000 and 2002 public sector wages declined by 21.8 per cent and private sector wages declined by 25.2 per cent.

In short, unlike the claims made in the STE, wage increases are not significant enough to justify the envisaged strict wage polices. When wage increases are compared with the contribution made by labour to the value added since 1980, the falseness of the claim that wages are high becomes even more evident. Again, according to the calculations made by BSBIG (2001:20–22), while value added made by the labour in the manufacturing industry increased 2.5 times between 1980 and 1997, increases in real wages have always fallen behind. In fact, wages in the manufacturing industry in 1997 were at 1980 levels. Despite huge increases in the productivity of labour, wage increases have not followed the same pattern. The STE claims to have aimed to follow a rational wage policy, but if this is so then labour productivity should be the criterion. Furthermore, the envisaged wage policy is to be applied to the formal sector of the

Table 3.1   Real wages indices (1994 = 100)

Net wages and salaries	1994	1995	1996	1997	1998	1999	2000	2001	2002
Net public sector wages	100	82.9	62.2	74.1	73.1	103.8	111.0	98.2	89.2
Net private sector wages	100	91.7	93.4		90.6	105.9	118.2	119.4	95.3	94.3
Net public sector wages	100		95.3	102.5	119.3	117.7	123.1	108.9	104.8	110.8

Source: Central Bank of Turkey (2004), *2003 Yillik Rapor* (2003 Annual Report), Ankara, p.32.

economy. BSBIG (2001) indicates that since 1980 there has been a tendency towards the informalisation of the economy and between 30 and 45 per cent of the workforce is employed in this way. Given the nature of the economic crisis in Turkey it can be expected that the flexibilisation of the labour market will be intensified. Yet there is nothing in the STE's wage policy to address the problems of flexible labour markets.

Recent figures on GDP growth led the Government to claim that economic recovery started in 2002 and will continue into the future. Yet close scrutiny suggests that the situation is not as rosy as the Government suggests. The 7.8 per cent growth in GDP in 2002 was a good sign of recovery compared with the −7.5 per cent in the year before. Yet BSBIG (2003) and Yeldan (2003) show that of the 8.5 trillion Turkish Lira increase in GDP, 7.7 trillion Turkish Lira (90 per cent) has been used in production for stock replacement. Thus positive growth in the GDP in 2002 has not been reflected in people's living standards. Throughout 2002 and until the end of the third quarter of 2003 the long-lasting negative trend in real wages has continued. While real wages depreciated by 1.3 per cent the real income per worker in the industry and service sectors declined by 4.6 per cent. Yeldan illustrates that the growth tendency in the economy since 2002 is not due to 'successful crisis management' but directly to reductions in wage costs and increases in imports generated by exchange rate appreciation. The depreciation of wages and import prices has stimulated production for piling up stocks. The rate of unemployment gradually increased from 5.6 per cent in 2000 to 9.9 per cent in the third quarter of 2003. Therefore, the great majority of people have not benefited from the recent economic growth. The Prime Minister Mesut Yilmaz's prediction in 1997 that the fight against inflation in Turkey, in the absence of unemployment insurance or job security schemes, will have serious social repercussions has become reality since the February 2001 crisis (*Milliyet Daily*, 5 December 1997). The legitimacy of the state in Turkey has been seriously challenged as a result of the policies followed since 1980. The state's legitimacy depends not only on the extent to which it establishes 'the rule of law, electoral accountability or national popular support' but also on its ability to ensure conditions of accumulation which will maintain better living standards for the majority (Jessop 1990:216).

It can be concluded that the main aim of the STE is to attract foreign capital by establishing the necessary conditions for sustained and stable economic growth. The STE promises to take radical steps to carry out structural reforms in order to persuade foreign capital to come to Turkey. The preferred policy measures include reducing the state, the separation of politics and economics through the transfer of the state's economic functions to committees, and privatisation. Yet the programme is silent on the question of investment in the productive sector and domestic capital formation. Policies suggested concentrate on fiscal and monetary measures which would ensure free operation of international finance capital in Turkey. There are no measures to strengthen the economy in order that it is able to withstand external shocks. Only a powerful economy relying on its own resources for savings and investment can successfully confront changes in the world economy. The STE is certainly not conducive to such a strengthening of the economy. What it proposes to do is to ensure free movement of international firms in Turkey by providing a suitable environment. In the restructured economy it will be possible for foreign firms to export freely to Turkey, and use the country's human and natural resources cheaply and effectively. The policies envisaged look set to undermine industry and agriculture in Turkey and put them under the effective control of foreign firms.

The most significant contributor to the sequential crisis and growth cycles, which has been the main characteristic of the Turkish economy since 1990, is the complete liberalisation of the exchange regime. Decree number 32 in 1989 lifted all restrictions on the mobility of international capital in Turkey. The artificial economic growth and crisis periods have shown close parallels with the direction in which capital is moving. The inflow of hot capital has preceded short periods of economic growth and its outflow has been followed by crises. Any loss of confidence in the economy due to internal or external shocks has led to the flight of international capital leading to new situations of crisis. Since 1990, capital movements in Turkey have become independent of the needs of the productive sector. Incoming capital has concentrated mainly on foreign currency markets, taking advantage of the overvalued Turkish Lira and real high interest rates. The increasing imports due the influx of foreign capital exacerbates the deficit foreign trade. This in turn sets forth a vicious circle which consists of a crisis of confidence and the flight of capital in its wake. Under the conditions of an economy unable to generate sufficient revenues through production and taxation, once the financial markets are deregulated, the economy faces a no-win situation. If the interest rates are increased, the inflow of capital generates huge trade deficits which lead to a crisis of confidence and hence capital flight. If interest rates are lowered, it becomes very difficult to attract foreign capital, thus leaving the state with huge problems of public financing. This instability generated in Turkey is structural in that the way in which the Turkish economy is integrated into the world economy is bound to lead to a cycle of crises. The fragility of the economy is caused not only by the weaknesses in the productive sector which is not internationally competitive, but also to the inability of the state to develop an effective taxation system to bolster state revenues. The result has been a huge increase in public debts. Policies introduced to fight the crisis have been ineffective and the targets set have not been achieved. For instance the year 2000 disinflation programme envisaged a US$2.5 billion current account deficit, but by the end of the year the figure had reached US$9.5 billion. It was inevitable that this would be followed by a crisis of confidence as far as short-term capital inflows were concerned.

The uncontrolled banking sector's contribution to the fragility of the economy has been huge in that in 2000 alone the amount of money brought in by the banking sector was US$209 billion and the amount of money repaid was US$204 billion. The amount of short-term capital in circulation in 2000 was equal to the total value of the production and service industries combined. According to Yeldan (2001c:30) these figures provided by the Central Bank illustrate the fact that the Turkish economy has been under severe attack by speculative international capital. Banks in Turkey have been instrumental in this by investing money in state valuable papers (a vehicle of internal borrowing) and consumer credits, thus making the biggest contribution to the fragility of the economy.

Kemal Derviş, the minister responsible for economic affairs from the February 2001 crisis until September 2002, declared that since 1980 US$195 billion had been squandered by the state. Derviş, an ex-deputy president of the World Bank who was brought in to resolve the crisis, blamed irrational state spending for the huge state debts without even mentioning any role that may have been played by the private sector. The fact is that the private sector in Turkey has been siphoning off public resources through the banking system and through state borrowing. Banks, whether private or public, have been entirely dependent upon the state's support for their incomes. The state has been underwriting uneconomic banks, and state borrowing has been the main source of income in Turkish banking. High interest rates paid by the state for its bonds and other valuable papers used in internal borrowing have been the bread and butter of the banking sector. The total internal state has debt increased from US$8.9 billion in 1980 to US$50 billion at the end of the year 2000. In the meantime the state has paid US$258 billion for the payment of interest and repayment of the principal (Akman 2001:32–45). Strangely enough, the state has borrowed externally at a cheaper rate in order to pay its internal debts with phenomenally high interest rates. The banking sector has been highly instrumental in this money squandering. The real interest rate has been so high that even the real sector investors have shifted their capital to the financial sector and siphoned off interest from the state through a mushrooming number of private banks. In order to meet the needs of the capitalist class, the state in Turkey has been using methods of 'primitive accumulation'. In the absence of a history of colonies and a slave trade, the underdeveloped Turkish capitalism has been making use of usurious state debts, inflation and excessive taxation for its accumulation needs (Akman 2001:36).

CONCLUSION

The long-term crisis and entrenched recession in Turkey necessarily raise questions about the validity and usefulness of liberalisation as a policy option to overcome economic and financial difficulties. Can the current crisis in Turkey and other emerging markets and less economically developed countries be reduced to mismanagement or are there theoretical and empirical weaknesses in arguments for liberalisation in general and for capital market liberalisation in particular? Were there any other policy options to overcome the economic difficulties faced by Turkey from the late 1970s? In answering these questions I would like to refer specifically to some of the recent writings of Joseph Stiglitz, who was one of the most prominent World Bank experts. Stiglitz openly blames financial and capital market liberalisation for the economic crises facing a number of East Asian and Latin American countries (Stiglitz 2000a:1075). The occurrence of approximately 80 to 100 crises since the 1950s is indicative of a fundamental weakness in global economic arrangements. Stiglitz explains that the IMF zealotry to insist on capital market liberalisation was predicated upon an ideology rather than on 'careful analysis of theory, historical experience or a wealth of econometric studies' (Stiglitz 2000a:1076). He questions the value of the liberalisation of external economic transactions as well as the ahistorical nature of the Washington Consensus in that he acknowledges the value of the long-term planning (Stiglitz 1998b).

In his opinion there are serious theoretical and empirical problems with the arguments that justify capital market liberalisation. Advocates insist that the liberalisation of capital markets leads to the diversification of the economy and hence generates stability. But evidence suggests that, being pro-cyclical, capital flows exacerbate economic fluctuations which generates greater instability. Countries also become exposed to negative changes outside the country. Huge capital outflows become a function of changes in lenders' perceptions of countries as being risky, thus they contribute to the instability of a financial system (Stiglitz 2000a:1080).

Furthermore, Stiglitz maintains that short-term capital flows do not make a significant contribution to GNP, and provides evidence to show that they do not lead to greater investment in less economically developed countries. The opposite view that restrictions on short-term capital flows discourage foreign investment is not true either. In fact, capital market liberalisation leads to economic volatility and this in turn makes investment less attractive. Liberalism makes countries vulnerable to the pressures of financial capital to reduce corporate capital tax and increase interest rates. This in turn makes it very difficult for governments to follow a beneficial investment policy.

The negative consequences of short-term capital flows for economic growth, employment and incomes make it necessary for the state to intervene and introduce restrictions on capital inflows, capital outflows and the banking system (Stiglitz 2000a:1083–1084). Taxes on short-term inflows can be used as regulators of capital movement: in the case of an over-abundance of inflows taxes could be increased, and in case of a shortage of capital inflows negative taxes may be used. Mexico learned its lesson from its financial deregulation which led to the volatility of capital markets and to the 1994 crisis. Corrective action was taken in the aftermath of this crisis and led to the realisation that financial deregulation needs to be accompanied by an effective and efficient superintendence of banks and curbs on short-term speculative capital (Gwynne and Kay 2000:145).

In criticising the Washington Consensus the World Bank's senior vice president and chief economist Stiglitz emphasises the fact that policies suggested by the Washington Consensus are incomplete and misguided:

> Making markets work requires more than just low inflation, it requires sound financial regulation, competition policy, and policies to facilitate the transfer of technology, to name some fundamental issues reflected by the Washington Consensus. (Stiglitz 1998a:1)

It is significant to note that Stiglitz's aim in criticising the Washington Consensus and in proposing a post-Washington Consensus is to acknowledge and address the imperfections of the market. He develops arguments that are diametrically opposed to the main tenets of the primacy of market forces and the reduction of state intervention and expenditure to a minimum. He sees state intervention in economic policies, basic education, health, roads, law and order, and environmental protection as vital. Focusing on these fundamentals would require for the state to play an important role 'in regulation, industrial policy, social protection and welfare' (Stiglitz 1998a:25).

Following neo-liberal prescriptions, Turkey has followed what Weisskopf (1981) calls the conservative strategy. This strategy was also used in the US in the 1980s to overcome economic crisis. The conservative strategy aims to pass the burden of restructuring on to the poorer and weaker classes in its attempt to maintain the economic power and privilege of the dominant capitalist class. Policies followed intend to revitalise economic growth by stimulating corporate profitability. This necessitates not only a direct attack on workers' wages and salaries but also a reduction of welfare services provided by the state. Social security, health, education and help to small businesses and firms are the targets of this market-based conservative strategy. A specific aim of this strategy is both to slow down the growth of wages and to reduce the state.

It is not clear whether the conservative option based on suppressed wages and reduced state expenditure on welfare services will necessarily stimulate productive investment and growth. Furthermore, such a policy is bound to lead to social and political tension and instability. The market-based conservative policies have been implemented in Turkey specifically to create suitable conditions to encourage corporate capital to move into speculative financial activities. The state has not made any serious attempt to include measures to persuade capital to move into productive investment. The restructuring of the Turkish economy has been carried out in accordance with the requisites of global capitalism. It has served to help the capitalist system to slow down its generalised crises by opening up a profitable market for globally floating finance capital. Locally operating capital has also jumped onto the bandwagon and shifted most of its investment from production to speculative lending to the state. The transformation from modern capitalism to globalised capitalism allows less economically developed countries neither to complete the project of modernity nor to isolate themselves in order to modernise at their own speed.

4

Agrarian crisis

The speed of rural transformations in Turkey has accelerated dramatically since the late 1990s and this has generated disbelief, bewilderment, anxiety and tension in the countryside. Turkish farmers today are experiencing a fate similar to that which Mexican farmers have been facing since 1992. Policies introduced under the close control of the Bretton Woods institutions are unleashing processes that are unfamiliar to farming populations in both countries as well as a large number of other less economically developed countries. Governments simply close their eyes to the reactions of farmers and continue with their liberalising mission, which brings about a process of what may be called 'de-agrarianisation', resulting in an increasing loss of livelihood for the great majority of rural producers. The policies followed since the 1980s are diametrically opposed to the developmentalist policies which characterised the period between 1950 and 1980. In this period the state acted as the guardian or manager of national development. Direct or indirect involvement of the state in productive and distributional relations ensured the commercialisation and commodification of agriculture.

Although the intensity of the state's involvement varied from time to time, the centrality of the state was the main feature of policy design and implementation in agricultural and rural development in this period. In close co-operation with international donor agencies, the state aimed to extend and intensify commodity production through a variety of policies and programmes. They included the provision of inputs, credits and extension services, promotion of modern farming technologies, introduction of new crop varieties, establishment of state farms, parastatal marketing and distribution agencies.

In its attempt to control agricultural and rural development, the state actively promoted the establishment of agricultural associations and co-operatives. While in appearance these organisations gave the impression of independent farmer organisations, in reality they were instrumental in the vertical integration of farming under state control. Through institutions like producer and marketing co-operatives, agricultural banks, etc., the state ensured its supremacy in the countryside and controlled the conditions of production of millions of farmers, big and small alike. By dictating what and how to produce, in what quantity and to what quality, the state determined the modality of integration into the world economy.

Agrarian policies of the developmental state in Turkey in the period between 1950 and 1980 were shaped in close co-operation with international development agencies such as the World Bank. Huge infrastructural development projects, the promotion of modern farming through technical innovation, mechanisation and export orientation of agriculture were all financed largely by international finance institutions and all of this facilitated Turkey's integration into the world economy. Such integration would not have been possible without better social and economic infrastructure (schools, health clinics, electricity, roads, bridges, dams, irrigation, etc.). Funding from multilateral organisations and the US was deployed to ensure that Turkey's integration into the global economy took a particular form.

The same international agencies have been imposing new policies since the 1980s on Turkey and other less economically developed countries and demanding liberalisation in every sphere of life. Implementation of neo-liberal policies means the abandonment of developmentalist policies and the curtailment of the role of the state in economic development. In agriculture, liberalisation has meant de-agrarianisation and de-peasantisation in the countryside, as well as withdrawal of state support for farmers. Why is it that since the 1980s international donor agencies and more economically developed states have changed their policy agenda which has since had serious repercussions on Turkish agriculture? Our main contention here is that the Turkish agrarian transformation cannot be understood in isolation from the internationalisation of agriculture. In order to gain a better understanding of the major policy shift from developmentalism to neo-liberalism in Turkish agriculture it is necessary to see how agriculture has become internationalised under the control of US transnational corporations (TNCs) and how they have shaped world agriculture to serve their own interests.

As in all less economically developed countries, Turkey's agrarian transformation has been shaped by changes in the world economy, which has seen the increasing internationalisation of agricultural production and trade since the turn of the nineteenth century in which the US has played a vital role (Bernstein 1994, 2000; Friedmann and McMichael 1989). The roots of the internationalisation of agriculture can be traced back to the 1870s. The competition between Europe and settler economies such as the US, Canada, Australia and Argentina to control world food markets has shaped the global division of labour since 1870. The colonialist expansion to Africa and Asia throughout the nineteenth century contributed significantly to the integration of agriculture into the global food chains. In order to meet world market demands for a variety of cash crops, colonialism gradually destroyed the old forms of production and replaced them with new ones. From this time onwards the rise of the agro-food complex in the US paved the way for US hegemony in the twentieth century. The most significant feature of US hegemony was the rise of transnational food companies which gradually mechanised and industrialised agriculture. Until the Second World War US agriculture exported dietary staples and helped develop the industry by providing cheap food for the labour force and constituting an internal market for industrial products. After the Second World War industrial capital started to control US agriculture (Friedmann and McMichael 1989).

INTERNATIONALISATION OF THIRD WORLD AGRICULTURE

The gradual internationalisation of Third World agriculture since the Second World War has been strongly influenced by the US model of development. The emphasis placed on the complementarity of agricultural and industrial development meant the pursuit of import-substitution policies in both agriculture and industry with the help of foreign aid. Import-substitution policies required an integrated national economy in which agriculture was to be a source of demand for domestic industry. In order to ensure that agriculture produces surpluses and exportable commodities to generate foreign currency for industrial use and to constitute an internal market for the industry, policies were designed to transform pre-capitalist structures and to speed up market orientation and the capitalisation of agriculture. The contention that a modern agriculture would better serve national development paved the way for the transfer of Green Revolution technology to less economically

developed countries. The consequent specialisation and industrialisation of agriculture contributed significantly to its internationalisation. In the first Green Revolution less economically developed
countries were encouraged and helped to concentrate on the production of wheat and animal protein, using the US model of capital
and energy intensive agriculture (McMichael and Myhre 1991:92–93).
The transformation of agrarian structures in the South was speeded
up during the long post-war boom. International agencies gave
strong support to developmentalist states to invest in rural projects
and programmes and infrastructural development schemes in order
to facilitate commercialisation and commodification of agricultural
production, especially production based on small-scale peasant
family farms. International efforts also concentrated on developing
and diffusing new high-yielding 'miracle crops'. With the adoption
of new varieties of wheat, rice and maize by millions of farmers in the
South, the increased market dependence of farmers for seeds and the
chemical package, which is an absolute necessity for productivity
increases, ensured their incorporation into the world market.

Gradually US agriculture's main function changed from producing final products for consumption to supplying inputs to corporations which manufacture and distribute foods internationally. With
the exception of wheat and dairy products, US transnational corporations increasingly intensified their efforts both to substitute raw
materials for one another and to find global sourcing of new materials for the agro-food sector. This necessitated the restructuring of
agriculture in all countries. In accordance with the demands of
transnational agro-food corporations for inputs, manufacturing and
distribution networks, nation states have been forced to restructure
their agriculture.

> The restructuring not only shifts sectoral balances within
> nations, but also disaggregates large sectors, such as agriculture,
> into minute divisions, and reintegrates each division into a com-
> plex web of inputs and outputs to increasingly complex and dif-
> ferentiated food products. Not only is agriculture no longer a
> coherent sector, but even food is not. It is linked, for instance, to
> the chemical industry at all phases from fertilisers to preserva-
> tives. (McMichael and Myhre 1991:112)

The transnational accumulation process controlled by US corporations undercut the independent capacities of states to regulate

domestic production and trade. The ability of US transnational agro-food companies to develop new crops to substitute tropical products with temperate or synthetic products undermined the ability of newly independent ex-colonies to establish balanced and articulated national economies. Furthermore, technological improvements in agricultural production led to specialisation in agriculture which became dependent upon chains of inputs controlled by the US agribusiness companies. With these two processes, 'agriculture became incorporated within accumulation itself, and states and national economies become increasingly subordinate to capital' (Friedmann and McMichael 1989:95). In the new food regime in operation under the hegemony of US transnational capital, peripheral countries imported wheat mostly from the US at the expense of domestic food production and tended to lose their export markets in sugar and vegetable oils due to import-substitution in advanced capitalist countries (Friedmann and McMichael 1989:103). Agriculture became more and more industrialised and intensified in advanced capitalist countries and food processing became a dominant feature of the new food regime. This necessitated inter-sectoral integration at international level. The new agro-food chains created became increasingly dominated by agro-capitals which ensured the shift 'in agricultural products from final use to industrial inputs for manufacturing foods' (Friedmann and McMichael 1989:105).

THE END OF DEVELOPMENTALISM

Developmentalism came to a close by the end of the 1970s. Without entering into the endless debates on the reasons behind the collapse of developmentalism and the rise of globalisation it may suffice to note a few changes in agricultural production and trade in the 1970s which had a significant impact on the internationalisation processes at work. In the 1970s exigencies of the changing international political order brought about the collapse of the post-war international food regime. US foreign and domestic policies no longer required the exports of cheap grain surpluses to the South. Second, development of agricultural export capacity in other countries constituted a major threat to US supremacy in the world grain markets (Friedmann 1978, 1982, 1993). The collapse of the post-war food order and the weakening of the US's hegemonic power generated possibilities and opportunities for TNCs to operate globally and organise the production and distribution of agricultural commodities (Friedman 1993:52).

Since the 1970s, particularly with the increasing indebtedness of less economically developed countries, a 'new international division of labour in agriculture' has been emerging (McMichael and Myhre 1991:93). Less economically developed countries are forced to produce and export luxury foods and durable food components such as oils and sweeteners in order to meet their debt. In the emerging 'new international division of labour in agriculture' the South is given the role of providing labour-intensive off-season fruits and vegetables, beef, poultry, fish and flowers, etc., while the North assumes the role of producing and exporting capital-intensive 'low-value' raw foods such as grains.

> This configuration is fundamentally asymmetrical. While the South's agro-food production is reoriented to higher value markets overseas, the North exports (indeed 'dumps') its domestic surpluses. The former compromises or pre-empts a coherent national agricultural sector, while the latter expresses the highly protected agricultural sectors of the metropolitan nations. (McMichael and Myhre 1991:93)

Mexico is a case in point where the recent Mexican crisis has 'led to the removal of food policy from the public realm, and the reorientation of the food sector to providing inputs for a transnational agro-industrial network' (McMichael and Myhre 1991:93). Under the tutelage of IFIs agricultural production has been reoriented and restructured in such a way as to ensure that the local labour force becomes very cheap in the process of global rationalisation in agriculture and industry (Sanderson 1986a:11–23; 1986b). In this new global shift the local states are reduced to authorised agents of the international system as they offer choices largely beneficial to international capital at the expense of the rural masses.

In the new international division of labour in agriculture the demands of transnational capital play a crucial role in the policies followed by less economically developed states. In the 1960s states promoted capitalist agriculture which used inputs produced by international capital. Production of standardised crops for internal and external markets constituted the backbone of the process. From the 1970s onwards the demands of international capital necessitated the pursuit of 'export-substitution' policy by less economically developed states who had been losing their control over the composition of their agriculture. The promotion of agro-export production has meant the replacement of traditional primary commodity production and exports (McMichael and Myhre 1991:94). The tendency has been that the traditional food crops are replaced by products that either tend to go to feed animals to boost meat production in order to satisfy the demands of high-income classes or to luxurious markets in the forms of fresh fruits, vegetables and flowers.

The pace of the replacement of traditional crops with agro-food production varies in less economically developed countries. In some places the promotion of agro-export or agro-industry has complemented the traditional crops, while in others it has replaced them rapidly. The speed of the replacement process depends on the state's willingness and ability to implement measures to ensure the structural transformation towards a fully market-oriented economy integrated into the global system. For this purpose rapid institutional changes are introduced and implemented and obstacles for the operations of transnational agribusiness companies are removed. The new agro-industry becomes involved in the production and export of standardised goods for high-value markets.

As Barkin *et al.* (1990:107) highlight 'with this process, social structures disintegrate as their rural productive basis erodes and people are inexorably driven into unproductive urban quicksands'. It is not surprising that since 1970 many less economically developed countries have become increasingly dependent upon the imports of basic foodstuffs while their agricultural exports have increased. Hathaway (1987), Tubiana (1989), Wagstaff (1982), Raikes (2000) and Morrison (1984) have all strongly emphasised this tendency. The speed of this process does, of course, vary from country to country. Less economically developed countries are forced to specialise in export crops to meet their debt obligation. IFIs have been instrumental in the transformation of Third World countryside to promote agro-export production. Through structural adjustment loans the IMF and the World Bank shape agro-food policies of indebted states. Sooner or later indebted countries face the IMF and World Bank impositions to speed up the internationalisation of their agricultural sector. Mexico experienced this in 1986 when the World Bank forced the Mexican Government to eliminate food subsidies, privatise or liquidate parastatals to liberalise the trade, input prices and domestic agricultural prices, and to streamline the Ministry of Agriculture through decentralisation and rationalisation. All these liberal policies contributed to the outward orientation of agriculture in Mexico and limited the state's ability to construct policies and institutions to meet internal demands for food (McMichael and Myhre 1991:99).

International organisations and TNCs mastermind the changes in Third World agriculture, which becomes specialised under TNC domination and moves away from food production. Exports of luxury cash crops, high-value food and animal feed in less economically developed countries do not keep up with the rising imports of agricultural commodities, most importantly food. Therefore the share of agricultural exports held by less economically developed countries declines and generates huge trade deficits. The extent to which TNCs control or exert influence over agricultural policy and practice in particular nations and the extent to which the consequences of that influence affect the potential for rural development in these nations obviously differ according to the particular socio-economic and political contexts in which agribusiness operates. The consequences of the participation of TNCs in a particular nation's agro-exporting sector also depends on the relative abilities of national governments, bourgeoisies, labourers and peasants to interact with the TNCs in ways that meet their own personal or broader domestic interests.

Given these provisos, there are some aspects of the global socio-economic context that have similar effects on all national interest groups in all less economically developed countries. The development aid agendas of the major international finance institutions are designed to push the agricultural sector in the less economically developed world into partnership with TNCs. Yet the economic and logistical realities of the world agricultural commodity markets, for which they produce and from which they hope to gain the desperately needed foreign exchange, bring the less economically developed world into a clash of interests with TNCs. The multilateral lending institutions encourage the activities of TNCs in the agricultural sectors of less economically developed countries in several ways. As a condition to lending money to less economically developed countries, the World Bank and the IMF require borrowing nations to implement particular economic policies that transform their economies. Through economic and political conditionalities the IMF and the World Bank are able to control the national agricultural and development policies of less economically developed countries. The lending decisions of these two institutions are vital for less economically developed countries, as other lenders also require their seal of approval before lending any money.

In the newly generated structures, export-oriented agriculture gradually becomes dominated by TNCs and Third World governments are forced to phase out or eliminate all the restrictions toward free trade. Due to the essentially low value of basic foodstuffs the governments in less economically developed countries do not see any problem in shifting their policies to the production of high-value crops. Thus they are easily persuaded to comply with 'the new politics of global capital accumulation', and not to 'employ their considerably reduced capacities to enhance food security through national programs to reinvigorate peasant agriculture' (McMichael and Myhre 1991:100).

Traditional export commodities such as coffee, tea, sugar, tobacco and cocoa have been increasingly displaced by high-value foods (HVFs) such as fruits and vegetables, poultry, dairy products, etc. since 1980. Watts and Goodman (1997) see this as part and parcel of a process which has irretrievably replaced the traditional international division of labour within the agro-food systems. Consequently, while the share of cereals, sugar and tropical beverages in world trade has declined significantly, the share of HVFs showed a dramatic increase (Watts and Goodman 1997:10). Some less economically developed countries like Brazil, Mexico, Argentina, China, and Kenya have become 'new agricultural countries' (NACs) comparable to the newly industrialising countries (NICs). A number of authors including Friedland (1994), Friedmann (1993, 1994), Jaffee (1994), Raynolds (1997) and Watts (1994) analyse various aspects of the new agro-food systems and show how the old food regime has been replaced by the new agro-food system in which certain countries have become specialist producers of HVFs.

A fundamental feature of HVF agriculture is its reliance on cheap labour to keep the cost of production as low as possible. Contract farming is the main mechanism of organising the production of HVFs for niche markets. International capital plays a significant role in promoting the production of HVFs, the suitability of the produce for the required tastes in niche markets, and linking farm-level production to international trade. However, international capital is highly selective in its investments in high-value agriculture. It prefers to go to places where the necessary groundwork is in place. It moves into countries where state policies under the directives of the IMF, the World Bank and the World Trade Organisation gradually eliminate traditional agriculture, and establish the prominence of free marketism in production, trade and distribution. As we will see in the following section this is what has been happening in Turkey since the 1990s. The structural adjustment policies (SAPs) in place since the 1980s have gradually eroded the viability of family farming specialising in traditional crops such as cereals, tobacco and sugar beet. Marginalised and desperate, farmers are being forced to move into the production of HVFs. While, through deregulation and SAPs, agriculture is being starved of investment and family farms are being pushed to the brink of extinction, the production of HVFs is presented as an alternative livelihood. Rampant poverty experienced in Turkish agriculture in the last decade parallels the global tendency in which a decreasing number of people are deriving their livelihood from agriculture and an increasing number of rural people are living below the absolute poverty line (Bingswanger and Deininger 1999).

The new food regime has been predicated upon the restructuring of national agricultures (Raynolds *et al.* 1993:1106). Under the dominance of transnational agro-capital, diets have become standardised and conditions of production have become homogenised. De-regulation of food production and distribution under the watchful eyes of the multilateral lending agencies and international institutions like the World Trade Organisation have generated a new international division of labour in agriculture. Agricultural production has gradually become regionally specialised and national states have lost a significant proportion of their autonomy. Agrarian internationalisation has taken multiple trajectories due to the central role the state plays in varying degrees in the restructuring of domestic economies.

GENERAL AGREEMENT ON TRADE AND TARIFFS (GATT) AND THE WORLD TRADE ORGANISATION (WTO)

International organisations play an absolutely vital role in the transnationalisation of agro-food systems. The rules and regulations accepted since the 1980s by the WTO and its predecessor, the GATT, have accelerated the internationalisation of agricultural commodity chains controlled by transnational biotechnology and agribusiness companies. In ensuring the transnationalisation of agro-food systems one of the most crucial policies imposed on less economically developed countries is the liberalisation of the trade in agricultural goods which represents the biggest challenge to food security and agricultural production in these countries. Liberalisation in agriculture is pushed as a feature of the new global division of labour that demands production for export. One significant objection has been that trade liberalisation leads to an almost instantaneous increase in food imports in less economically developed countries without a corresponding increase in their exports, which leads to the marginalisation of small producers and a rampant increase in unemployment in rural areas. A case in point is India which implemented a partial liberalisation of agriculture in 1995 and realised by 2001 that liberalisation had generated problems in the economy. For instance, between 1995 and 2000 the imports of agricultural products in India increased from 50 billion Rupees to 150 billion Rupees. Consequently, in 2001 India demanded that more economically developed countries should also adopt tariff bindings to ensure a substantial reduction in tariffs. Furthermore, India insisted that both the US and the EU should abandon direct income support to their farmers under the name of deficiency payments, as they are equivalent to subsidies which distort trade patterns to the detriment of less economically developed countries (Muradilhan 2001:32). While less economically developed countries are being asked to liberalise their agriculture, the total support given to farmers by OECD countries has increased from US$308 billion in the 1981–88 period to US$347 billion in 1997–99. In 2001 the total estimated support in OECD countries stood at US$360 billion, which was more than double the entire US$170 billion agricultural output of the less economically developed world (Muradilhan 2001:32). It is evident that less economically developed countries cannot compete with the highly subsidised agricultural products of the OECD countries which now control the global markets.

The hegemonic 'Quad' powers (the EU, the US, Canada and Japan) apply double standards to trade in agricultural products: while preaching liberalisation for less economically developed countries, they use protectionism in their home markets. The Uruguay Round of the GATT negotiations reflected the preferences of the Quad powers who insisted on the liberalisation of agricultural trade. The WTO, which replaced the GATT in 1995, became the main target of anti-systemic movements for not representing the interests of less economically developed countries and promoting the interests of the more economically developed world.

In its 'Proposal for Comprehensive Long-term Agricultural Trade Reform' the US defines food security in terms of trade liberalisation. The US Government states that:

> [T]he United States believes, [... that] further liberalisation of trade in agricultural products and promoting legitimate assistance programs are important elements in strengthening food security [...]. In addition to specific disciplines which expand sources of supply and encourage efficiencies in agricultural production trade reform will result in economic growth and spur innovation, expanding global food security. It is important that liberalisation alone will not address food security needs in all developed and least developed countries. As a consequence, the negotiations need to take into account the continuing rule of international food aid and credit programmes in providing for food import needs. (WTO 2000:2–3)

A purely market-oriented approach is not appropriate for achieving food security in less economically developed countries where the great majority of farmers are smallholders who cannot cope with unpredictable international prices. The US definition of food security is predicated upon the premise that food aid and financial aid would always be there to provide food for the needy in less economically developed countries. A familiarity with international political economy would reveal that financial aid and food aid to less economically developed countries are not available without stringent conditions attached to them.

Free trade in agricultural commodities creates unfair competition between producers in more economically developed countries who receive subsidies and those in less economically developed countries whose subsidies are increasingly being phased out. Particularly expensive export subsidies used by more economically developed countries to support their farmers are not an option for governments of less economically developed countries, which lack financial resources. State intervention in more economically developed countries has a direct bearing on food security in less economically developed countries where farmers are forced out of food production in the face of cheap imports of food. The Uruguay Round on Agriculture, which was signed in 1994 and came into force with the emergence of the WTO in 1995, prevented countries from introducing export subsidies in agriculture and stated that countries that already had export subsidies should reduce them. In 2000 only 25 countries out of the total 137 WTO members had export subsidies in operation while the EU had a direct subsidy system in operation. As world market prices reflect export subsidies and direct subsidies, producers in less economically developed countries are forced to sell their foods below cost of production. Export subsidies and direct income support do not internalise cost and as such they promote production for sale in world markets. Increased global supply leads to decreasing prices internationally, and rural producers in less economically developed countries who are not in receipt of export subsidies and direct income subsidies lose their competitive edge.

The Uruguay Round of the GATT negotiations (1986–94) laid the foundations of the rules which were to govern international agricultural trade and production. Although the Agreement on Agriculture (AoA) seems to be somehow lenient in allowing countries to determine their own support measures for agriculture, this is only allowed as long as such policies do not countervail the liberalisation and integration of agriculture into the world market. In this vein less economically developed countries are allowed to support their low-income and poorly resourced farmers financially and invest in the provision of infrastructure and public food stocks at world prices. The AoA envisages the elimination of tariffs in all countries within a given timescale. Likewise, export subsidies are to be phased out in countries where they are already in place and they cannot be introduced in countries where they do not exist. The AoA is based on the assumption that a free market in agriculture is the key for achieving food security. But the contradictory context of the agreement makes this very difficult. Article B prevents governments from taking measures to protect themselves from dumping, yet other articles of the agreement legalise export subsidies where they already exist. In other words, in the name of free trade, less economically developed countries are prevented from raising tariffs against countries like the US which already have export subsidies in place, thus they have to sell crops below the cost of production. This is a good example of double standards on the part of the US and the EU which strongly influenced the final form of the AoA. While they protect their agricultural export sector at home they insist on liberalisation of agriculture in less economically developed countries.

The reduction of import tariffs in conjunction with the AoA, the World Bank and the IMF conditionalities has provided TNCs with an opportunity to dump products strategically on less economically developed countries below the cost of production. In this way, TNCs which control particular commodity markets eliminate competition and secure markets for their own products by ruining local production. The AoA clearly favours agricultural exporters rather than producers. It does not allow countries to opt for self-sufficiency in any agricultural products. It is interesting to note that the AoA does not question whether cheap commodities contain export subsidies, while at the same time it insists that no country should prevent an exporter who is willing to sell cheap from doing so.

The Food and Agricultural Organisation (FAO) found that the AoA increased the food dependence of less economically developed countries. Research carried out in 14 less economically developed countries revealed that the value of food imports in the period 1995–98 exceed those over the 1990–94 period. While India and Jamaica's agricultural exports were higher than their imports before 1994, this trend reversed after this date. In 11 of the 14 countries included in the research, food imports increased relative to agricultural export earnings (FAO 2000). The FAO concludes from its 14 country case studies that there is:

> a growing trend towards the consolidation of farms as competitive pressure began to build up following trade liberalisation. While this has generally contributed to increased productivity and competitiveness, it led to the displacement and marginalisation of farm labourers, creating hardship that involved typically small farmers and food-insecure population groups, and this is in a situation where there are few safety nets. (FAO 2000:3)

Trade liberalisation and globalisation of agriculture do not necessarily increase food production or the efficiency of food production, thus they are not conducive to improving the economic situation of farmers. On the contrary, participation in global markets leaves the great majority of the poor in rural areas without sufficient purchasing power to access food. The Philippine Government predicted that agricultural export earnings would increase by 20 per cent if the WTO rules were applied. In reality agricultural export earnings fell by 12 per cent in the 1995–98 period. Again, unlike the prediction that trade liberalisation would create 500,000 extra jobs between

1996 and 1998, in reality 710,000 jobs disappeared in the Philippine agriculture (Yabut-Bernardino 2000).

While claiming to be striving for food security, defined as adequate safe and nutritious food for everyone, what international agencies and rich nations do in fact is endanger food security for the great majority in less economically developed countries. Policies imposed by the World Bank, the IMF and the WTO lead to displacement of farmers from agriculture and prepare the groundwork for the TNCs to move in to establish corporate super-farms for luxury production for international markets. Corporatisation of agriculture is well underway in India and Mexico where impoverished farmers are forced into new forms of bondage through unequal and unfair contracts. The saga of Punjabi farmers in India is a case in point. The farmers in Punjab received only 0.75 Rupees per kg for their tomatoes from Pepsico while the market price was 2.00 Rupees. Pepsico, the firm who contracted the farmers, refused to increase the price and eventually left the region by selling its tomato processing plant to a subsidiary of Levers (Shiva, Holla and Menon 1997). Food security in India is being undermined by trade liberalisation policies and land previously under food cultivation is being increasingly allocated for luxury food crops or non-food crops.

In Mexico the principles of the 1910 revolution were discarded and the land law was changed in order to speed up liberalisation. The so-called Second Agrarian Reform has left Mexican farmers at the mercy of international companies and free trade. Consequently Mexico's 9000 years of food security was wiped out after 14 years of liberalisation under structural adjustment and two years of NAFTA (North American Free Trade Association). Under the Second Agrarian Reform the state has abandoned its responsibility for food security. The Executive Director of the National Association of Peasant Maize Producers, Victor Suarez Carrera, suggests that Mexico has become dependent upon importation of maize which originated in Mexico. Mexico's food imports more than doubled in the four years following the new agrarian reform and NAFTA, increasing from 20 per cent of its food requirements in 1992 to 43 per cent in 1996. Eating 'more cheaply on imports is not eating at all for the poor in Mexico'. One in every two peasants is not getting enough to eat. In the 18 months since NAFTA, the intake of food has been slashed by 29 per cent. 2.2 million Mexicans, have lost their jobs and 40 million are in extreme poverty (TWN 2002).

THE PROMOTION OF SMALL-SCALE HOUSEHOLD PRODUCTION AND THE MODERNISATION OF TURKISH AGRICULTURE

In the post-war period peasantry in newly independent states became a significant political force. Modernising elites in Asia, Africa and Latin America formed alliances with the peasantry in order to speed up the process of development. Developmental states in less economically developed countries showed willingness to address peasants' demands for land. Land reform policies in many areas of the less economically developed world not only reduced the power basis of rural elites but were also conducive to agricultural modernisation. The needs of import-substituting industries for large internal markets led governments to take serious actions to improve the productivity of the predominant small-scale farmers. As large landownership has never been a serious issue in the history of the Turkish Republic, between 1923 and 1980 the Turkish State emphasised policies that would create conditions for family farms to increase their productivity. The alliance formed between the urban elite and the broad masses of rural producers until the 1980s helped strengthen the owner-occupier medium-sized farmers who relied mainly on family labour (Aydın 1986; Keyder 1983; Sirman-Eralp 1988). Peasant production gradually became capitalised as a result of the agrarian reforms involving government credit, input provisioning and guaranteed state purchasing of main crops. The threat of land reform, on the other hand, forced the big feudal and semi-feudal landlords of eastern and south-eastern Anatolia to modernise and capitalise their farming practices. 1950 marked the beginning of a specific integration of the Turkish economy into the world economy, which assigned Turkey the role of producing raw materials. The modernisation of Turkish agriculture through mechanisation, helped by the importation of a large number of tractors in conjunction with the Marshall Aid, facilitated this process (Boratav 1988:xi–li). Mechanisation not only allowed intensive farming but also enabled the rapid opening up of previously uncultivated areas for agricultural production. In a sense Marshall Aid represented a continuation of the state support for agriculture. The first attempt to support agriculture emerged as a reaction to the world economic crisis of the 1930s to prevent the collapse of production due to falling prices. Throughout the 1930s the state had intervened to stabilise cereal prices and established a number of institutions including the Soil Products Office and Agricultural Sales Co-operatives to procure crops and provide credits and inputs. Agricultural support became an integral part of development plans which envisaged a balanced growth based on agriculture and industry. In the planned period between 1960 and 1980 the aims of agricultural policies were multifaceted and included such things as productivity, price stability, increased exports, prevention of inflation, quality enhancement and competitiveness. In accordance with the diversity of these aims, the policy instruments were also varied (TÜSİAD 1999; Işıklı and Abay 1993). The most common policies were support buying at floor prices decided by the state, input subsidies and subsidised credits. The number of crops included in the support procurement went up to 30 during the 1970s but dropped to 24 in 1980 when liberalisation policies started.

On the whole, throughout the 1960s and 1970s the modernisation of the agricultural sector via state policies, including the Green Revolution, credit and input schemes, and integrated area development programmes, invigorated the internal market for producer and consumer goods, and generated opportunities for wage labour both in urban and rural areas. During this period the Turkish State received enormous help from international agencies, particularly the World Bank. With the recommendations and impositions of the World Bank, Turkey emphasised policies that gave priority to small-scale agriculture and enhanced the market orientation of family farms. Following McNamara's 1974 Nairobi speech, the emphasis on small family farms represented a shift in the World Bank's approach to rural development in the less economically developed world. The shift in the World Bank's lending policies in the 1970s from the support of large-scale infrastructural development projects to the promotion of small-scale agriculture with the rhetoric of reaching the poor was not accidental. There were two main concerns behind this shift: the first was to counter mounting criticism of the Bank's support for Green Revolution policies, ease the social tension and militancy caused by extreme class differentiation and inequalities in rural areas in the less economically developed world and prevent the spread of communism; the second was to expand the market for agricultural inputs produced by transnational agribusiness companies through the commercialisation of peasant agriculture. This also fitted well with the demands of import-substituting industrialisation in Turkey between 1960 and 1980. Turkey received its fair share from internationally-supported development schemes designed for small-scale family farms (Aydın 1993).

Significant productivity increases took place in Turkish agriculture in the 1960s and the 1970s due to the increasing use of modern technology and considerable state support for agriculture through five-year development plans. While mechanisation and commercialisation of agriculture led to increased productivity, they also enabled the developmental state to extract surpluses from the agricultural sector through price controls and marketing arrangements. The agricultural sector was used as a black box from which cheap food for the urban populace and commodities for export could be taken. While at a rhetorical level the state claimed to be promoting the interests of the peasantry through the provision of subsidies, credits, infrastructure, health and education, it also appropriated surpluses through the control of the market and prices. However, on the whole the period between 1950 and 1980 can be characterised as being relatively beneficial to agriculture with significant welfare gains for producers (Köymen 1998; Akşit 1993). Particularly the introduction of a multi-party political system in 1947 signified a process in which political parties sought an alliance with the peasantry through populist policies. By 1980 the rural population had received significant welfare gains through state subsidies (TÜSİAD 1999).

ECONOMIC HARDSHIPS AND NEO-LIBERALISM

The late 1970s and the 1980s witnessed the beginning of the gradual evaporation of farmers' previously accomplished material gains. The crippling economic, political and social problems were compounded by the oil crisis in the second half of the 1970s. This signalled the beginning of the elimination of subsidies to agriculture and the gradual reduction of public investment in the agricultural sector, as SAPs and conditionalities imposed by the IMF meant the withdrawal of the state from the economic sphere.

As emphasised earlier, the adoption of neo-liberal policies in Turkish agriculture needs to be considered in conjunction with the emergence of the new international division of labour in agriculture and the control exercised over the new food regime by transnational agribusiness companies. From the post-war period until the 1970s transnational agribusiness companies were attempting to eliminate the pre-capitalist forms of production in less economically developed countries in order to be able to expand the market for agricultural inputs. Therefore, with the mediation of international aid agencies they supported import substitution policies which saw agricultural and industrial development as complementary. However, since the 1970s developments in agricultural technology have enabled the transnational agri-food companies to control the world food chains and force less economically developed country governments to restructure their agriculture so that suitable conditions would be in place for these companies' activities. In this new global food order, less economically developed countries' governments gradually lose their control over their agricultural sectors through the implementation of neo-liberal policies.

Neo-liberalist organisations and states consider Turkey's existing farming practices as impediments to the restructuring of agriculture. In particular, the state subsidies to farmers, which were instrumental in the sustainability of traditional agriculture, are seen to be the key impediments to the introduction of high value foods. The belief that subsidies help maintain the household-based production of traditional crops has been the basis of policies which intend to increase the vulnerability of household producers. Therefore policies imposed on Turkey aim to abolish the support to farmers in order to open up possibilities for international agro-capital to penetrate into the areas previously engaged in traditional crop production. At the rhetorical level, neo-liberal policies are justified on efficiency grounds, yet in fact they speed up the impoverishment of rural areas. In reality it is expected that increased impoverishment of traditional crop producing farmers will allow international agro-capital to introduce new mechanisms of co-ordination and control of production, to ensure product standardisation and just-in-time production. The form of the relationship between the direct producers and the national and/or international firms that establish direct or indirect control of the production process may vary, but the most preferred form is contract farming through which farmers are integrated into the international commodity chains. The process of impoverishing the farming community in Turkey and thus generating conditions for the introduction of new crop varieties in co-operation with international agro-capital has been a slow process. 1980 represents a turning point in the Turkish agricultural policies as neo-liberalism started to dominate Turkish policymaking. In the 1980s Turkey joined a number of less economically developed countries which embarked upon a new experiment in economic policy. The first and foremost aim of the new policy has been to leave the protectionist, state-guided import-substitution industrialisation (ISI) model and replace it with measures that emphasise the free play of market forces. This has been considered to be the only way to eliminate the problems of inflation, balance of payments deficits, inefficiency, lack of international competitiveness and increasing international debt.

The dominant monetarist school of thought blamed excessive state involvement in the economy and extensive public spending for the existence of inflation and unsustainable growth. In the 1960s and 1970s the critics of the ISI model argued that inflation discouraged private saving and growth because of its impact of lowering real internal rates. Furthermore, overvalued exchange rates fired by inflation promoted great inefficiencies in resource use. Under such circumstances the survival of industries depended upon the rent-seeking mentality encouraged by state protection and subsidies. Monetarist solutions to these problems emphasised stabilisation policies in the 1960s and 1970s but have favoured SAPs since the 1980s. The thinking behind the SAPs is based on neo-classical economic theory which is concerned primarily with the efficient allocation of scarce resources. This relies on the effective operation of the price mechanism in the market. In other words, the neo-classical liberalisation policies emphasise the supremacy of the market and maintain that if market forces are left to operate freely only then will resource allocation take place more efficiently and the economy will run smoothly. The *sine qua non* of this is the cutting back of the state in the economy. The SAPs in the 1980s aimed to transform the productive structures through complete liberalisation. In a liberalised economy the expectation was that with the reduction of the state, the economic efficiency and the potential for long-term growth would be restored. The expectation was that individual economic agents would make more efficient resource allocation decisions in a free economic atmosphere where the state's role is reduced to ensuring property rights and maintaining macroeconomic stability.

Since the introduction of the neo-liberal policies in the 1980s the agricultural sector has posed a serious problem for the free marketeers. While by definition they needed to reform the agricultural sector in order to cut back state expenditure in the process of 'rationalisation', the exigencies of multi-party politics forced political parties to give concessions to a large number of agricultural producers in order to establish legitimacy in the countryside. Policies implemented in agriculture have oscillated between the pre-requisites of the minimisation of the state and legitimacy concerns in the countryside. A full-scale attack on agriculture has just started. In the liberalist crusade in rural areas there has been close co-operation between the theologians of the IMF and the state officials.

Given that the agricultural sector employed a significant propor-tion of the workforce and that political parties had been in compe-tition to recruit support from the countryside, neo-liberal policies were not entirely implemented during the 1980s and the first half of the 1990s. The complete elimination of subsidies to farmers has been a serious source of friction between the IFIs and the Government. For instance, the World Bank has withheld credits to the Government on a number of occasions as a result of Turkey's insistence on subsidising fertiliser prices in the late 1980s. Political expediency prevents governments, who intend to avoid a crisis of legitimacy, from taking drastic measures on subsidies. Particularly in the years prior to elections no government dared to attract the wrath of agricultural producers by introducing sudden and sharp cuts in subsidies, wages and services.

The 5th of April decisions taken in the aftermath of the 1994 financial crisis were the first systematic effort to attempt to restruc-ture the agricultural support system in accordance with the promises made to the IMF. With the 5th of April decisions, the state restricted guaranteed procurement of crops only to cereals, sugar beet and tobacco. Likewise, the Union of Agricultural Sales Co-operatives were left to their own devices in the procurement of crops like hazel-nuts, sunflowers and cotton. The Seventh Five-Year Development Plan (1996–2000) envisaged further rationalisation of support to agriculture in order to ensure compliance with the WTO's agricul-tural agreements and the EU's agricultural policies. The plan specif-ically stated that the main targets were: to intervene in crop prices; to put an end to state guarantees in farm gate prices; to eliminate guaranteed crop procurements by the state and parastatal organisa-tions; to gradually phase out input subsidies and replace them with a direct income support scheme to farmers; to limit the plantation of some crops of which there is over-capacity; and to encourage the introduction of new crops for which there is international and domestic demand (DPT 1996:57–60). During the seventh plan a number of publicly owned agricultural industries including the Milk Industry Association (Türkiye Süt Endüstrisi Kurumu), Meat and Fish Association (Et Balık Kurumu) and Fodder Industry were privatised without proper consideration of the implications for producers in terms of production, organisation and distribution.

In the first decade of liberalisation, agriculture experienced a severe blow in terms of incomes as the number of crops receiving support prices declined sharply (Boratav 1988:135). However, due to political expediency and electoral concerns, governments were not able to follow a coherent liberalisation policy in the 1990s and on the whole the agricultural sector recovered some of the unprecedented losses it made during the 1980s. It could easily be argued that the 1990s represented a period in which the state bureaucracy prepared the necessary legal ground and institutional justification for a comprehensive restructuring of agrarian relations in line with the wishes of the IMF and the World Bank. The 1994 fiscal crisis gave an opportunity to the state to try out some liberalisation policies to find out the reaction of rural producers who constitute 45 per cent of the labour forces. The 5th of April decisions implemented under the guidance of the IMF included measures to reduce the number of supported crops, reductions in input support and the removal of the Unions of Agricultural Sales Co-operatives (UASCs) from the scope of support. The reactions of rural producers and UASCs were not strong enough to challenge the attempts of the State Treasury and the State Planning Organisation in the Seventh Five-Year Development Plan (1996–2000) to take significant steps to transform the agricultural sector congruent with the demands of the IMF and the World Bank.

STANDBY AGREEMENTS SINCE 1999 AND TURKISH AGRICULTURE

Prior to the December 1999 letter of intent, the agricultural sector was given a long leash as far as full liberalisation was concerned. This was largely because the state was not capable of liberalising the economy on all fronts; while the financial and industrial sectors were given priority treatment, the agricultural sector had been subject to piecemeal treatment. By the end of 1999, when the liberalisation of the international trade and capital accounts was completed, efforts were concentrated on a comprehensive restructuring of agriculture. A series of letters of intent submitted to the IMF since 1999 laid down medium and long-term policy objectives for transforming the agrarian structures. The first two letters of intent submitted on 9 December 1999 and 10 March 2000 prioritised a gradual elimination of the existing support policies and replacing them with direct income support for the poor in the medium term (Hazine 2000a:xiv) and breaking with past policies once and for all in the longer term (Hazine 2000b:52).

The fourth letter of intent foresaw the elimination of all indirect support policies and their substitution by the direct income support system by the end of 2002. Not only did the state promise to abolish the subsidies to farmers and their organisations but it also promised to privatise and commercialise public assets in agriculture and related activities (Hazine 2000b:54). The far-reaching reforms promised in four consecutive letters of intent since 1999 were incorporated into the much debated '2001 Economic Reform Program' (ERP). The stipulations of the Economic Reform Loan (ERL) agreement signed with the World Bank in June 2000 were the main inspiration behind the ERP. In return for receiving US$760 million, Turkey was to implement the pledges made in the 1999 standby agreement.

The ERL envisaged a number of structural changes in the public finance administration, social security, telecommunications, energy and agriculture. In the agricultural sector the ERL envisaged a complete phasing out of the support system, a strengthening of the direct income support system, the transition to new cropping systems and changes to the administrative structures in agriculture. Accordingly, the rolling back of the state was to include no state involvement in agricultural production or the agricultural industry, the speeding up of the privatisation of agricultural institutions such as TZDK, Çay-Kur, Tekel and Şeker Fabrikaları, and the reformulation of the co-operatives law according to the directives of the World Bank.

The US$600 million ARIP (Agricultural Reform Implementation Project) agreement signed with the World Bank in July 2001 provided the Bank with the authority to monitor the extent of the implementation of the pledges made by the ERL agreement, during the 2001–05 period. The ARIP allows direct intervention into the agricultural support system, hazelnut and tobacco production. It aimed to abolish tobacco support purchases from the 2002–03 production year onwards, to privatise the TEKEL (state monopoly of cigarettes and beverages) selling all its assets from 2001 onwards, and to provide support for the adoption of alternative crops. The so-called new support model consists of direct income support for the farmers for five years and alternative crops project support for one year to help with the cost of inputs, care and harvest of the newly adopted crops. The project aims to ensure a shift from the production of over-supplied hazelnuts and tobacco to under-supplied new crop varieties. From the alternative crops project's total budget of US$161.6 million, US$146 million has been allocated for the reduction of the areas under hazelnut production and US$15.6 million for the reduction of tobacco production. The justification for the reduction of tobacco production is based on production figures provided by the State Treasury for 1998 and 1999 when more was produced than the state monopoly, TEKEL, could buy. However, according to the data produced by the State Institute for Statistics and TEKEL, the total tobacco production stood at 144,000 tons in 2001 and 153,000 tons in 2002. These figures are well below the annual domestic demand of 180,000 tons announced by the State Treasury itself (<www.treasury. gov.tr>). The main purpose of reducing tobacco production then, is to open the Turkish market to international tobacco companies. At the moment TEKEL controls 70 per cent of the 180,000 ton cigarette market. With the completion of TEKEL's privatisation, international tobacco firms such as PM, JTI and BAT will be able to increase their share in the vast Turkish market.

The requirements of Turkey's accession to the EU, the regulations of the GATT and the WTO, and the conditionalities imposed by the IMF and the World Bank work together to force the country to restructure its agriculture. Consequently, the policies for transforming Turkish agriculture have been accelerated since January 1996 when Turkey signed a Customs Union agreement with the EU. While the EU insists that Turkey should introduce the necessary institutional and structural policies to streamline Turkish agriculture to be compatible with the EU's Common Agricultural Policy, the GATT Uruguay Round agreements require measures to liberalise agricultural trade and to gradually eliminate production subsidies and reduce export subsidies. In recent years the WTO which replaced the GATT in 1994, has been at the forefront of attempts to integrate Third World agriculture into the global system. As a signatory to the WTO, Turkey has to comply with the stipulations of the Agreement on Agriculture (AoA) which came into force in 1995 outlining the main directions of policies to be followed by less economically developed countries. The AoA promotes the removal of protectionist policies from the trade in agricultural products to ensure freedom of entry to markets. It emphasises the liquidation of incentives and subsidies for agricultural exports and the elimination of domestic support for agriculture. The WTO sets different time-tables for different groups of countries, giving longer periods of adaptation to less economically developed countries and shorter periods for the more economically developed ones. Thus, radical change to agricultural support policies in Turkey is only one of the many examples of how the less economically developed world is having to adapt to meet the requirements of the AoA.

Clearly, Turkey has been pushed by the IFI to sacrifice its agriculture in order to receive additional financial resources to combat its recent fiscal crisis. The standby negotiations since 2000 have marked the final stage of Turkey's submission to external pressures to liberalise its agricultural production and trade. It is not a coincidence that this comprehensive economic programme was introduced at a time when Turkey was trying extremely hard to meet the requirements set by the EU prior to the country's accession to the union. The reforms that have been promised to the World Bank and the IMF since 1999 fit in very well with the EU preconditions. A large number of new laws have been quickly passed by the Parliament in order to establish the legal framework within which the restructuring of the economy will take place. Measures were also taken fairly quickly to establish an institutional framework for the reforms. Accordingly, a 'Restructuring Board' was established in 2000 to oversee the streamlining of UASCs in accordance with the promises made in various letters of intent to the IMF.

Furthermore, two significant laws concerning sugar beet and tobacco production were passed in 2001 to comply with the wishes of the IMF, the World Bank and agribusiness firms involved in the production and distribution of sugar and cigarettes. Justification for the 'rolling back of the state' in agriculture is provided through the need for rationalisation in agriculture as the existing price and sup-port policies are seen as irrational and burdensome on the State Treasury, benefiting mainly rich farmers rather than the poor (Letter of intent 2, Hazine 2000a).

Oyan (2003) finds the claim shared by the Turkish State and the IMF that agricultural support only benefits rich farmers and puts a heavy burden on the Treasury unfounded and exaggerated. If holdings above 20 hectares of land were considered to represent rich farmers then their numbers would be about 200,000 in 1991. Yet the number of agricultural holdings was about 4.2 million, most of whom are members of some 700,000 Agricultural Sales Co-operatives which administer at least one third of the support given to agriculture. Thus the suggestion that only rich farmers benefit from support policies at the expense of poor farmers is a distortion of the reality (Oyan 1997, 1999, 2003). Furthermore, such claims are based on exaggerated estimates and unreliable statistics. The office of the under-secretary for the Treasury, whose figures constitute the basis of such argument, contradicts itself by claiming in one place that agricultural support represents 10.2 per cent of GNP and in another that it makes up only 3 per cent of GNP (Letter of intent 1, 9 December, Hazine 2000a). Oyan's calculation that in 1999–2000 agricultural support was equal to only 0.8 per cent of GNP makes a mockery of the IMF, World Bank and State Treasury's claims that support funds are a huge burden on the state.

The four letters of intent given to the IMF detail the types of arrangements to be used to phase out agricultural support. First, they envisage eradicating support purchases, which involve not only guaranteed prices for products but also other items like input support, credit support and premium support. Once this is realised, it is believed that there will not be a need for the UASCs which have been the institutional basis of the support system. The sale of the assets, including production and distribution networks of agricultural co-operatives, to private interests is seen as the best step in the direction of rationalisation. In the past the state was not able to force the UASCs to privatise their assets as UASCs were co-operative societies and subject to private laws. Due to the enduring pressure from the World Bank the Government passed a law in June 2000 to transform UASCs from co-operative societies to joint stock companies. The 'Restructuring Board' established in tandem with the World Bank demands oversees that all industrial plants belonging to the UASCs are converted to joint stock companies and run on private enterprise. What are left to UASCs are primary processing facilities that will not receive any support from the state. The law specifies that no financial support can be provided to co-operatives and unions by the state or other public loyal bodies. The law specifically ensures that the state washes its hands of UASCs by granting them the so-called 'full autonomy'. Accordingly, the state will no longer support UASCs in crop procurement from member farmers.

The attempt to make UASCs 'autonomous' is nothing more than a clever plot to liquidate them without inviting public reactions.

The law intends to prepare the ground for the privatisation of factories and production units belonging to farmers' organisations. Without such income-generating institutions, farmers' organisations cannot survive to maintain their functions of extending credit, and providing facilities and help to their members. The law intends to undermine the principle of co-operation. The law was passed in conjunction with the IMF's imposition and intends to increase farmers' vulnerability to the encroachment of the private sector and corporate interests into farming. The draft law concerns 16 UASCs and 400 co-operatives with 3 million rural people, 15,000 wage labourers, and 4.5 million agricultural holdings which employ 45 per cent of the labour force. The law is adamant that while UASCs will not receive any financial help from the state, the state will have a free hand to interfere in the organisational and administrative structures of UASCs when it deems necessary. This heralds the liquidation of all the industrial and processing assets held by UASCs who will be left on their own in the market as far as prices, processing and procurement are concerned. However, they will be strongly controlled by the state through the appointments of state inspectors to the auditing bodies of the UASCs. Without the financial support of the state it will become virtually impossible for the farmers to compete with their western counterparts in the world market.

Furthermore, the letters of intent guarantee that wheat prices will be allowed to be only 5 per cent above the Chicago Exchange prices (supplementary letter of intent). This is a huge drop from being 35 per cent above the Chicago Exchange prices in 2000. The assumption is that the Chicago Exchange prices represent objectively and competitively formed 'world prices'. Yet it is well-known that Chicago Exchange prices reflect the hidden subsidies given to US and EU farmers and thus are distorted. If Turkish farmers are forced to accept wheat prices based on Chicago Exchange prices they will not be able to meet their production costs and thus will be pushed out of production by cheaper wheat imported from outside. This will have serious implications for food security, balance of payments problems as well as social tension in the countryside. On the other hand, it will open up lucrative business opportunities for transnational food giants to export grains to Turkey and to attempt to redirect producers to produce high value foods and other cash crops over which they have monopolies (Oyan 2003).

The IMF and the World Bank's insistence on the elimination of import restrictions on agricultural products in the South works in tandem with the monopolistic control by transnational agribusiness firms over seeds, animal feeds, inputs, stock breeding, etc. The way the Turkish Government has been pushed to restructure its sugar and tobacco production is a good example of how the IFIs act on behalf of TNCs and help create conditions for their expansion into the South.

THE SAGAS OF SUGAR AND TOBACCO

Sugar

Turkey has been forced to restructure its sugar regime as a combined result of the four standby agreements with the IMF since 1999, the pledges made to the World Bank in return for fresh loans, and the promises made at the Helsinki Summit to ensure Turkey's candidacy for full membership of the EU. For this purpose the Sugar Law was ratified by the Parliament on 4 April 2001 and became an integral part of the New Economic Programme announced on 14 April 2001 in the aftermath of the November 2001 and February 2001 financial crises.

The Sugar Law stipulates the privatisation of 27 publicly owned sugar factories and the establishment of a Sugar Agency and Sugar Board furnished with powers relinquished by the Ministry of Industry and Trade. The Board is entrusted with extensive responsibilities and the authority to decide who will serve on the Board and how much sugar beet and sugar should be produced for both the internal and external markets. The Board is intended to work as an arbitration board whose authority, duties and period of service are to be regularly reconsidered and revised by the Cabinet in conjunction with new agreements to be signed by international agencies. The law ensures that from 2002 onward the price of sugar beet will be determined not by the state but by negotiations between private sugar factories and producers. The aims of the new Sugar Law include the stabilisation of sugar production, the establishment of the principles of free market and competitiveness in the sugar sector, the enactment of a judicial infrastructure to facilitate privatisation and meeting the obligations imposed by agreements signed with the WTO and the EU. All this means the introduction of quotas in the share of sugar factories in the internal market, the opening up of the internal market to competition and the minimisation of the state's influence on the sugar sector.

Considering that there is over-production of sugar globally and that sugar prices have been in decline since 1995 (the price of sugar in the Sugar Exchange of London declined from US$396.6 in 1995 to US$200.5 in 1999), it appears extremely likely that the Board will impose ever decreasing production quotas. This would lead to the abandonment of sugar beet production by 350,000 small producers. Given that more than 90 per cent of them cultivate land below two hectares the amount of direct income support (set at about US$7 per decare) they will receive will be too small to enable them to sustain their agricultural activities.

It is clear that the liberalisation of the sugar will have far-reaching consequences for 500,000 sugar beet producing households and 27 publicly owned sugar factories which provide a livelihood for 30,000 workers. The Sugar Law does not specify how thousands of sugar beet producers will be protected against cheaply imported sugar which receives state subsidies in the US and EU. In the US the cost of production for sugar is 60 cents per kg and sugar is sold at 120 cents per kg in the US market but it is exported at 30 cents. In other words, the cheap export price reflects a huge subsidy which in turn enables US farmers to maintain their production. Likewise, the EU has made a special deal with the WTO to protect its sugar beet producers. Without state protection the so-called free market will ruin the Turkish sugar beet farmers and the sugar industry as a consequence of distorted import prices.

The main purpose of the Sugar Law is to ensure the dominance of transnationals in Turkey where artificial sweeteners produced by transnationals from imported sweet corn is already threatening sugar production as a result of the lack of protective regulation. The US limited isoglucose production to 2 per cent of sugar produced from sugar beet in 1999–2000. Due to luck of protective legislation, isoglucose capacity reached 292,000 tons in the same year representing a massive 14.6 per cent of the total 2 million tons of sugar produced from sugar beet. The sole purpose of the Sugar Law imposed by the IMF/World Bank is to open up the huge Turkish market to sweeteners produced from maize by TNCs at the expense of generating further unemployment in rural areas.

Tobacco

The infamous Tobacco Law speedily passed on 9 January 2002 (that generated tension between Parliament and the President, who vetoed the law but was overridden by Parliament in the second round of voting which is not subject to presidential approval) is another example of the IMF/World Bank imposition that aims to open up Turkish markets for the TNCs.

The Tobacco Law does not have any specific stipulations about how the production of tobacco is to be organised and regulated. This is left for future legislation. The only statement about tobacco production is the decision to stop support buying by the state. Instead, all tobacco will be traded through auction or contractual production. The law has been prepared in congruence with the desires of the Treasury to please the IMF and the World Bank without taking into consideration the warnings of either the Ministry of Agriculture or the state monopoly, TEKEL. Therefore the fate of several hundred thousand tobacco producing families is left to the operations of the market.

While the Tobacco Law is silent about the marketing problems faced by tobacco producing farmers, the implementation of the ARIP and the ERP actively seek to reduce the production of this traditional Turkish crop by 36,000 hectares in Adıyaman, Batman, Bingöl, Bitlis, Diyarbakır, Hakkari, Mardin, Muş and Van (Ministry of Agriculture 2003). The fate of another traditional cash crop, hazelnuts, is similar to that of tobacco. Another World Bank financed project, the Alternative Crops Project, aims to reduce the area under hazelnuts by 100,000 hectares in the provinces of Artvin, Bartın, Bolu, Giresun, Kastamonu, Kocaeli, Ordu, Rize, Sakarya, Samsun, Sinop and Trabzon. The project suggests that in the areas 'recovered', alternative crops such as sunflowers, rape seed, soy beans, vegetables, greenhouse vegetables and flowers, fruits, ornamental plants and aromatic and medical herbs could be grown.

The Tobacco Law puts an end to the monopolistic position of TEKEL, a state-owned regulating agency which has had nearly complete monopolistic control over tobacco production. The newly established Regulating Agency and Board for the Tobacco, Tobacco Products and Alcoholic Beverages Markets is authorised by the Tobacco Law to ensure a smooth transition to privatisation of the tobacco industry. This Board is intended to act like an arbitration board by assuming the powers of TEKEL and the council of ministers in issues related to the tobacco and cigarette industry. Under the new arrangements, TEKEL will no longer exist to act as a regulating agency, setting the conditions of purchase and tobacco prices. This means a complete elimination of support purchases and price setting in the tobacco market.

The Tobacco Law is the pinnacle of the long-term international pressure to open up the Turkish market for the international tobacco corporations. The process, which ended with the complete elimination of state intervention into the tobacco business, started in 1984 when the Özal Government lifted the ban on cigarette imports. This was followed by the liberalisation of tobacco imports in 1989. Since then the Turkish cigarette industry has been penetrated mainly by US TNCs. This is evident in the fact that in the ten years between 1989 and 1999 the share of imported tobacco in locally manufactured cigarettes increased from 6.7 per cent to 40 per cent. Given the greater dependence-creating features of Burley and Virginia varieties of tobacco, domestic demand for cigarettes rose from 59,000 tons in 1980 to 115,000 tons in 1999. Consequently, Turkey lost its large share in the world tobacco market and exports decreased from US$601 million in 1997 to US$395 million in 2000. Self-sufficient in tobacco and tobacco products until very recently, the country spent US$2 billion on tobacco imports between 1996 and 2001.

DIRECT INCOME SUPPORT

With a special decree in March 2000 the Government introduced the direct income support system (DIS) with the aim of abolishing all the existing support and subsidies for agriculture. It declared that the main aim of the DIS was not to fully compensate every farmer for income lost by the removal of subsidies, but to provide help to overcome the short-term losses and to encourage farming activities. It was stated that payments under the DIS would be recurrent but would eventually be explicitly targeted at and harmonised with the EU system under the Common Agricultural Policy. The second aim of the DIS policy was to encourage farmers to move away from crops currently over-produced towards alternative crops. The DIS started on an experimental basis in a small number of pilot regions such as Ankara-Polatlı, Trabzon-Akçaabat and Sürmene, Adıyaman-Cental and Kahta, and Antalya-Serik and Manavgat. Since 2002 the DIS system has been implemented countrywide and landowners have been registering their land with the state in order to qualify for the DIS. Yet as of December 2003 no payment was made to areas other than the pilot areas. The state's medium-term target is to completely get rid of state support for agriculture. The extent and speed of this shift has no match anywhere in the world. Although the EU and the

US also use the DIS they do not use it as the sole support mechanism in agriculture. For instance, in the EU the DIS represents only 30 per cent of the overall support given to agriculture while the market price support constitutes 55 per cent and the input support 8 per cent (Özkaya *et al.* 2000). On the other hand, in the US the DIS's share in the total agricultural support is 10 per cent while the shares of market price support and input support are 50 per cent and 10 per cent respectively.

The aim of the DIS in the EU and US is to support farmers who may have lost income due to production quotas; in other words the DIS is closely linked to production. In Turkey, on the other hand, no connection is made between production, efficiency and the DIS. Despite the problems of administration and implementation discovered in the pilot schemes, the state has extended the DIS to cover the whole country. However the State does not provide any timetable as to when the DIS will be abolished. The World Bank admits that the DIS scheme has been introduced as a stopgap measure to ease the rising tension in the countryside in relation to the losses made due to the abolition of subsidies (World Bank 2001:11). The impact of the abolition is so severe that no one wants to be left out of the scheme, however short a period it may last. For instance, the untenable cost-price squeeze in Turkey has forced the farmers in south-eastern Anatolia to demand to be included in the DIS immediately. According to the daily *Özgür Politika* (25 February 2002) 162,292 farmers applied to the provincial Agricultural Directorates to receive direct income support (10 million Turkish Lira per decare) to ease their financial difficulties. The applications were made in order not to be left out of the DIS programme which had been implemented in only a few pilot areas.

One of the main problems with the DIS is that the payment is very small and made to landowners rather than farmers. The amount paid is so low (about US$7 per decare) that of the 4.5 million farming families only 2.3 million have applied for it. As there are no complete cadastral records the state aims to obtain a complete land and farmer registry through the DIS. This has created serious problems as in some places people do not apply for the DIS and in other places it is not possible to determine the ownership of land due to multiple claims over it. Up to 200 decares of private land qualifies for the DIS. As the title deed to the land is the basis for qualification, a large number of sharecroppers and tenant farmers are excluded, and this is in contradiction to the supposed poverty alleviation aim of the DIS. Furthermore, as the Ankara-Polatlı pilot experiment showed, there is a strong possibility that absentee landowners, land speculators, building co-operatives and professionals may register to claim support from the scheme.

Direct income support policies are justified by their non price-distorting nature and their ability to guide farmers' production decisions according to supply and demand, independently of support prices. It is assumed that DIS will lead to a more productive and efficient allocation of resources and thus the economy as a whole will benefit from it. In theory neither the producers nor the Treasury will lose out as the producers will receive about the same income from the state as before.

Yet a recent study by Doğruel and Yeldan (2001) suggests otherwise. They analyse alternative agricultural support policies for the Turkish economy through the use of a dynamic general equilibrium model based on intertemporally optimising agents. The model is based on the assumption that excessive public sector borrowing requirements generated by the cost of domestic interest bring about distortions in the economy. Furthermore, farmers' decisions to continue farming are highly responsive to changes in policies concerning subsidies and income support. They estimate that the shift in the agricultural support policies from price subsidies to direct income transfers will generate deflationary results. Doğruel and Yeldan (2001) expect that within 15 years agricultural production will decrease by 5.5 per cent. The elimination of price subsidies and the invigoration of direct income transfers will lead to a 2 per cent decline in aggregate GDP. The authors clearly slow that under the new agricultural support regime the ratio of debt to GDP will increase and put further limitations on capital investment. It is expected that the burden of the fiscal debts will worsen due to the relative contraction of the GDP. Furthermore, the income transfer from the central budget will have a detrimental impact on the fiscal balance (already in the red for a long time). The increased financial fragility will contribute further to the unsustainability of the economy. The increased fragility of the domestic financial system coupled with the protracted confidence crisis is likely to lead to distortion in investments.

Doğruel and Yeldan (2001) draw the conclusion that the current attempt to reform agricultural pricing in an environment characterised by failure and unsustainable fiscal targets is an extremely difficult task and will achieve neither more efficient resource allocation nor an improved social welfare in the country. What Turkey needs is effective planning for its agricultural production. The DIS is far from achieving this as it encourages farmers to move into crops which will produce high yields with minimum expenditure. This in turn will lead to over-production of some crops and shortages of others. Removal of subsidies to agriculture threatens not only the profitability but also the viability of agricultural production. It is not possible to ease the Treasury's financial burden through the provision of DIS for all agricultural land in the country, unless either the payment is kept very low or it is limited to areas under selected crops.

LIBERALISATION AND FOOD SECURITY

The champions of free trade argue that increased international trade leads to specialisation and higher productivity as a result of access to global markets. They maintain that when exposed to international competition, producers make more efficient use of resources by moving into crops in which they have a comparative advantage. However, such expectations for increased participation in international trade do not generate the expected results among small producers. When state support is removed from agriculture in the form of input price liberalisation and the disappearance of state procurement of crops, small agricultural producers tend to adopt risk-avoiding strategies by diversifying their economic activities rather than simply shifting to a new and specialised commercial crop. The expectation that increased liberalisation of agricultural production and trade will lead to more efficient resource use through specialisation and improved use of technologies is far from realistic, in that small farmers in less economically developed countries do not possess the necessary financial power and know-how to use the new technology and analyse the international market situation. Globalised agriculture puts all sorts of stringent quality specifications on the internationally traded crops and most small producers in less economically developed countries are not capable of meeting them. They do not have sufficient command over land, finance and knowledge to respond to market opportunities and increased competition.

Liberalisation of trade in agricultural goods represents the biggest challenge to food security and agricultural production in less economically developed countries. The International Convention of Economic, Social and Cultural Rights considers the right to food or food-producing resources as a basic human right. Food security is defined as 'food available at all times, to which all persons have means of access, that is nutritionally adequate in terms of quantity, quality and variety, and is acceptable within the given culture' (FAO 1996). In recent years the US and other industrialised countries of the North have ceased to subscribe to this long-standing definition of food security. Participation in global markets has now replaced the concept of food security as a fundamental human right. The FAO's well-accepted definition stated above has been removed from the draft of the World Food Summit held in June 2002 (FAO 2000).

The UN Food Summit's contention that 'trade is vital to food security' reflects the nature of the change in the interpretation of food security. International agencies like the World Bank, the IMF and the WTO are pushing the governments of less economically developed countries to establish structures that will secure free trade in agriculture. Liberalisation in agriculture is pushed as a feature of a new global division of labour that demands production for export. Changes in the agricultural sector have far-reaching implications for rural producers who constitute a large proportion of the population in less economically developed countries. Export-oriented agriculture necessitates changes in land-use patterns which are inimical to the livelihoods of farmers and the environment. Most farmers lose the ability to produce their own food and become dependent on imported food. The fact that hundreds of farmers' organisations and NGOs from all over the world went to Rome to hold their own forum, the World Forum on Food Sovereignty as an alternative to the FAO's World Food Summit between 10 and 13 June 2002, demonstrates the failure to meet the targets of the previous World Food Summit held in Rome in 1996. Despite the 1996 Plan of Action there is immense evidence that world hunger has been on the increase and that it will be impossible to eliminate it by 2015 unless there is drastic reorientation of policies. Rampant poverty and hunger in less economically developed countries in particular cannot simply be explained, as the official documents prepared by the UN for the June 2002 World Food Summit suggest, by the lack of will to allocate sufficient resources.

Deregulation in the agricultural sector has meant that rural producers have to compete in the global commodity markets without any help from the state and without much preparation for the transition. Having lost their access to productive resources such as inputs, credits, and marketing facilities, and having been starved of state investments in agriculture, rural producers are not only losing their competitive edge but are also facing the danger of being unable to sustain their production. The deregulation of national markets has been accompanied by increasing costs of production in agriculture, farmers' inability to find markets for their crops, fluctuating agricultural commodity prices and increasing farmer indebtedness. These have led to the exhaustion of farmers' survival strategies (Aydın 2002). In the early years of liberalisation poor farmers were able to develop survival strategies to counteract the welfare-decreasing impacts of liberalisation. The extent and speed of liberalisation in Turkish agriculture in the last five years has left very limited scope for farmers to intensify their 'self-exploitation' in the form of survival strategies. The more the state washes its hands of the poor and middle farmers, the more they attempt to diversify their economic activities in order to sustain a basic livelihood. This has meant lesser and lesser reliance on agriculture as the main source of livelihood. The withdrawal of state support from agriculture has occurred in stages and after each wave of new deregulatory policies more and more farmers have been pushed into the deep end. The Turkish bourgeoisie's desire to join the EU as quickly as possible, the debt crisis, and the recent economic crises have left the state powerless *vis-à-vis* the demands imposed by the IFIs, the EU and the US. Neither the farmers nor the state were prepared for the immediate consequences of the IMF and World Bank-engineered liberalisation policies. The implementation of each new deregulatory decision has caused immediate bewilderment and hopelessness among the farmers. Income diversification strategies used by small-scale and medium-scale farmers are no longer geared towards supplementing agricultural income but towards supplanting them. There has been a strong tendency for the agrarian labour force to move towards non-agrarian activities (Aydın 2002). The hope of finding other non-agricultural sources of income has led many rural dwellers to move to urban areas. The inability of urban areas to absorb the ever-increasing number of migrants and to meet their demands for employment, housing and other social services force some of the migrants to return back to rural areas. The movement of people between urban and rural areas indicates the complexity of the transformations taking place in the country. Such complexity in turn adds to the analytical difficulties surrounding the nature of transition in rural areas. The permeation of rural societies by the state and the market has irretrievably altered the nature of family farms and village communities, so much so that the farmer's relationship to the soil has changed.

The recommendations of the IFIs that farmers should move into the production of new crops for the expanding global fresh fruit, vegetable, flower and GM crops markets are far from realistic in terms of resolving their immediate livelihood problems. To obtain knowledge of new markets and gain expertise in the production of new crop varieties requires time, organisation and capital, which the disorganised and non-unionised farmers in Turkey lack. Although the state intends to provide help in the future, in the interim period farmers simply cease to farm and tend to migrate to cities to diversify their sources of income.

HISTORY REPEATS ITSELF: MEXICO AND TURKEY

The Turkish liberalisation of agriculture is fairly new and therefore there is not sufficient research to provide definitive conclusions about the impact of globalisation on the rural poor, but Mexico's experience with liberalisation since 1992 has produced convincing results to suggest that both the rural poor and food security have suffered greatly. Mexico's entry into the GATT in 1986 and NAFTA in 1994, together with extensive 'Second Agrarian Reform' since 1992, have marked the transformations in Mexican agriculture. Entry into the GATT and NAFTA have meant a reduction tariff and non-tariff barriers in trade, particularly in agricultural commodities. Together with agrarian reform, this has played a vital role in the way Mexico has become integrated into the international commodity production and distribution system and in the shaping of the local economy. Economic liberalisation and the privatisation of the agriculture sector have had far-reaching consequences for the *ejidatoria* agricultural production throughout Mexico (Stanford 1998). As the services and subsidies were dismantled and privatised as part of the Second Agrarian Reform and liberalisation, the vacuum created has led to a stagnation and decline in the *ejidal* production. Contrary to expectations, the *ejidatarios* have not been able to compete in an open economy which has been plagued by market failures. Under neo-liberal reforms smallholders have experienced failures of information, credit, input supply and output markets and thus the great majority have not been able to switch to commercial crops for export markets (Marsh and Runsten 1998).

The DIS, introduced in 1994 under the name of PROCAMPO in order to compensate farmers for the elimination of guaranteed prices on support crops, simply failed to achieve the expected results (Sadoulet and de Janvry 2001, 2002). On the whole the liberalisation policies have had a negative impact on food security and poverty in Mexico. For instance, grain production, particularly of sorghum and maize, declined in the *ejidal* sector in response to drastic reductions in agricultural credits between 1986 and 1991. In Tierra Coliente irrigation district *ejidatarios* have been facing two major constraints in their efforts to shift to commercial agriculture: 1. low levels of productivity due to a lack of financial investment; 2. international companies establish indirect control over fresh fruit and vegetable production through their expansion of activities into shipping, marketing and distribution. Local capital is forced to take responsibility for direct investment in agriculture and go into joint ventures with international companies in order to be able to export their products. Small producers who do not have investment capital are increasingly being marginalised and denied access to commercial opportunities. Thus they are being pushed out of agriculture and away from their land (Stanford 1998).

It seems that the Mexican scenario is being replayed in Turkey, as there are significant similarities between the liberalisation policies put into practice in both countries. Yet the way the Turkish experience is set up suggests that no lessons have been learned from the Mexican case. Early signs suggest that the liberalisation of agriculture in Turkey is setting up irreversible tendencies, and despite repeated warnings from farmers' organisations, the Chamber of Turkish Agricultural Engineers (<www.tmmobzmo.org.tr>) and academics (Aydın 2002; Boratav 1988; Doğruel and Yeldan 2001; Oyan 1999, 2003; Özkaya *et al.* 2000) the state is determined to continue with full liberalisation in agriculture. The great majority of farmers in Turkey responded to the decreasing viability of cash crops like cotton, tobacco and sugar beet either by abandoning agriculture and entering into non-agricultural income diversification activities in urban areas or, to a much lesser extent, by withdrawing from the market by producing subsistence crops.

In the last two decades, Turkey has been experiencing a trend of de-agrarianisation defined as a long-term process of occupational adjustment, income earning reorientation, social identification and spatial relocation of rural dwellers away from strictly agricultural-based modes of livelihood (Bryceson *et al.* 2000). This has been actively propelled by the state in recent years, as the politicians, policy-makers and development think tanks identify development with the decline of the relative share of agriculture in the national income. Consequently, state and private investors have neglected the agricultural sector. A contributing factor to this has been the deteriorating terms of trade for major agricultural export commodities such as cotton, tobacco, hazelnuts and sugar. The loss of a productive base poses a serious danger for subsistence food production and the production of traditional commodities by small- and medium-scale farmers. This is evident from the fact that while the export of agricultural products increased 1.5-fold between 1980 and 1999, the import of agricultural products increased 20-fold (from US\$51 million to US\$1062 million) in the same period (Ministry of Agriculture 2003). Self-sufficient in terms of food security, Turkey has become a net importer of food in recent years.

Another significant factor in the process of de-agrarianisation in Turkey is the availability of cheap imported foodstuffs from more economically developed countries which continue to subsidise their own farmers. The farmers in Turkey, who feel the scissors effect of rising import prices and declining product prices, are gradually reducing the domestic production of wheat and other cereals.

The vacuum created by de-agrarianisation and de-peasantisation is being filled by TNCs which move into less economically developed countries to produce just-in-time crops using bio-technology. Agricultural production in Turkey is still largely carried out by small family firms but TNCs such as Nestlé, Danone, Lamb-Weston, Kraft-Jacobs and Suchard are gradually moving into the food sector (Yenal 2001). In the last decade investments by agri-food TNCs showed a significant decline in the Middle East, Africa and the Mediterranean. However, in the Mediterranean region Turkey has been an exception as direct foreign investment in the food sector quadrupled between 1980 and 2000 (Yenal 2001:44–45). The process of the corporatisation and industrialisation of agriculture in Turkey is still in its infancy, yet such changes are predicated upon the restructuring of agriculture. This has profound implications for small, undercapitalised peasant family farms in Turkey. Market deregulation and liberalisation at work since the 1980s have eroded the resource base of small- and medium-scale farmers and their ability to compete in the world market. Given the inability of the urban economy to provide sufficient sources of livelihood for the rapidly increasing impoverished and proletarianised rural labour force, conditions have become ripe for the TNCs to move in and take advantage of this huge cheap labour force through various arrangements including contract farming.

In conclusion, it is pertinent to say that Turkey has become increasingly incorporated into the global economy. In this process the state has been gradually losing its control over the economy under the influence of outside players including more economically developed capitalist countries and their agencies as well as the international finance institutions. The increasing indebtedness of the country has facilitated the process of Turkey's integration into the global economy. As far as the agrarian economy is concerned, globalisation has meant the restructuring of agrarian structures and policies away from developmentalism to a free market economy which ensures that agriculture is put in the hands of modern technology owned and controlled by large multinational corporations whose primary interest is to generate profits for themselves, and not the welfare of the people, or something as social-oriented as food security (Tandon 1999:22).

The policies implemented in Turkey in the last few decades under the guidance of international organisations have undercut farmers in general and small farmers in particular. The foremost of these policies is trade liberalisation which has been pitting small family farmers in Turkey against highly subsidised corporate farms in more economically developed countries. Likewise, policies that are being enforced on Turkey in the form of the elimination of price supports and production subsidies, the privatisation of credits, and the excessive promotion of exports put small family farmers into an increasingly vulnerable position. Consequently they find it extremely difficult to continue farming as their costs of production increase and their markets contract.

Small farmers in Turkey are becoming more and more helpless as a result of the concentration of agricultural commodity chains in the hands of TNCs which are capable of pushing large numbers of small farmers out of agriculture. Not being able to compete with the monopolistic prices set by the TNCs, farmers have been slowly abandoning agriculture *en masse*. Food producers have been hit particularly hard by the increasing costs and decreasing crop prices. This process, well advanced in Mexico, has just started in Turkey, and if history is to repeat itself the future for small producers in Turkish agriculture looks bleak.

The changes put into practice in Turkish agriculture since the 1980s, and particularly since 1999, are ill thought-out. They do not reflect any serious thinking about the long-term consequences on the economy. The concern to please the IFIs, the EU and Turkish business interests lies behind the state's rapid action to implement comprehensive policies concerning product and input prices, sectoral credits, breeding stocks and seed production. The haphazardly taken decisions propel the integration of the Turkish economy into the global market economy without giving any serious thought to the social, political and economic consequences. The three-year programme between 2000 and 2003 might have far-reaching consequences and serious implications for Turkey's political, economic and social stability.

Given that these policies are leading to the contraction of agriculture, food security issues have been emerging. Taken together with other serious difficulties generated by SAPs, such as rampant unemployment, bankruptcies, unaffordable prices, high inflation and declining incomes of the masses, the destruction of agricultural production will only exacerbate Turkey's problems. Rapidly increasing mass unemployment in rural areas will speed up migration to big cities which are already incapable of coping with urban problems and unprecedented social pressures.

5
Political Islam in Turkey

The fact that the Welfare Party (Refah Partisi) managed to increase its share of votes from 7.2 per cent in 1987 to 21.4 per cent in 1995 is an indication of how powerful political Islam became within a short period of time. Considering that at least three political parties' participation in a coalition government was necessary to obtain a vote of confidence shows the key role that the Welfare Party had to play in Turkish politics.[1] The fact that Islamic parties have been closed down four times since 1971 also indicates how sensitive the state is about the rise of Islam as a political force. A series of Islamist parties have been established, each in defiance of the closure of the previous one. The importance of the Islamist Party in Turkish politics and Parliament continued in the April 1999 general elections, as the successor of the Welfare Party, the Virtue Party (Fazilet Partisi), still managed to get 15.41 per cent of the total votes winning 111 seats in the Parliament.[2] The army's serious concerns about the Virtue Party's anti-secularism coincided with similar concerns of secularist political parties who managed to hold some parliamentary seats. The longest lasting coalition government in Turkish history, consisting of three parties (the Democratic Left Party, the Motherland Party and the extreme right National Action Party), was formed with the specific aim to leave out the Islamist Virtue Party. The militant and uncompromising attitude of the *de facto* leader of the Virtue Party, Necmettin Erbakan, led to a revolt within the party under the leadership of Abdullah Gül. This resulted in the formation of two parties: the Felicity Party (Saadet Partisi), headed by Recai Kutan under the guidance of Erbakan who was banned from politics, and the Justice and Development Party. Both parties solicited the votes of Islamists and pious citizens. While the reformist Justice and Development Party (JDP), established in 2001, surged into power in the November 2002 general elections by obtaining 363 seats in the 550 member Parliament, the hawks in the Felicity Party faced a heavy defeat, managing to get only 2.5 per cent of the total national votes.

Although the JDP claims to be a secular party, a considerable proportion of its rank and file are the same people who came from the ranks of an Islamist party.[3] The JDP is the first Islamist party in Turkish history to come to power on its own. It is early to judge whether the actual policies of the JDP are going to be as mellow as their party programme. At the rhetorical level the opposition to the West seems to have come to an end as the Islamist movement has seemingly transformed itself from within, and moved towards being a 'conservative modern party of Democrat Muslims'. The political discourse of the JDP, which managed to poll 34 per cent of all the national votes, no longer includes anti-western slogans.[4] Instead, it preaches for liberal democracy, globalisation and incorporation into the European Union. While the rise of the Welfare Party in the 1980s was seen as paradoxical in a country where a strong official secularist ideology has been dominant since the 1920s, equally the weakening of Islamism and gradual secularisation of Islamist parties appear baffling to outside observers. Both the rise of Islam and the phenomenal tendency towards secularisation of Islamic parties need to be explained, and a political economy approach is necessary for an effective analysis. The Weberian and Marxist problematic of asking whether religion is conservative, moderate or revolutionary is no longer useful in trying to understand the role of religion in society. An approach that looks at the structural conditions which raise the importance of religion in the organisation of societies and in the mobilisation of people to attempt to change the existing societal order is more pertinent (Levine 1986). In order to understand the rise of political Islam it is necessary to look at socio-economic processes operating in Turkey as well as global processes which have significant impacts on Turkey.

POLITICAL ISLAM AS A REACTION TO MODERNISATION

One of the earliest but most influential explanations for the rise of political Islam has been provided by Binnaz Toprak (1981, 1993). For her it is the incompatibility of Islam and the Christian West that lies behind the rise of Islam. She explains this by comparing and contrasting the roles played by ideology and religion when faced with the transformational forces of modernisation. In her opinion, in traditional societies religion is the dominant value system and as such has a significant impact on economic, social, political and cultural spheres. On the other hand, in modern societies religion does not have a regulatory function in these spheres. In transitional societies where the institutions of modernity are still in the making and not fully functional, religion tends to fill the gap and acts as a buffer mechanism (Toprak 1981:9–15).

She suggests that in the face of turmoil generated by the process of modernisation, the attempts to find solutions to newly emerging problems give religion an ideological role. Ideology is a system of symbols which helps individuals to regulate their relations with the environment and to define themselves within various social and political role categories. Religion too has the function of ideology in explaining non-religious phenomena at an individual level. It can also provide a frame of reference for individuals to perceive, understand and explain their environment and the world. Furthermore, religion attempts to keep elements of social structure unchanged. As such, religion as an ideology comes into direct conflict with the process of modernisation (Toprak 1981).

Industrialisation, nationalism and secularisation take place concomitantly. With industrialisation, nationalism takes root and religion loses its significance as a unifying identity. With nationalism, secularisation starts to emerge. Both nationalism and secularism conflict with religion as far as the unifying function is concerned. The institutions of the state take over this function, thus religion is pushed out of the political sphere. The gradual process of secularisation does not influence everybody or every behavioural pattern in society. Therefore the existence of individuals and groups who attempt to stop the process of secularisation is inevitable. The intensity of the conflict is determined by the nature of religion and socio-economic and political structures. If the dominant religion in society claims to be a political one, in that it wants to regulate individual social and political life, then the nature of the conflict is bound to be strong. Islam claims to be a political religion and thus it is vehemently opposed to nationalism and secularism. Islam lays claim on everything from individual private life to the legal, social, political and economic spheres (Mardin 1969:52; Sencer 1971:236; Toprak 1981:20).

Toprak suggests that the comprehensiveness of Islam leads to a confusion as to what falls within the domain of religion and what does not. The individual's inner world and every sphere of life come under the strict control of Islam. It thus inevitably conflicts with nationalism and secularism, which regulate social and political life according to different principles. The fact that nationalism and secularism are products of the West and the history of Islam is characterised by its conflict with the West necessarily makes the opposition to the West an intrinsic feature of Islam. However such conflict is defined, the emphasis is on the fact that Islam and the West do not have anything in common.[5] Toprak's view finds echoes in the analysis of other Islamic societies as well. Marty and Appleyby (1991), Riesebrodt (1993) and Wuthnow (1991) also interpret the rise of political Islam in terms of Islam's reactions to modern systems of thought which fail to provide adequate meaning systems for people. Here religious movements are reduced to the defence of tradition and to the search for meaning and moral order. Tuğal (2002) has a point when he criticises this approach and maintains that religious movements do not simply strive to return to an idealistic past but also actively create their own modernities by revising and adapting the traditions. In his analysis of the debates on the role of Islam in Turkey, Tuğal (2002:107) arrives at the conclusion that 'the meaning of Islam is always remaking itself through the conflict of *materially situated actors*'. The tension between how Islam should be and how it could serve different interests underlines the struggle between various elements within the Islamic movement to establish their hegemony. This is very clear in the struggle for hegemony within the Islamic movement in the aftermath of the closure of the Virtue Party in 2001. A moderate group, which later formed the kernel of the JDP, has separated itself from the centre of the Islamic movement, by believing in the internalisation of democracy within Islam and thus taking a conciliatory position. Their relatively moderate attitude towards the dominant Kemalist ideology has been at the root of their emergence as a splinter group from the moral anti-capitalist Islamic movement. The JDP intends to stay to the right of centre and refrain from agitating the military and the bureaucracy which have historically opposed radical Islamism. The leadership of the new liberal Islamic Party has moved away from the idealistic imagery of Islam and incorporated a capitalist imagery into its religious outlook in order to be accepted by the dominant power block and to be able to work towards its own hegemony without antagonising this power block. Tuğal's analysis is useful but limited in that it fails to explain the forces that are behind the changes within the Islamic movement. There is a need to elaborate on the nature of the 'materially situated actors'. Who are they? What are their relationships to the state and business communities? How are they linked to the global order? (Öniş 1997).

The evaluations of the November 2002 elections indicate that it was not just the Islamists who voted the JDP into power. People from all sorts of backgrounds chose the JDP. Therefore the rise of Islam to power cannot simply be explained in terms of the internal dynamism of the Islamist movement. Such explanations need to be supplemented by an analysis of the external processes that prepared the ground for the flourishing of the more moderate Islam.

The view that the rise of Islamic radicalism in the Middle East is due to a long standing anti-western sentiment stemming from the traditional conflict between Christian and Islamic civilisations is inadequate to explain the Islamic radicalism in recent decades (Gülalp 1992:15). Nor is it sufficient to attribute it to the internal dynamism of Islam alone. The explanation has to be sought in the specificity of Third World modernisation, not in a traditionalist plea to return to a pre-modern era. In order to understand the historical timing and specificity of the Islamic revival in Turkey it is necessary to analyse how Turkish modernisation has unfolded and why this has attracted a reaction from the Islamists. There is a need to investigate the ways in which the internal contradictions of the Turkish development experience have contributed to the Islamic resurgence in Turkey. It is also necessary to find out the social bases of political Islam in Turkey. Who supports it? Why do they support it? Answering these questions would also necessitate a consideration of the forces of globalisation. In other words, questions need to be answered about how and in what ways the intense process of globalisation in the economic and cultural realms is undermining many of the established contours of political activity. Such an analysis will allow us to go beyond the historically specific features and locate such historical specificity within a broader process of transformation. This will allow us to link explanations emphasising the internal tension within the Turkish Republic with those highlighting the processes that generate tensions globally (Öniş 1997).

KEMALISM, ISLAM AND IDENTITY POLITICS

The discourse of globalisation emphasises the fact that identity politics is gradually replacing class-based politics. The argument is that due to the development of technology we are witnessing a tendency of homogenisation of tastes and values across the world. Particularly the ideas of democracy and human rights have been spreading across the globe by leaps and bounds. An inevitable consequence of this has been the emergence of cultural pluralism, the effect of which has been a process of fragmentation leading to the rise of identity politics (Öniş 1997). The atmosphere of tolerance created by the spread of democratic values and respect for human rights as a reflection of the homogenising tendency of globalisation has been at the root of identity politics. However, as Buğra (2002a, 2002b), Gülalp (1997, 2001) and Öniş (1997) maintain, the rise of identity politics cannot simply be reduced to the cultural impact of globalisation alone; the economic aspect of globalisation needs to be taken into consideration as well. Rapid transformations in production, finance and distribution systems and de-regulations have produced new forms of relations between capital and labour, between people and the state and have led to the marginalisation of the masses who are left bewildered. Class politics no longer seems to be sufficient for the workers, the peasants, and the artisans etc. who feel insecure and unprotected in the epoch of globalisation. The crisis of identity generated by the combined impact of economic and cultural globalisation has opened new political forms of expression facilitated by the dissemination of democratic values and by the acceptance of diversity and pluralism. Although the traditional politics based on left and right wing ideologies has not disappeared, varieties of identity politics based on diverse elements such as religion, ethnicity, linguistics, regionalism and environment have made class politics extremely complicated.

However, the rise of political Islam as a form of identity politics in Turkey cannot simply be explained by the development of globalisation. The explanation should also include the rise of Turkish nationalism as a form of identity politics because the rise of Islamic identity politics has been largely a reaction to it. The renaissance of political Islam as a legitimate political force in Turkey in recent decades has given a new dimension to the debate over Turkish identity.

TURKISH IDENTITY AND ISLAM

Since the inception of the Turkish Republic in 1923, Islam has played a vital role in the creation of Turkish identity and Turkish nationalism. The origins of Turkish identity can be traced back to the late Ottoman period. Since the Tanzimat reforms, there have been various efforts to modernise society in the image of Europe (Kubicek 1999:157). While the Tanzimat reforms were specifically aimed at modernising Turkish society along French lines, the Young Turks in the early years of the twentieth century aimed to establish a constitutional society similar to the West. Likewise, since 1923 Kemalism has been trying to engineer a western-style society. The efforts to adopt the 'image' of European society have inevitably generated social tensions, as many characteristics have not been compatible with the existing features of Turkish society.

Ziya Gökalp has been the major influence behind the efforts to create Turkish nationalism and a Turkish identity. The concept of nation constituted the basis of his argument. He argued that a strong state should be based on a nation and that the new Turkish state built on the ashes of the Ottoman Empire should promote the concept of Turkishness and the Turkish nation. His proposed Turkish nation should adopt western civilisation and technology while maintaining Turkish culture which would fill the spiritual and moral vacuum present in western society (Berkes 1965:276). The aim was to manufacture a notion of nationalism which would blend western technology and Turkish culture, in which Islam was a significant constituent. What Gökalp and his followers did not realise was the impossibility of separating culture from its material basis, and thus there was no guarantee that the borrowed modernising elements from the West would not spill over into the cultural sphere. The expectation that the masses would accept this manufactured notion of nationalism and the new brand of identity in fact displayed a lack of understanding that people would not be prepared to change their way of life overnight. Ziya Gökalp's Turkish nationalism and identity, which have been put into practice by Kemalist social engineering, have been at the root of a long lasting social tension in Turkey and form the basis of today's complicated question of Turkish identity.

The main aim of Kemalist reforms was to generate a Turkish nation of people who would feel first and foremost Turkish. The Republic's secular Kemalist ideology found Islam as a thorny and paradoxical issue to tackle. Paying attention to the fact that almost 99 per cent of the population are Muslim, Kemalism had to incorporate Islam as an integral part of Turkish nationalism, yet the very essence of Kemalist westernisation necessitated a strong rupture with the Islamic Ottoman past. A series of reforms was set in motion, including the replacement of the Arabic alphabet with Latin scripts, Islamic Shariat Law with a European Legal Code, and the introduction of western-style institutions, dress code and universal suffrage. Religion and religious institutions were the main targets of the reforms which aimed at putting an end to society's reliance on Islamic foundations to provide guidance in all matters of life. Turkish nationalists had to redefine Islam as an integral part of national identity in order to avoid the pitfalls of national identity based on ethnicity. This way it was possible to curtail the identity claims of the Kurds while at the same time controlling Islam and Islamic movements (Yavuz 2000b).

The 1922–50 period was characterised by two competing conceptions of Turkish nationalism: secular ethno-linguistic nationalism and religious communal nationalism (Yavuz 1998, 2000a). The state used all means available to create an ideology of westernisation which necessitated the establishment and regulation of a state-monitored public sphere. Kemalist reforms introduced far-reaching changes in every sphere of life including the social, cultural, economic and political spheres. 'By organising the public sphere around the ideology of westernism, the state was able to incorporate whatever it imagined constituted western-ness into its display' (Yavuz 2000b:2).

Despite the reforms, the Islamic cultural heritage survived in the countryside as the people identified themselves with the local community and religion. The reiteration of Islam as the official religion of the state in the Constitution did not appease their feelings of disparity. The number of rebellions of Islamic and Kurdish flavour throughout the 1930s was an indication of some people's hostile feelings about the Kemalist project to establish a western-style Turkish society.

Kemalism's vast secularisation project since 1920 has permeated every sphere of life including education, law, jurisprudence, ethics and social norms. While forcibly restricting the influence of religion, the state has followed a secular education policy which helped to expand secularism mainly among educated people in urban areas. Although religion survived in family and small community life, it was no longer determinate in public life and institutions (Ayata 1990). Until the 1950s the official ideology and its educated supporters considered religion as a symbol of backwardness, opposing modern science, technology, progress, development and the unity of the Turkish nation state. Excessive official opposition to religion meant that religion became a diffused ideology for individuals who felt that the westernised elite was culturally alien. The cleavage generated by the westernisation project since the 1920s between religious masses in rural areas and the educated urban elite continued to grow throughout the Republican period (Ayata 1990).

The secular Kemalist state was based on six principles: republicanism, secularism, populism, *étatism*, nationalism and revolutionism. These principles were quickly accepted by the elite and bureaucrats but found strong opposition from the religious and Kurdish circles. The Kemalist westernisation project sought to establish a society whose guiding principle was not religion but Turkishness. The Turkish nation was to be constituted by citizens with a common language, culture and ideas. If necessary, force was to be used to ensure the homogenisation of society along the Kemalist and western lines. While Kemalist reforms were able to transform Turkish society radically, they have not been able to eliminate totally the tension among competing national identity claims. Secular nation-building efforts of the westernised Kemalist state elites initiated a process of 'othering' Islam (Yavuz 2000b). The stamp of the paradoxical situation created in the early years of the Republic to a certain degree still characterises Turkish society and polity: while using Islam to unify diverse ethno-linguistic groups the state defined its westernisation ideology in opposition to Islam. Islam was used as an integral part of the newly created Turkish identity while ethnicity was left out of this notion.[6] Concepts like *millet* (religious community in the Ottoman Empire), *vatan* (homeland), *gazi* (victorious in battle fought for Islam), and *şehit* (Islamic martyr) were incorporated into the discourse of creating Turkish identity. However, the early trend of nationalisation of Islamic identity based on the Islamic conception of community was counterpoised by other attempts to generate a secular, ethnic Turkish nationalism. The Kemalist secularism and westernisation projects have been anti-Islamist in their world outlook which has been the basis of Turkish nationalism (Yavuz 2000b:23).

The Kemalist reforms gradually found supporters mostly in urban areas, whereas the reaction of rural areas was apathy at most, and thus the divisions between the elite and the masses were deepened. While westernisation and modernisation laid down a framework for a democratic society, people in rural areas continued to maintain their traditional lifestyle in which religion and religiosity played a significant role. The great majority of ordinary citizens felt excluded from the public sphere created by the state elite and consequently informal networks and education systems emerged to protect and preserve their sacred realm.

The Republican state was adamant to separate religion and the state through secularism. Therefore, religious orders which strove to establish an Islamic order had to operate clandestinely. The complete transformation of the relationship between the state and religion almost overnight generated a huge distance between the state, bureaucrats and the masses. The state's heavy-handed approach towards the old institutions and religious practices generated disenchantment among certain sections of the society (Ayata 1990).

The mystical *Nakşibendi* and *Nurcu* sects provided an alternative arena for the evolution of the popular Islamic identity. Religion and various religious orders like the *Sufi* and the *Nakşibendi* emphasise purification of the soul, superior morality, personal integrity and self-control (Ayata 1990). Their promise of other-worldly salvation necessitates refraining from materialistic desires and hedonism. They capitalise on the problems created by the rapid changes brought about through capitalist western modernisation. Religious movements bank on people's sufferings and traditionalism to mould them into pious, devout individuals who would give high esteem to morality, faith and submission to God and the religious order. The *Sufi* and *Nakşibendi* orders have been able to mobilise people for their religious cause through their hierarchical structures which give high priority to humility and submission to the religious order and its sheikhs. The notion of a communication of hearts is the key in the *Nakşibendi* order. Through this notion the sheikhs have been able to enlist people's loyalty and establish a wide network of influence and solidarity beyond local communities. Through its strong religious observance and rituals the *Nakşibendi* order has been able to exercise control over every sphere of life of its members. The *Nakşibendis* indoctrinate their members about the superiority of their moral and value systems at the expense of any other competing ones. Their target is usually the self-employed and the artisans in bazaars and small communities in urban areas. They regulate every sphere of life in accordance with the divine ordinance and continuously introduce new rules to fit the changing situations. The *Nakşibendi* order is supranationalist and aims to raise Islamic consciousness and solidarity globally. It is Islam, not the nation that is the appropriate political unit. However, the *Nakşibendi* does not refrain from operating within the nation state in order to strengthen the Islamic influence. *Nakşibendi* supporters go about their aims quietly, paying specific attention to avoiding confrontation with the state and its secularist institutions while invading them from inside (Ayata 1990:52–54).

The Islamic movement in Turkey is a form of resistance and challenge to the homogenising policies of Kemalism. It consists of legal and illegal networks and organisations that seek to establish an alternative moral order based on various interpretations of Islam. However, the Islamic movement in Turkey is in no way a homogeneous one. Shepard's (1987) differentiation between neo-traditionalist and radical Islam is particularly useful here. Neo-traditionalists are moderate in their attitude towards modern science, technology and modern civilisation while radicals take an uncompromising attitude towards anything that deviates from the ideal Islamic society. The main representatives of neo-traditionalism are the religious orders like the *Nakşibendi*s and *Nurcu*s, which emerged after the establishment of the Turkish Republic. Neo-traditionalists see the need to operate within the existing order and influence society gradually and peacefully in order to counterbalance the challenge posed to traditionalism by westernisation (Shepard 1987:318–320). On the other hand, radical Islam is nothing more than an ideology as numerous splinter groups tend to cut their ties with the traditional and neo-traditional Islamic orders. Radical Islamists are well versed in the modern ideologies and world-views from which they intend to dissociate themselves. The ironic thing about the radicals is that they tend to dissociate themselves from past and current forms of Islam as well as from current ideologies. They are enmeshed in an act of politicising every aspect of life by idealising their past in order to establish a society in the future. This highly politicised version of Islam does not have strong support from ordinarily religious people. Therefore there is a need to differentiate between religiosity and the Islamic radicalism which has been penetrating into the public institutions since the 1980s, although there is also an inevitable connection between the two (Ayata 1990).

The common denominator between many factions within the Islamic movement is their opposition to the Kemalist project and hegemony since the 1920s.[7] The *Nurcu* movement, arguably, is the most powerful Islamic oppositional movement which seeks to preserve and reconstruct the Muslim personality. The writings of Said Nursi provide the basic principles of the *Nurcu* movement. Said Nursi (1876–1960) was of Kurdish origin and spent his life trying to institutionalise a new moral language which puts a high premium on the interpretation of the Quran in the light of modern science and rationality (Yavuz 2000b). The reconciliation of science and the Quran is the foremost aim of the *Nurcu* movement which also sees democracy as the best form of governance. *Nurcus* seek to raise the level of Islamic consciousness through education which pays attention to the connection between reason and revelation (Eickelman 1999).

The writings of Said Nursi, *The Epistles of Light* (*Risale-i Nur Külliyatı*) are discussed, interpreted and applied to everyday life by his disciples through discussions in what they call *dershanes* (reading circles). The aim of regular meetings and discussions by the followers of Said Nursi is to raise Islamic consciousness against westernisation and alienation exemplified by Kemalism (Yavuz 2002). Individuals' inner feelings are the key in this movement that sees worldly and other-worldly salvation in establishing a strong link between reason and revelation by raising the level of Islamic consciousness.[8] Currently there are more than ten *Nurcu* movements operating in Turkey due to their clandestine nature and regional variations. The most significant of these is the Fethullah Gülen *Nurcu* movement. The belief that highly spiritual and intellectually developed individuals with a high Islamic consciousness will be better equipped to struggle against oppressive economic and political forces leads this movement to take the individual as the focal point (Yavuz 2000b). Gülen believes that individuals with Islamic consciousness will be even stronger against the oppressive system if they also take science and technology as their guide. He is adamant that the True Islam of Anatolian Sufism, which synthesises reason and revelation, religion and science, individuals and community stability and change, and globalisation and nationalism, is not inimical to science, nor is it in contradiction to modernity and progress. Gülen's version of *Nurcu* uses the power of persuasion to attract more supporters committed to the creation of a more humane and better society and polity. Being aware of the power of the established order and the army, the Gülen-led movement has taken a gentle approach and sought legitimacy at the state level. Due to the fears of the Kemalist and secularist army, the Gülen movement has been forced to follow contradictory policies. Their mostly covert activities to expand a resistance movement against Kemalism and secularism have been at odds with their search for legitimacy at the state level by behaving in an accommodating manner (Yavuz 2000b:27–28). The concentrated efforts of the Gülen movement to expand their social base through educational institutions have aroused the strong suspicions of the army and of an influential media group, West Working Group. Both vehemently argue that the Gülen movement constitutes a serious threat to secularism and the Kemalist state and their organisational expansion should be stopped. The Gülen-led movement has established a large number of foundations, associations and educational institutions both in Turkey and abroad to expand its support base by attracting more and more people from secular backgrounds. In doing so they have highlighted the view that their aim is to achieve a new form of modernity that is compatible with the fundamental precepts of Islam: democracy and human rights (Yavuz 2000b:28).

Unlike the *Nakşibendi* and *Sufi* orders, radical Islamists do not hide themselves and openly oppose the state, secularism and secular institutions. Most radical Islamists are urban professionals, who glorify the Golden Age of the Prophet Mohammed and judge contemporary times in terms of deviations from and aberrations of the ideal Islamic society (Ayata 1990:56). Radical Islam takes a militant stand against nationalism, as nationalism and nationalist boundaries are seen as artificial creations devised to divide and weaken the unity of Islamic people. Militant Islam, furnished by the values of the glorified 'Golden Age', adopts 'confrontationist, antistate, antisystem' strategies. Although the intellectual Islamists emphasise changing people's minds through education, action-oriented militants see the use of physical force as a legitimate method to achieve their aim of establishing an Islamic state. Radical Islamists constitute a small minority within the fundamentalists in Turkey. However, there is a fear that they could become a powerful urban movement in the face of rising socio-economic problems and reduced possibilities of upward social mobility (Ayata 1990:57).

Kemalism, the official ideology of the state, has considered unofficial religious organisations, movements and their notion of identity as a danger to the unity of the state. Specific efforts are made to keep Islam and Islamic factions at bay. There is no room for other identities in Kemalism and thus any identity claims based on either religion or ethnicity will bring the wrath of the military. Cultural and ethnic differences are considered to be sources of instability that might threaten national unity. The attempts of the Kurdish and Islamic movements to emphasise the difference of their identities from the nationalist Kemalist ideology are met with suspicion by the state (Yavuz 2000b:23–24).

The introduction of a multi-party system and western-style elections in 1946 provided a forum for people with Islamic tendencies to raise their voices. The Democrat Party capitalised on the tension between the secular state elite and the religious masses in its 1946 election campaign. It deliberately manipulated people's religious sentiments by using religious slogans and symbols counterpoising elitist laicism with religion (Ayata 1990:63). Following the fall of the Republican People's Party from power in 1950, the strong state control over religion, a main characteristic of the single party period (1923–46), ceded to a more relaxed and conciliatory attitude towards religion. Since the adoption of a multi-party system almost all political parties have in one way or other attempted to appeal to people's religious sentiments. Some parties have even gone beyond this by developing open and/or secretive connections with organised religious groups. Organised religious groups, for their part, also make every effort to co-operate closely with those political parties which strive to enhance the power of Islam in society. Consequently their ties are stronger with the conservative, right of centre parties which place a significant importance on Islamic principles and practices. In the 1980s the Welfare Party (WP) and its predecessor the National Salvation Party (NSP), were the two prominent examples of Islamic parties whose main aim was to create a society based on Islamic principles. In the period between 1973 and 1979, when the NSP became a coalition partner in the government, organised groups found the right conditions to penetrate state institutions. This trend continued during the 1980s when the Motherland Party ruled the country. The determination of the military rule to fight the left after the 1980 coup led it to follow policies that allowed the Islamic world-view to infiltrate state institutions. Particularly significant was the opening of a large number of clergy schools whose increased number of graduates failed to find suitable jobs in religion-related institutions. The fact that the vocational clergy schools (*İmam Hatip Okulları*) were granted the status of ordinary high schools allowed thousands of their brainwashed graduates to enter universities to study any subject they wished to. This in turn helped to create professionals with strong Islamic beliefs who could easily infiltrate state institutions in the relatively conducive atmosphere provided by the military rule, and could use these institutions for their ideological cause. The military, while still following the Kemalist tradition of keeping religion under state control, relaxed its attitude towards Islam during the 1980s with the belief that religion had a significant place in people's social life and could act as a conservative element in the fight against the spread of leftist ideas that were considered to be the main culprit for the social and political instabilities of the 1970s. Therefore the policies followed by the military in the 1980s reflected their concern with finding a happy marriage between controlling religion and at the same time allowing people and religious organisations to operate relatively freely. Religion was used as a legitimising tool by the military during the years of its oppressive policies. The promotion of Islam as a countervailing element by the army was rather surprising considering the secularist nature of the military as an institution in Kemalist Turkey. Although the direct military rule lasted just over three years, between September 1980 and November 1983, the changes brought about were to have far reaching and long lasting consequences for every aspect of life including the economy and politics. The measures introduced by the military to consolidate the post-1980 regime are referred to as the 'Turkish–Islamic synthesis'. The most significant policy as far as the rise of political Islam is concerned was the introduction of compulsory religious education in primary schools (Öniş 1997:750). Ironically, the Directorate of Religious Affairs, the government body established by the Kemalists to ensure the separation of religion from affairs of the state, was furnished with considerable financial support and authority to enable it to open up a large number of religious secondary schools (*İmam Hatip Okulları*) which have now proved to be a hotbed for religious fanaticism. A great majority of the Islamic intelligentsia who make up the leadership of Islamic parties have emerged from the ranks of *İmam Hatip Okulları*, including the leader of the JDP, Tayyip Erdoğan.

Furthermore, in the 1980s international conjuncture led the governments to relax their policies towards religion. The increasing trade partnership and diplomatic alliances with other Islamic countries in the 1980s when relations with the West were deteriorating is a significant factor behind the rapprochement between the state and religion. The 1980s were characterised by a paradoxical approach to religion in that while concrete steps were taken to increase the religiosity of people, at the same time measures were taken to stop the strengthening of fundamentalism (Ayata 1990:64). One significant consequence of this has been the penetration of state institutions by neo-traditionalist Islamic groups.

Many official departments became vehicles for the promotion of fundamentalist ideas and interests. In some ministries personnel departments fell into the hands of the fundamentalist networks, which used the opportunity to draw upon the graduates of *Imam Hatip* schools and students who had religious ties to the 'dormitories'. (Ayata 1990:64)

The revival of Islam in Turkish politics with the intention of controlling the state through the democratic election system has always provoked the army, which sees itself as the guardian of the Kemalist state. The army's position has been an ironic one since the establishment of the Kemalist Republic: the officers claim to safeguard the democratic regime and aid the process of democratisation but at the same time they will not allow political Islam to come to power through democratic processes (Karaosmanoğlu 1993:32). It is clear that the democratisation process revealed weaknesses in the Kemalist social engineering project. Islamic beliefs and culture were still deeply ingrained in Turkish society after some 40 years of systematic efforts to create a Turkish identity devoid of Islamic values and attitudes. With the introduction of the multi-party system old notions of Turkism which did not separate Islam and Turkishness were re-surfacing. The aims of Islamic parties to establish an Islamic state constitute a major challenge to the secularist Kemalist state (Kadıoğlu 1996). It is not surprising that Islamic parties are closed down regularly by the state under the clear direction of the army, and the famous 1997 intervention by the army is a case in point. This occurred despite the introduction of the, in some respects, more liberal 1982 Constitution which put an end to elite domination of the state and made governments become more responsive to the people's needs. The people's demand that religious education should be compulsory was met and the expression of religious beliefs in any form became freer. Consequently, local identities began to surface, challenging the state's ideal of a homogeneous Turkish identity and emphasising different sects of Islam and ethnic differences (Kadıoğlu 1996:13).

A number of factors have been effectual in the creation of Turkish identity: Islamism, western culture, Kemalism and the Ottoman roots. The attempt of the Kemalist state to move away from Islamic influences towards the West has been at the root of the recent identity crisis in Turkey. However, western and Islamic identities have been the most dominant influences in the identity crisis in recent years as various local identities express themselves through these two opposing poles. Kemalism has tried to create a unified culture at the expense of Islamic identity, but local identities have attached significant importance to Islam. Most political parties since the 1950s have attempted to reconcile the two in the expression of a Turkish identity. The result has been the emergence of multiple identities in which people jump at their convenience between local identity, Islamic identity, westernised identity and national identity. Kemalism's intention to generate a coherent culture and unity through social engineering has not been very successful, as new cleavages have emerged in the democratic structures set in place. People have been able to express themselves through representative democracy and institutionalised civil society. Political leadership has reflected the identity cleavages. Since 1990, two forms of strong leadership have surpassed the others: westernised and Islamist elites who have different views about national identity and have a powerful influence on the rest of society in terms of identity formation.

Turkish army officers represent the most powerful section of the westernised elites. They see themselves as being protectors of the Turkish State against its enemies, particularly the internal enemies who reject westernisation (Karaosmanoğlu 1998:32). The officers are given a strict secular education in tandem with the principles of Kemalism. For the officers, democracy means the promotion and protection of the state and reconciliatory politics is foreign to them. Consequently, they do not understand party politics which pursue group interest before national interest. The National Security Council (NSC) is the pinnacle of the army hierarchy and consists of five generals and six civilians. The officers in the NSC make sure the consensus reached is the one the army favours. Although the decisions of the NSC are of an advisory nature, no government dares to challenge their views or advice (Rouleau 2000:106). As the army has strong support from the public their views about Turkish identity have a considerable influence on people's perception of identity. The army espouses to the belief that Turkish nationalism, secularism, modernisation and clear separation of religion and politics are the building blocks of identity. Although in recent years the NSC has made sure that no government follows policies which will conflict with Kemalism, the Kemalist project's attitude towards Islam has been somewhat ambiguous and paradoxical: while it has attempted to move Islam from the public political sphere, at the same time it has felt the need to institutionalise a state-approved version of Islam (Buğra 2002b). The introduction of the 'Turkish–Islamic synthesis' as the pillar of state ideology in the aftermath of the 1980 military coup served to ensure social unification was instrumental in the ascendance of Islam as a constituent element in Turkish national identity. The military expected to use Islam as a unifying element to consolidate state power, but once Islam received recognition from the military the former used the state to question the state's traditional relations with religion, politics and society. Under various governments in the 1980s, Islam managed to penetrate state institutions and extend its organisational basis. In its electoral campaigns political Islam raised the issues of social inequality, unemployment and injustice in order to attract votes from different socio-economic classes including the poor, the urban middle class, the newly emerging entrepreneurs of Anatolia, as well as Islamic intellectuals and professionals. The Islamist Welfare Party (RP) achieved quick successes both in the municipal elections (in 1994) and national elections (in 1995) as a result of the 'politics of recognition' (Buğra 2002a:189).

THE MODERATION OF POLITICAL ISLAM

Faced with the might of the military, Islamic forces in Turkey can no longer openly seek to establish an Islamic state based on Shariat. Instead of confronting modernisation head on they concentrate on its negative influences and emphasise the protective nature of Islam. This is a clear shift from the traditional Islamist discourse that has been tied up in a conflict of Islam vs. the West (Toprak 1993:244). The legitimacy and respectability that the Islamist intellectuals have found in Turkish society since 1980 and particularly in the 1990s are partly due to the multi-party system which has been tolerant of differences of opinion, and partly to the intellectual development of Islamist thinkers who have gained 'clarity of vision' through secularist education. Contemporary Islamist intellectuals have been able to develop a rational discourse, compared to the irrational jargon produced by earlier Islamist writers, and thus have been able to gain acceptance in academic circles and political elites. Islamist intellectuals no longer emphasise the conflict between the West and Islam or civilisation and technology in a dogmatic fashion and they reflect a better awareness of the changes. They have taken a pragmatic approach rather than a dogmatic one in the interpretation of society and its transformation. The emergence of concepts like 'Islamic liberalism' or 'Islamic socialism' is a testament to the pragmatism of the current Islamic discourse in Turkey. The intellectuals' attempt to reconfigure Islam in response to contemporary changes and problems has increased the popularity of Islamic politics in the eyes of some sections of society. A number of political parties have utilised the reinterpretation of Islam through western concepts. For instance the Motherland Party is a case in point in their efforts to create 'a curious mix of parochial conceptions of Islamic identity with liberal values' (Toprak 1993:243). Islamic intellectuals are well aware of the link between cultural change and industrialisation. They no longer directly blame the West for the weakening of the Islamic identity but explain it as the inevitable outcome of industrial growth and technological progress. Recent Islamic discourse concentrates more on issues concerning human rights, civil society and democracy rather than focusing on historical and cultural differences between Islam and the West. It is quite difficult to gauge how much of this is due to secular pressures and how much is due to a genuine move within the Islamist intelligentsia. The tendency of religious discourse to become more 'mainstream', especially among Kemalist democrats, has been behind the wider support for Islamic views. Some authors argue that in recent years there has been a negative correlation between the popularity of political Islam and its radicalism (Rouleau 2000:113). This can be explained by the strength of the Kemalist army which would not tolerate any movement both popular and radical in nature. It can easily be argued that the army is almost in full control of the Islamic movement and would not hesitate to liquidate any movement that could pose a challenge to the Kemalist system. For instance, the Islamist Refah Party was closed down in 1998 and in February 2001 generals openly threatened to take action against any Islamic movement demanding an Islamic state. The army sees the rise of political Islam as a direct consequence of democratisation and thus regularly takes action to curb its ascendance. Despite the fact that Islamic identity has gained acceptance as one of the multiple identities that contribute to a Turkish national identity, the continuing sensitivity of Kemalism still creates problems and social tension.

The rise of political Islam can partly be explained by the inability of political parties to run the economy. Poverty and unemployment have been on the rise for a long time but the rate of increase has grown since 1980, the starting point for neo-liberal policies. The great majority of the poor have become disenchanted with the coalition governments formed mostly by the mainstream centre,

centre-right and centre-left parties. The political system has been revealed as corrupt and inept in the last three decades (Kuniholm 2001). The public has lost trust in the 'corrupt and fossilised political system' and politicians have started to give support to political Islam. Given that the army does not tolerate radical Islam, most political parties have attempted to incorporate Islamist discourse into their party programme and find a compromise between the two opposing poles: Kemalism and fundamentalist Islam. However, it seems that the more liberal oriented parties that have shared various governments in recent years have not been very successful in attracting more votes, despite their attempts to occupy a middle ground between Islam and Kemalism. Disenchantment with rising poverty and unemployment has increased the popularity of Islamic political parties, particularly that of JDP (Justice and Development Party). Furthermore, Islamists' readiness to discuss things rationally and act via the established democratic institutions have contributed to their political popularity among the unemployed (both urban and rural), the peasantry, artisans, small businesspeople and merchants.

POLITICAL ISLAM, CLASS POLITICS AND BUSINESS INTERESTS

Political Islam in Turkey has emerged as a form of identity politics and 'fills the void left by the decline of the orthodox or secular democratic politics of the left. In other words it emerges as a political movement expressing the grievances of the poor and the disadvantaged in both rural and urban areas in a social democratic guise' (Öniş 1997:748). This is not specific to Turkey as there has been a global shift from the politics of distribution to the politics of recognition (Fraser 1995, 1997). In other words the focus of politics has moved away from the economic issues related to equality towards the cultural issues that highlight differences. Despite my reservations about the disappearance of the politics of economic redistribution I think it is still important to note the rise of identity politics in the fight against injustice. Obviously there is certain truth in Fraser's assumption, also shared by Featherstone and Lash (2001), Maffesoli (1996) and Phillips (1999), that the recognition of ethnicities, religion and gender is replacing class-based projects for equality. The question to be raised is whether engagement in identity politics is tantamount to the abandonment of redistributive politics or whether it is a reflection of efforts on the part of certain groups to achieve their goals of redistribution of resources. In other words, is not the politics of recognition the handmaiden of the politics of redistribution? (Walby 2001). The way political Islam has been transformed in Turkey verifies this point very well. Ever since the 1970s political Islam has been using the language of recognition. This has led authors like Keyman (1995, 2002) and Buğra (2002a, 2002b) to analyse political Islam in Turkey in terms of the decline of class politics and the rise of identity politics. In their parlance, forms of communal belonging which are of a cultural nature and cut across class lines have taken the central stage in the political struggle. However, what these authors do not realise is that despite the cultural colouring of Islamic discourse and the language of recognition politics, political Islam has been promoting the interests of the petty bourgeoisie. Elements of class politics have always been hidden in their agenda. The language of recognition has been used by small and medium businesspeople mostly of Anatolia, small merchants, artisans and traders within Islamic parties to end the hegemony of the western-oriented big businesses of the Istanbul bourgeoisie. The main concern of these marginalised groups was to penetrate the state in order to promote their own economic interests. The language of recognition was used as the handmaiden of the politics of redistribution. Islamism was used to mobilise political support for a particular form of distributional politics. It is not a coincidence that within a few years of gaining political strength and being represented in Parliament, a huge section of the National Outlook Movement (NOM) reorganised itself under the leadership of Tayyip Erdoğan within the JDP. It is instructive to notice that while anti-westernism and anti-secularism were the main tenets of the essentialist Islamist project the JDP did not hesitate to denounce them by preaching for secularism and joining the EU. While in power Islamists were able to utilise 'personalised politics', to use Offe's term (1999), to ensure transfer of state resources to the business circles known for their support of Islamism. Once in a position to benefit from operating internationally, the rising Islamic capitalists did not hesitate to sacrifice their ideological commitment to oppose the West. The first thing the JDP did after the election results were out was to declare their allegiance to the West and international financial institutions, particularly the IMF. This transformation of the national outlook was not something that took place overnight but a slow process in which economic interests within it were realigning themselves in congruence with Turkey's integration to the global economy. In the 1990s, the leadership of the Welfare Party was at pains to promulgate the idea that Islam was compatible with the global capitalist economy and democracy and to try hard to integrate the hitherto alienated majority into socio-economic and political life. Specific care was taken to appear to be representing the masses while the members of the Islamic networks that supported the Welfare Party's political Islam were being helped to make economic gains. The Welfare Party's economic programme was designed in such a way as to persuade the members of Islamic networks that the party was there to promote their economic interests. Such an apparent contradiction was compounded by the militant position taken by Erbakan, the unquestionable leader of the National Order Movement, on the question of secularism and the West.

THE NATIONAL OUTLOOK MOVEMENT (NOM)

Political Islam found its most salient expression in the National Outlook Movement (NOM) that followed its political aims through the establishment of successive political parties from the 1970s onwards. The National Order (Milli Nizam), the National Salvation (Milli Selamet), the Welfare (Refah), and the Virtue (Fazilet) parties were closed down by the state for their anti-secularist stand. However, the existing constitution cannot prevent the emergence of a new political party as the successor of a previously closed political party. Therefore each of the above listed political parties under the leadership and/or influence of the charismatic Professor Necmettin Erbakan emerged as a successor to a party closed by the state under the overt or covert guidance of the army.

The NOM idealises the classical Ottoman period rather than Prophet Mohammed's time. However, the NOM has not been static in its goals, as its targets have changed over time. Originally a mixture of Ottomanism, nationalism, modernism and Islamism, the NOM emphasised ethics and industrialisation in the period 1973–80, justice and identity in the 1983–98 period, and democracy and the rule of law after 1998 (Yavuz 2000b). The roots of the NOM can be traced back to a dissident movement within the centre-right Justice Party (AP) in 1969. The establishment of the National Order Party under the leadership of Necmettin Erbakan in 1970 marked the beginning of the NOM (Buğra 2002a, 2002b). The National Order Party emerged in 1970 as the first Islamist party as a result of the disenchantment of small businesses operating in Anatolia. The NOP came out to promote the interests of small businesses, small traders and artisans who felt left out by the ISI policies which promoted big businesses (Gülalp 2001). The cosy relationship between the state and large corporations situated mainly in Istanbul contributed to the marginalisation and peripherialisation of small to medium-sized businesses in provincial towns. Members of such businesses have historically been members of religious brotherhood orders since Ottoman times and have been conservative in their world-views. A succession of Islamic parties since 1970 has attempted to articulate the feelings of the people who have felt marginalised by the state's policies. In order to enlarge their constituencies the Islamic parties have gradually become populists through the advocacy of the rights and interests of various groups and classes (Gülalp 2001).

The NOP was banned by the military in the aftermath of the 1971 military coup. The Islamic Party resurfaced under the following names: the National Salvation Party (Milli Selamet Partisi), the Welfare Party (Refah Partisi), the Virtue Party (Fazilet Partisi) and the Felicity Party (Saadet Partisi) following the closure of the previous parties by the state. In each case charismatic Necmettin Erbakan emerged as the unchallenged leader of the Islamic Party. The highly volatile and unstable political atmosphere in the 1970s allowed the National Salvation Party (NSP) to participate in various coalition governments (Öniş 2001). However, the NSP was not able to please all Islamists, some of whom blamed the party for being too conciliatory and moving away from the basic tenets of Islam through close integration with secular institutions. This alienated some of the *Nurcu* and *Nakşibendi* groups which did not lend support to the NSP. The political and electoral behaviour of organised Islamic groups has not been homogeneous. Some supported other centre-right political parties during the 1980s. For instance Suleymancis and some sections of the *Nurcu* supported the True Path Party, while *Nakşibendi*'s votes were divided between the Motherland Party (MP) and the Nationalist Work Party, Fethullahci and Kadiri supported the MP and Rifai voted for the Nationalist Work Party (Ayata 1990:62). The NSP remained a small, marginal and parochial party compared with its successor, the Welfare Party (Sunar and Toprak 1983; White 1995; Sayarı 1996; Öniş 1997). The fact that the Welfare Party emerged as the leading party from the 1995 elections polling 21.4 per cent of the national votes was a sign that political Islam was on the rise and this could have serious implications for the secular constitutional democracy.

THE RISE AND FALL OF THE WELFARE PARTY

The ideology of the Welfare Party (WP), the vanguard of the NOM between 1983 and 1998, was based on the historical opposition of the East and the West. The Welfare Party strongly opposed the West by claiming that it represented colonialism, oppression, unjustness and ultimately Christianity. The Welfare Party saw Kemalism as 'the West within' and thus sought to obtain power to replace the 'Turkish identity' created by Kemalism with its own version of identity based on a mixture of Islamic, Ottoman and Turkish features (Yavuz 2000a, 2000b). The national outlook ideology flourished on the dichotomic notions of superiority and inferiority characterising Islam and the West respectively.

It is difficult to pigeonhole the Welfare Party as its programme includes features that fit in with the programmes of political parties with diverse ideological persuasions: the centre, the right and the left. It emphasises both tradition and modernity at the same time. While it takes a traditionalist position on cultural issues, it adheres to the idea of using modern science and technology in the economic sphere. Its attack on the West and western values as representatives of imperialism does not fit in with the glorification of western science and technology. Furthermore the economic order labelled as the 'Just Order' mixes and matches elements of western capitalism, socialism and Islam. In Öniş's words the Welfare Party represented 'a model of hyper-populism based on morally justified cross-class compromise, designed to form a broad coalition of political support ranging from private business to the poorest segment of society' (Öniş 1997:754). In the mixed economy envisaged by the 'Just Order', private enterprise was to constitute the motor of development while the state was to provide the necessary conditions for its enrichment. The 'Just Order' insisted that Turkey could become a prominent force in the world economy by using science and technology and by changing its orientation from the West to the East, particularly to the second generation of the NICs with Islamic populations (i.e. Indonesia and Malaysia), to the Islamic Middle East and to the Turkic states of the ex-Soviet Union. The rejection of the West and therefore Turkey's integration into the EU, was one of the issues that contributed to the emergence of the moderate reformists who later formed the JDP. On many counts the WP differed from the traditional political parties and this increased its popularity among the people. The WP saw all the other parties as imitators of the West and thus presented itself as the only party representing the national and moral view. It represented a movement led by Islamist middle and upper classes who attempted to mobilise the urban poor against the established order represented by Kemalism (Gülalp 2001). The grassroots strategy of establishing face-to-face contact with potential voters, listening to their problems, providing food and shelter for the needy and the destitute, and promising to find employment were some of the organisational features of the WP's success in the elections (Ayata 1990). The social democratic discourse used by the WP seemed to be more convincing when material help was provided to the poor in shantytown areas of big cities like Istanbul and Ankara. With the use of computers, big cities were surveyed and potential voters were given financial help in return for their votes. Therefore it was not surprising that the WP won the local elections in Istanbul and Ankara in 1994 while disorganised social democratic parties could not persuade the people to vote for them. Once in office the WP mayors used their power and authority to show that their party was a radical alternative to traditional secular social democracy. While the WP was extremely organised and systematic in its approach, the traditional parties, both on the right and on the left, were in organisational disarray. The dividing line between such parties had become quite blurred in conjunction with Turkey's integration into the global economy and the world-wide predominance of neo-liberalism. The public became tired of endless bickering in Parliament among coalition partners as well as between the Government and the opposition parties. Apart from the leadership cadres there did not seem to be any difference between the orthodox parties as far as their programmes were concerned. The clash of personal interests among leaders had led to the creation of a large number of parties with similar policy orientations. The fragmentation of the left and the right into many similar parties contributed significantly to the rise of the Islamic Welfare Party (Öniş 1997:756–757). Furthermore, the Social Democratic Populist Party's (SDP) concentration on democracy and human rights issues in isolation from economic problems during its reign as a coalition partner with the right of centre True Path Party in the early 1990s, as well as the allegations of corruption, inefficiency and incompetence against the local governments controlled by the SDP ruined its image. The SDP was no longer seen as a party which could meet the aspirations of the poor who traditionally constituted its electoral base. Therefore the success of the WP can partly be explained by the failure of the SDP.

Political Islam in Turkey aims to institute an Islamic society by addressing economic and class issues under a religious guise. In this sense the political Islam promoted by the WP was a multi-class movement unified by the attraction of the superiority of Islam. The NOM has drawn its support from the Anatolian bourgeoisie, the urban poor and the excluded Kurds, and as such it has become the ideology of opposition. It managed to poll a significant portion of the votes in the 1996 national elections, but was not allowed to form a government as the army pressurised two rival right of centre parties, the True Path Party and Motherland Party, to form a government. However, the incessant squabbles between the two for the leadership of the centre right generated a breathing space for the WP which became a coalition partner with the True Path Party in June 1996 in the aftermath of Prime Minister Mesut Yılmaz's resignation. Necmettin Erbakan, the leader of the Islamist Party, became the first Islamist Prime Minister in the history of the Republic.

The army reacted to this by ignoring the Government and refusing to co-operate with it on some issues. Through the National Security Council[9] the army established a supervisory role over government decisions concerning all major domestic and foreign policy issues. An unspoken coalition of the army, businesspeople and the media declared a war against Islamists as they saw them as the enemy of the secular state and society. Any identity claims based on religion and ethnicity were met by a powerful reaction from the state through the State Security Courts. The WP was eased out of the Government by the military in February 1997. Criticising secularism became a crime punishable by imprisonment. For instance, Necmettin Erbakan was sentenced to imprisonment for one year in 1994 for saying that Turkey had moved away from its Islamic roots. Similarly the leader of the JDP (Adalet ve Kalkınma Partisi), Tayyip Erdoğan, was sentenced to four months in 1998 for reciting a poem with the lines 'mosques are our barracks, minarets our bayonets, domes our helmets, the believers our soldiers'. This conviction kept him out of the office of Prime Minister for a few months in 2002 as convicts cannot be elected to Parliament. However, the JDP managed to reform the laws and hold a by-election to ensure Erdoğan's membership in Parliament and thus his appointment to the office. Erdoğan's party won the elections with a landslide majority on 3 November 2002. The JDP emerged as a result of a division within Erbakan's WP which was closed down by the constitutional court in January 1998. Having realised that being in overt opposition to secularism would prevent the Islamists from maintaining power, a group of politicians from the ranks of the Saadet Party (Felicity Party) – which carried the banner for the NOM as the successor of the WP – decided to form a moderate splinter party in 2001. The phenomenal success of the JDP in November 2002 was not simply due to the power of its ideology but to a combination of factors. The most significant included the weaknesses of other political parties and the inability of the existing coalition government to stop the economic crisis, rising unemployment, high inflation and corruption and to provide a platform for true democracy. Voters sought vengeance on old party leaders who would never let go of the leadership regardless of how poor their election results. Election after election, the same old faces would appear before the public seeking their votes while not responding to their demands and not acting democratically within their own parties. Recession, unemployment and political stalemate led the voters to punish the three ruling parties who were not able to pass the 10 per cent threshold required nationally to hold seats in Parliament. The JDP has been very careful not to include any anti-secularist rhetoric in its political campaigns. The Turkish electorate eliminated all the parties who had been part of a government since the middle of the 1990s, putting an end to the incessant bickering among coalition partners, incompetence and corruption. The voters punished all the political parties whom they thought were responsible for the economic and financial turmoil, and all party leaders who had clung to their position for a long time despite failure after failure, and who had disconnected themselves from the wishes of the people. With around 34 per cent of the votes, the JDP managed to obtain more than two thirds of the parliamentary seats necessary to receive a vote of confidence. Time will tell whether the JDP is just a centrist conservative party, as its leader claimed in his speech following the 3 November election (Milliyet 2002, 4 November), or an Islamic party with a hidden agenda. In his speech, Erdoğan, the former mayor of Istanbul, specifically emphasised the fact that his party intended to respect everyone's lifestyle, to speed up integration into the EU and global economy and to remain respectful of the rule of law. He was very careful to employ a moderate, pro-western rhetoric that avoided conflict with the secular state. The JDP claims to be a Muslim democratic party espousing the principles of liberalism and supporting pro-western and pro-IMF policies. It is well aware of the fact that it was the anti-secularist discourse of previous Islamist parties that got them into trouble with the state courts and finally led to their closures.

It may be argued that the military's attempt to cleanse the public sphere of Islamism was one of the major factors behind the emergence of the JDP in 2001 and its rise to power in 2002. The army's intolerance of identity claims based on religion and ethnicity was behind its action to push the pro-Islamic WP out of the coalition government in 1998. In 1997 the army asked the Government to take stringent measures to stop the infiltration of Islamic groups into state institutions. The army's directives included the closures of religious seminaries and preacher schools, via the implementation of the Uniformity of Education law. Furthermore, the army wanted measures to stop the recruitment of Islamists into government jobs and to control the economic activities of Islamic economic groups. Despite the WP's subservience, in January 1998 the constitutional court shut the party down and banned its leader Necmettin Erbakan from politics. Claims have been made that apart from the army's intent to cleanse the public sphere of Muslim presence, the interests of the Istanbul-based media cartel and bourgeoisie were behind the closure (Yavuz 2000b:33–34). The bourgeoisie saw the WP as a serious obstacle to their gaining financial benefit from the privatisation of state companies, and therefore engineered its replacement with a more dependent government. It must be emphasised that Erbakan's challenging style and the welfare-led government's attitudes concerning secularism speeded up the downfall of the WP. The WP's closure signified the end of the military's policy of using Islam as a counter-force against the left and the Kurdish ethnic movements. It also signified a shift in the strategies of all major Islamic groups towards the West and westernisation. Both the traditionalist and modernist versions of the NOM, embodied in the Erbakanist Felicity Party headed by Recai Kutan and Erdoğan's JDP respectively, have started to show the signs of being pro-western. It could easily be argued that the continuous harassment of the NOM by the state has been largely responsible for the transformation of its world outlook, culminating in seeing modernity, democracy and multiculturalism as universal values, not as the outcome of western domination. The weakening of the NOM started with the attempts of some of the

Virtue Party members to distance themselves from the legacy of the WP. This led to the disgruntlement of some of the individuals and organisations who provided open or tacit support for political Islam. The reformists within the Virtue Party intended to emphasise the significance of economy, technology and progress rather than concentrating on the cultural issues that had been the basis of the WP.

The centre's intolerance to any other identity than Kemalism is certainly a significant factor behind the disillusionment created within political Islam, but other factors stemming from the workings of global processes and class configurations have equally contributed to its downfall. Perhaps one or two factors could be briefly mentioned here. One is the rise of an internationally oriented business class from the ranks of Anatolian merchants, wholesalers, shopkeepers and small-scale producers. Second is the emergence of Islamic capital, raised from the Turkish migrant workers in Europe and from Saudi Arabia, and this capital's willingness and desire to be integrated into the global market. Third is the real world situation which compounds the first two. September 2001 and the West's reaction to it brought it home that, at least in the foreseeable future, anti-western political Islam would be detrimental to the rising business interests in Turkey that strive hard to be completely integrated into the West by becoming a full member of the EU. September 11 played a vital role in the election victory of the JDP. It forced political Islam to reassess the possibility of its coming to power in Turkey. Their awareness of the strength of secular forces in Turkish society, including the army, in the aftermath of the unearthing of the horrible murders committed by the Turkish Hizbullah, 'God's faction', in the name of political Islam was intensified by September 11. They had already lost the support of the Turkish democrats who tolerated them for the sake of democratic rights. It was this realisation that militant Islam had no chance of coming to power in the aftermath of September 11 that made the revisionists within the ranks of the Islamist party decide to further distance themselves from Erbakan and his militant anti-secularist approach and preach for democracy, secularism and human rights.

The 'reform' movement, which started within the ranks of the Virtue Party (Fazilet Party) under the leadership of Abdullah Gül, specifically raised the opinion at the first convention of the party in 2000 that political Islam was doomed to fail and the party should have a secular stand. The defeat of the reformists in the general assembly sowed the seeds of the JDP which surged to power within

14 months of its establishment in August 2001. Immediately after the election, the declaration of Erdoğan, the leader of the JDP, that his party is a conservative but modern party of Muslim Democrats is a good indication that the 'reformist' faction of the NOM is gradually moving away from Islamism to become a part of the system.

GLOBALISATION AND THE RISE OF POLITICAL ISLAM IN TURKEY

The resentment to state policies that pushed Islam to the private sphere and that only allowed the officially recognised version to flourish was not the only factor that contributed to the rise of political Islam. The explanations of the WP's success that revolve around either the party's appeal to the poor or the inherent contradictions of modernity and secularism are of limited value. They need to be complemented by explanations that consider the socio-economic transformations undergone by Turkey in conjunction with contemporary changes in the world economy which provided suitable conditions for the rise of political Islam (Buğra 2002a, 2002b).

Three prominent Turkish academics, Buğra, Gülalp and Öniş have made significant contributions in this field. They emphasise the fact that internationalisation of production and the spread of flexible specialisation have provided economic opportunities for the most significant supporters of political Islam: the Anatolian artisans, businesspeople and merchants. The challenges of globalisation have prepared the ground for attempts to use Islam as a strategic resource by business and political circles. The forces of globalisation have brought about transformations on many fronts. First of all, in the social and political arenas, in parallel with the decline of the power of the nation state, identity politics emerged and replaced the concepts of national identity and belonging with those of cultural, regional and religious forms of identity (Buğra 2002a, 2002b; Öniş 1997). The global supremacy of neo-liberalism, greatly helped by the policies imposed by international organisations on less economically developed countries, has been instrumental in the loss of the sovereignty of nation states. Globalisation has instituted the internationalisation of production which allows the TNCs to escape from state control and follow their own interests globally. The mobility of capital and developments in information systems, technology, communications and transportation have all contributed to the supremacy of the TNCs *vis-à-vis* the nation state.

Furthermore the conditionalities imposed on less economically developed countries by the IMF, the World Bank and the WTO, acting on behalf of corporate capital, contribute further to the erosion of the sovereignty of the nation state. The pressures to relinquish the state's sovereignty to either supranational organisations and/or to local or municipal organisations exacerbates the process of loss of sovereignty on the part of the nation state which finds itself increasingly unable to meet people's expectations (Öniş 1997).

Parallel to the decline of the nation state is the decline of the traditional left both in more and less economically developed countries. The establishment of neo-liberalism as the dominant ideology and the supremacy of the US in the world economy and politics coupled with the collapse of communism in recent decades, inevitably led to the decline of the left as a whole including social democracy. Therefore neither the nation state nor the traditional politics operating within the left–right axis has been able to meet the aspirations of the impoverished masses in less economically developed countries. Globalisation has been accompanied by rapidly increasing inequalities among social classes and the loss of state legitimacy and authority, as continuous conditionalities imposed by the supranational organisations have generated a crisis of governance on the part of the state. The implementation of neo-liberal policies in less economically developed countries has meant the abandonment of the post-war developmentalism which proved to be inefficient in most of these countries.

Developmentalism, which characterised the Turkish policies from the 1920s until the end of the 1970s, was not able to meet the desire of the masses for a better life. The modernity project initiated in 1923 with the establishment of the new Republic brought about fundamental changes in society within a very short period and produced a stronger reaction from the Islamists in the form of radical Islam. The new Republic's nationalist and state developmentalist project ensured a particular form of integration into the world economy in the aftermath of the Great Depression. Nationalist and statist emphasis on import-substituting industrialisation (ISI) was not sufficient to deliver what they promised. In the atmosphere of relative freedom created by the world recession, Turkey was able to follow a nationalist development strategy with the state taking a leading role in capital accumulation. Soon the nationalist developmentalist project, with its focus on ISI, ran into a crisis which coincided with the vicissitudes of post-war world capitalism. Having overcome the Great Depression, the capitalist world economy revised new ways of reintegrating the Third World which had managed to follow inward-looking nationalist industrialisation policies. In the new international division of labour productive capital from the advanced capitalist countries found investment outlets in the Third World and thus laid the foundations of a new industrialisation strategy: export-oriented industrialisation. This shift took place at the end of the 1970s in Turkey and marked 'the collapse of the welfare-statist economic policies and the populist democratic regime, with corresponding crisis in secular nationalist ideology' (Gülalp 1992:20). Neo-liberalist economic and social polity that came to dominate Turkey after 1980 established the predominance of the market economy in the economic sphere and allowed the opposition forces in the political sphere to raise their voices and organise themselves along religious, ethnic and local community lines. The collapse of the nationalist project undermined the secularist legitimisation of the state, as it was not possible to protect the common national interest. In the relatively free atmosphere of market-oriented competitive individualism, Islamists openly started to show their commitment to religious ideology which intended to undermine the secularist basis of the state. The 1980s witnessed the replacement of the nationalist developmentalist state with neo-liberal competitive individualism. It was realised that the state had not represented the collective interest of the nation and the welfare of its citizens. Rising poverty and unemployment were the results of the nationalist developmentalist project which had been losing legitimacy since the late 1970s. Parallel to the replacement of nationalist ideology, 'secularism was displaced by the ideological refuge of other worldliness' (Gülalp 1992:22).

The deification of the market forces since the 1980s has further exacerbated social problems concerning employment, education, health and services. In particular the implementation of SAPs has limited the capacity of the state to deliver social services to the populace as a whole. Increasing privatisation of public services has compounded the impact of impoverishment on the great majority. While aggravated income distribution means the masses increasingly expect the state to alleviate the impact of rising poverty, the declining capacity of the nation state to meet these expectations has generated an atmosphere of disillusionment and mistrust among the masses. The inability of the nation state to implement Keynesian-style distribution policies has led to the erosion of the power base of social democratic parties. Extreme nationalist and religious ideologies have filled the gap created by the decline of social democratic and centrist political parties.

This has been evidenced by the rise of a number of Islamic parties such as the Welfare Party, Virtue Party, Felicity Party and the Justice and Development Party one after another; and the ultra right-wing National Action Party since the 1980s, as well as the ruination of the Social Democratic Party in the 2002 national elections. The WP argued vehemently for a multicultural society with the belief that only within such a society could oppression and discrimination be avoided by religious and ethnic communities (Refah Partisi 1992). Furthermore the WP claimed to represent the poor and the destitute and promised to bring about a 'Just Order' in which inequalities would be minimised. The successors of the WP in the 1990s and more recently have used the same rhetoric of identity politics and social justice (Buğra 2002b).

In the economic field, globalisation signified the end of Fordist production and the emergence of what is usually referred to as post-Fordist production. The aim here is not to discuss the debate in detail but to highlight some of the most significant features of post-Fordist production.[10] Fordism characterised advanced capitalist countries between 1930 and the 1970s. The main feature of Fordism was the mass production of standardised goods in huge factories owned by TNCs. Bureaucratically and hierarchically organised TNCs competed in the world market by using their full capacity and cost cutting. In the 1970s, Fordist mass production began to exhaust its potential as mass markets began to shrink due to consumers being tired of standard products. The economic system started to experience economic crisis. Industries exhausted their efficiency gains as the costs and timescale of investment became huge. Labour resistance built up in reaction to capital's efforts to achieve high rates of profit by keeping wages low. Flexible production and flexible accumulation emerged in response to the crises experienced by Fordist capitalism.

The term 'flexible production' refers to a new international division of labour within the global economy where new advancements in production, communication and transformation technologies have allowed the fragmentation of production and de-skilling of labour. In this new international division of labour, capital has become extremely mobile and has relocated itself in less economically developed countries to take advantage of cheap and organised labour as well as the privileges offered by national states. International capital has been able to organise production indirectly through sub-contracting arrangements with local firms in less economically developed countries. Given the fragmented nature of production it is no longer necessary to produce a whole product from start to finish in the same locality. Many different fragments of a product could be produced in different locations all over the world using the cheapest labour available as flexible production does not rely on a highly skilled labour force. Fragmentation of production has also allowed the descaling, downsizing and decentralisation of business firms. All these features have contributed to the weakening of the working classes *vis-à-vis* capital (Buğra 2002a, 2002b).

Flexible production enabled capital to overcome the crises faced throughout the 1970s. Post-Fordist flexible specialisation was based on interlinked specialised small firms with flexible organisation, a flexible work process and flexible output, producing smaller batches of customised goods. Thanks to developments in new technologies in production, design, transportation and communication, the rigidities of Fordist production have been overcome to a significant extent by flexibility in production sites, labour and products. By relocating segments of production to industrial districts all over the world, and by utilising the labour market flexibility, flexible firms have been able to minimise the cost of labour at the expense of worker protection rights and social benefits. The flexible firm uses a workforce composed of 'core' and 'peripheral' workforces. Most of the workforce used in less economically developed countries by international flexible firms consists of: regular employees engaged in low-skill, routine work with fairly low pay and limited job security; contingent employees with high skills working on short-term contracts or projects with high pay; and finally low-skill, low paid contract workers. The twin processes of de-skilling of labour and fragmentation of production have paved the way for small entrepreneurs in less economically developed countries to enter into sub-contracting arrangements to produce commodities and services for both the internal and world markets by using mainly cheap and non-unionised local labour.

The breakdown of traditional economic and social structures in less economically developed countries through such processes as the introduction of private land ownership and the mechanisation of agriculture have contributed considerably to the creation of a large 'industrial reserve army'. Local entrepreneurs with an intimate knowledge of local processes adventured to participate in the world market through subcontracting arrangements in simple and labour-intensive industries like textiles and shoes. De-skilling of labour and fragmentation of production also allowed small and medium-sized production units in less economically developed countries to produce only a part of a product under sub-contracting arrangements.[11] The rise of small businesses with export orientation in the so-called Anatolian Tigers (cities like Gaziantep, Kahramanmaraş, Kayseri, Çorum, etc.) has to be seen in this context of globalisation of production and the process of informalisation.

What Portes, Castells, and Benton (1989) call 'informalisation of the economy' is concretised in the form of undeclared, unprotected labour, small units of production, home work rather than factory work, segmentation of labour along age, gender and ethnic lines and dependence upon the absence of legal control to maintain job security. Informalisation is perceived as a deliberate strategy to create a fragmented labour force unable to guard its class identity, to the detriment of working-class organisations. Primordial relations are often invoked to regulate the relations between the labourers and the employers. In Turkey they include fictive kinship, membership of a religious brotherhood organisation and having the same spatial origins.[12]

The mobilisation and organisation of labour in export-oriented small businesses are governed by personal primordial relations rather than by institutionalised contractual relations. Given the high element of insecurity in labour relations and the lack of state regulation to protect the labourers against capital, networks of solidarity based on kinship, neighbourhood, ethnicity and religion have developed. In the case of Turkey, reciprocity relations in the last few decades have become prevalent not only in labour relations and in the protection of the vulnerable but also in 'subcontracting, outsourcing, information sharing and collaboration in matters of technology and marketing among smaller firms, as well as between' smaller and larger firms (Buğra 2002b:113).

It is difficult not to agree with Buğra (2002b:109) that contemporary global capitalism provided the most suitable context in which to justify a discourse demanding a multicultural society and the elimination of inequalities to improve the lot of the disadvantaged. The networks of social relations used by anti-secular and anti-state movements filled the gap generated by the decline of the state as a regulator of economic relations in the era of global capitalism. Business organisations, industries and interest associations have increasingly used Islam to create common values throughout their institutions and thus to ensure stability and governance. Segments of business circles have used Islam as an organisational resource in establishing networks, providing information and regulating capital–labour relations (Buğra 2002b). Networks of reciprocity relations based on personal trust and loyalty are strongly buttressed by Islam in Turkey.

In the era of globalisation, labour unions have lost much of their power in their dealings with capital. Furthermore, globalisation is said to have decreased the role of the state in economic life leaving the field open to the forces of the free market. Likewise, the boundaries between political, economic and cultural aspects of life have become blurred in the epoch of flexible specialisation. Deregulation of production and the relations between capital, labour and the state have undermined the basis of class identity and replaced it with other identities based on religion, culture and ethnicity. Businesses may evoke 'pre-industrial affiliations' in their dealings with labour and other similar businesses rather than being governed by impersonal rules and regulations, the characteristics of the context in which Fordism flourished.[13] This is what the MÜSİAD and member firms have been doing in Turkey since the establishment of the organisation in the late 1970s (Buğra 1998, 1999, 2002a).

Ayşe Buğra (1998, 1999, 2002a, 2002b) provides an excellent analysis of MÜSİAD (the Association of Independent Industrialists and Businessmen) and the Islamic labour union Hak-İş in highlighting how political Islam benefited from primordial relations. She maintains that the organisational abilities of MÜSİAD were an important factor behind the success of Islamic parties in the national elections of 1995, 1999 and 2002. MÜSİAD has been able to foster feelings of trust and solidarity among newly emerging and regionally dispersed small-scale enterprises all over the country (Buğra 2002a:192–193). The 3000 member firms consist mainly of small enterprises employing fewer than 50 workers. The way in which the Islamic business association MÜSİAD has responded to global changes has been instrumental in the rise of political Islam. The main consideration behind MÜSİAD's economic and social strategy is that the failure of the statist model of past development is due to ignoring Islam as an important component of organisational structures. Relying on the work of Kuran (1995), Buğra maintains that MÜSİAD actively supported the emergence of an Islamic sub-economy which has been committed to Islamic principles and which fulfils a psychological and economic mission. By emphasising informal ties of trust and solidarity between businesspeople and workers and among businesspeople, Islamic principles not only 'alleviate feelings of guilt associated with personal wealth accumulation in contexts where money-making activity is based on rather precarious legal arrangements and consequently lacks legitimacy' but also reduces uncertainty for businesspeople. In a sense the fostering of trust and solidarity among small businesses through informal ties gives a sense of identity to small firms which are continuously being pushed to operate in an unregulated informalised economy governed by flexible specialisation.[14] MÜSİAD has used the language of social exclusion and claimed that the state's support for large-scale businesses has disadvantaged newly emerging small businesses therefore there is a need for such businesses to establish solidarity networks based on Islamic principles.

There is a strong parallelism between the views of MÜSİAD and the Welfare Party as far as airing the voices of small to medium-size enterprises is concerned (Gülalp 2001:438). The idea behind MÜSİAD's endeavour to disseminate technology and market information, to provide training in modern management techniques and languages, to publish informative pamphlets and journals, to organise conferences and product fairs for small to medium-sized enterprises, and so on, is the contention that state policies have treated the small and medium-size enterprises unequally by favouring large firms in the allocation of resources and privileges. In doing so MÜSİAD places a high premium on establishing and maintaining networks and solidarity among its members and praises Islamic identity for achieving co-operation among businesses. Islamic solidarity is seen as absolutely vital for smaller businesses to be in a position to challenge the cosy relationship between the state and the 'rent seeking' big businesses who obtain unfair advantages. Through co-operation between hard-working, pious and humble business people it will be possible to end the hegemony of the 'rent seeking' classes who are responsible for the disruption of democracy and the removal of the Welfare Party from the government (MÜSİAD 1997).

MÜSİAD, the Welfare Party and Islamist intellectuals used the discourse of poverty to gain the allegiance of the working class. The big business circles which have leaned on the state for self-advancement were blamed for skewed income distribution, high inflation and corruption within the state. The social democratic and populist discourse used by the Islamic Party was instrumental in recruiting support both from some sections of the working class and from the majority of small and medium businesses. Islamists were able to channel popular opposition to the status quo towards the Islamist Welfare Party.[15]

Buğra's statement that the strategic use of both the network forming and guilt alleviating functions of religion by MÜSİAD is in tandem with the characteristics of international economy seems to be appropriate here. Once business relations among firms and industrial relations between employers and workers are based on mutual trust then there is no need for a formal labour code and labour unions. Also, solidarity and trust among the community of believers will lead to stable and productive industrial relations. What MÜSİAD is doing here is strengthening the class position of the business class who operate in an economy dominated by flexible production. The involvement of the association in activities such as input supplies, outsourcing, subcontracting, retailing and establishment of retailing agencies simply reduces uncertainty, minimises the cost of information gathering and monitoring as well as preventing the breaching of contracts (Buğra 2002a:192–193). These micro-level strategies of the association are closely related to its macro-level strategy of moving the country's economic allegiances towards East Asia by weakening the ties with the West. MÜSİAD has openly declared its admiration for the East Asian economies for achieving high levels of development and becoming information societies while maintaining their own cultures and traditions. Therefore it is not surprising that during its short life the coalition government led by the Virtue Party attempted to promote close relations with some ASEAN (Association of Southeast Asian Nations) and Islamic countries. MÜSİAD's vision of Islamic economy in Turkey is characterised by minimum state intervention and regulation but is different 'from a pure market economy[16] in that it is clearly embedded in social relations mediated by religious morality' (Buğra 2002a:194). Medium and small-size enterprises which pay the Islamic wealth tax, rather than the existing taxes based on secular principles, and operate according to Islamic ethics constitute the backbone of the Islamic economy.

MÜSİAD's insistence that large-scale state economic enterprises should be sold to dynamic medium-sized enterprises is in congruence with the informalisation of the economy as a reflection of flexible production in the international economy.[17] As Buğra (2002a) indicates, MÜSİAD favours industrial relations based on informal personal relations not on organised labour unions. The disappearance of labour organisations is also a significant feature of the contemporary international economy dominated by 'flexible production'. Dominant forces in society have continuously portrayed labour unions as inimical to efficiency and international competitiveness.

CONCLUSION

The above discussion indicates that the analysis of the Islamic resurgence in Turkey cannot be complete unless the contribution of Islamic business and Islamic capital are taken into consideration. The Welfare Party inherited the political constituency of the Islamic National Salvation Party which received strong support from small and medium businesspeople in Anatolia in the 1970s. All the parties which have succeeded the NSP have used Islamic language to attract the support of small town businesspeople. The liberalisation of the economy since the beginning of the 1980s has provided new opportunities for businesspeople with Islamic inclinations. Financial capital obtained from Saudi Arabia and from Turkish workers in Germany has made huge contributions to the business activities of Islamic brotherhood networks (*tarikat*) (Öniş 1997). The Welfare Party has been the most significant party to have strong links with Islamic brotherhood organisations. In the relatively free market-oriented atmosphere of the 1980s, Islamic capital expanded by leaps and bounds and established some of the most powerful businesses in Turkey. Two good cases in point are the Kombassan and Yimpaş which together have more than 50,000 shareholders mostly consisting of migrant Turkish workers in Germany and some other European countries. The rise of Islamic-oriented businesses is also evidenced by the increasing number of members of the principal Islamic business association, the Independent Association of Industrialists and Businessmen (MÜSİAD).[18] Unlike TÜSİAD (the Turkish Businessmen's Association), the majority of MÜSİAD members are not situated in major metropolitan centres like Istanbul, Izmir, Bursa and Izmit but in towns like Konya, Denizli, Gaziantep, Kahramanmaraş, Çorum and Urfa, referred to as 'Anatolian Tigers' due to their recent success in becoming new centres of export.

Although not all small and medium-sized businesses in Anatolia supported the Islamic Welfare Party, there are significant similarities between the views of MÜSİAD and the Welfare Party. Thus it would be no exaggeration to claim that MÜSİAD has given considerable backing to the Welfare Party. Both have been admirers of the success of the East Asian model of development. They were both against Turkey's accession to the European Union throughout the 1990s. Therefore the rise of the Welfare Party has to be seen in close connection with the rise of the Islamic bourgeoisie, particularly in the Anatolian Tiger areas. Islamic-oriented MÜSİAD members took advantage of their political affiliations mainly with the Welfare Party but also with other centre-right parties to benefit from the rents distributed by the State. MÜSİAD has also provided networking opportunities to its members in their attempts to accumulate wealth, capital and elite status (Öniş 1997; Gülalp 2001; Buğra 1998, 1999, 2002a, 2002b).

With Turkey's further integration into the global market through rapid liberalisation since the late 1980s, two significant challenges have emerged to the cosy relationship between the Welfare Party and MÜSİAD: one political and one economic. The political challenge refers to the Welfare Party's ultimate aim to establish an Islamic society governed by 'Shariat' law. This is diametrically opposed to the pluralistic liberal democracy that the Welfare Party has been utilising to consolidate its position and gain political power through peaceful mechanisms. Shariat is an all-encompassing rule which governs all aspects of social life and does not respect individual liberty and human rights. Shariat's vision of economics does not square with the liberal economy based on the principles of the free market. There have been two powerful challenges to the Welfare Party's hidden agenda to establish an Islamic society and polity in Turkey: the long tradition of secularism within the state and the army, and the fruits of the liberal economy for the rising business elites within MÜSİAD (Öniş 1997; Gülalp 2001).

Let us take the second first. The fact that certain sections of the Islamic business community managed to accumulate large sums of capital through participation in the international economy brought about the realisation that for further expansion it was necessary to establish links with Europe and the US. The opportunities to be opened up by Turkey's leaning towards the West were too good to be missed. To resist Turkey's strong attempts to be integrated into the West was futile as the state and society on the whole saw that this was where Turkey's future lay. Therefore oppositional voices within both the Virtue Party (the successor of the Welfare Party after its closure by the constitutional court) and MÜSİAD became boisterous in the late 1990s, and this culminated in the reformist movement within the party. After failing to control the party from within, the reformists broke away in 2001 to establish the JDP. The first thing that the JDP did was to declare its strong commitment to the IMF-engineered economic programme in operation since 2000 and to continue the policy of completing the necessary conditions for joining the EU. In a television interview with TV8 on 20 November 2002, the leader of MÜSİAD argued vehemently how keen his organisation was to support the government's efforts to join the EU. The convergence of the views of the Islamist MÜSİAD and its secularist counterpart TÜSİAD as far as Turkey's economic orientation is concerned is quite instructive. In the 1970s and 1980s, while MÜSİAD advocated close co-operation with the Islamic world and the NICs of South-East Asia and keeping away from the US and Europe, TÜSİAD insisted on further strengthening of the ties with the West. Now, with the JDP in power, both organisations are saying the same thing with the one difference that MÜSİAD is now in a favourable position as far as relations with the government are concerned. In short, the point to be made is that in explaining both the emergence of the JDP and its orientation towards the West there is a strong need to take into consideration the external influences. This is only possible by scrutinising the ways in which Turkey's integration into the global economy has been speeded up.

The political challenge stems from the existence of powerful forces of secularism entrenched within the state. The army in particular sees itself as the guardian of Atatürk's secular legacy concretised in the Constitution. The robustness of the state's reaction to anti-secular forces is exemplified by the four times closure of Islamic parties and the Welfare Party's expulsion from the government. The moderates within the ranks of the Virtue Party were all aware of the near impossibility of operating within the existing political and constitutional structures. They were also aware of the virtues of a pluralistic democracy which allows a breathing space for identity politics. Most importantly, big business interests in Islamic circles now recognised the importance of liberal democracy for their own class interests. This necessitates advocacy of democracy as well as close co-operation with the West. This is not just the result of helplessness stemming from the fact that since 1980 Turkey's international economic and political relations have generated an irrevocable situation which calls for a pluralistic democracy, but also that capital in Turkey, be it of Islamic or secular origin, has a vested interest in liberal democracy and economic integration into the global order. The JDP seems to represent this new orientation of Islam, while the old ground is left to the Felicity Party who had a disastrous election in November 2002. At the time of writing the Felicity Party was busy licking its wounds and time will tell what the orientation of the party will be once it manages to re-organise itself. Whatever orientation it may choose, the Islamic Felicity Party (FP) will be aware of the fact that the majority of the Turkish population is against a militant Islam that seeks to establish the Shariat. It may also be clear to the FP that being religious and conservative is in no way tantamount to espousing a view of the state based on religious principles. It is exactly this factor that was behind the success of the JDP in the November 2002 elections. Given the strong and entrenched tradition of secularism in Turkey, militant Islam is bound to become limited to a small and parochial movement while moderate Islam may convert itself into a democratic conservative movement reminiscent of western Christian democratic parties. It seems that the JDP has chosen cultural Islam in preference to political Islam. What the JDP has done is to use religion and religiosity to organise a protest movement while respecting the principles of democracy and secularism. In a sense this is similar to the election strategies of some of the past centre-right parties such as Demirel's Justice Party in the 1960s and 1970s and Özal's Motherland Party in the 1980s. The JDP has taken advantage of the recent economic crises which have discredited all the parties that had been in power since the beginning of the 1990s. It has been able to represent itself as the voice of the poor and marginalised through the use of social democratic election propaganda while also appealing to people's religious sentiments without antagonising the established bastions of the constitutional order. While it has emerged as a protest movement, it has not elicited severe resistance by attempting to institute any radical change in the foreseeable future. By concentrating on poverty and employment issues the JDP has moved away from identity politics and this has enabled it to attract votes from secular circles as well. It has also attempted to please the business class by declaring its allegiance to the West and the IMF. Again time will tell how successfully the JDP will reconcile the interests of the business class with those of the poor and the marginalised. Being able to take advantage of a multiplicity of factors such as the fragmentation of the existing party system, rising poverty and unemployment, skewed income distribution and the loss of the credibility of recent governments is one thing, but being able to resolve the problems is another. If the critical view that the main culprit for the current socio-economic problems is the specific way that the country has been integrated into the global system is correct, then the JDP is doomed to fail in its attempt to resolve Turkey's problems.

6
The Kurdish question

In Chapter 5 it was argued that political Islam in Turkey is a form of identity politics. The rise of identity politics was explained in terms of the contradictory tendencies within the process of globalisation. Two counter-tendencies seem to be at work; while globalisation intensifies and attempts to homogenise different cultures, some people, ethnic groups and social categories tend to emphasise the local in order to highlight their unique and distinct characteristics. While successful in the sphere of economics, globalisation has failed to achieve global ethnic and cultural integration. The cases of the Soviet Union and Yugoslavia clearly exemplify this; national identities in these countries have resisted monolithic and centralised power by holding on to several different nationalisms. Although the process of cultural homogenisation unleashed by globalisation tends to work against these localised nationalisms, as Hall (1991) argues, we have been witnessing 'increasingly militant demands for ethnic exclusivity, minority language, education, religious separatism and exclusive territorial entities' (Cohen and Kennedy 2000:342).

The fact that, with the collapse of the Soviet Union and communism in eastern Europe, so many ethnic-based conflicts have emerged, along with the fact that since the 1960s in Europe, Canada and Africa secessionist movements have been dominating national politics, suggests that the questions of ethnicity and nationalism will continue to occupy a significant place on the world agenda.

The tenacity of ethnic and religious differences and the widespread conflicts along ethnic and religious lines present a paradox for the theorists of globalisation. Stuart Hall attempts to explain the emergence and re-emergence of local identities in terms of people's tendency to search for and attach to the familiar. People feel threatened by the rapidity of change brought about by globalisation and react to it by emphasising their attachment to their own communities, returning to the faces, voices, sounds, smells, tastes and places that are familiar to them.

The face-to-face communities that are knowable, that are locatable, one can give them a place. One knows what the voices are. One knows what the faces are. The re-action, the reconstruction of imaginary, knowable places in the face of the global postmodern flux of diversity. So one understands the moment when people reach for those groundings, as it were, and the reach for those groundings is what we call ethnicity. (Hall 1991:35–36).

The forces of globalisation are seen to be deconstructing the known world and generating confusion and bewilderment such that people react by reinforcing their own cultural and ethnic ties. They develop protective strategies in the form of primary identities based on religion or ethnicity (Castells 1996, 1997; Woodward 1997). Therefore, the emergence or re-emergence of ethnicity and localism should be interpreted, not as an irrelevant anachronism to the process of globalisation that leads to economic, social and political homogenisation, but as an inevitable reaction to it. If the globalising forces are operating in a context where there is already a history of ethnic conflict and resistance to a dominant ideology or exclusionary politics, then ethnic reaction to it may be particularly strong. This is the case with the Kurdish question in Turkey, where the roots of the ethnic question pre-date the rapid post-war technological, economic and social transformations. Turkey's further integration into the global economy since the Second World War and its attendant political liberalisation have contributed to the ripening of the conditions under which the people have begun to make demands for religious and cultural rights. While rapid economic changes have increasingly marginalised the masses and contributed to their feelings of helplessness, at the same time the dissemination of democratic values and respect for human rights have created an atmosphere of tolerance for multiculturalism and identity politics. In particular the political conditionalities of the IFIs and the EU's demands that Turkey should meet the Copenhagen Criteria before entering the Union have played major roles in creating suitable conditions for the people to make demands for a multicultural society.

However, the reasons behind the Kurdish question and the rise of ethnic politics cannot be reduced to the forces of globalisation. Explanations involving the effects of global forces should be supported by an understanding of the dynamics specific to Turkey. The rise of Turkish nationalism in particular should be brought into the equation, as Kurdish identity politics have emerged largely in reaction to it. Kurdish nationalism in Turkey represents a new form of identity politics which stands in strong contrast to Turkish identity politics, as the latter uses the concepts of nationhood and common citizenship at a rhetorical level, but follows exclusionary practices in reality. The situation being faced in Turkey is the existence of mutually exclusive national identities vying for control of all or part of the territory.

The fact that the Kurds live mainly in the most underdeveloped part of the country, namely in the south-east, helps the fervent supporters of Kurdish nationalism to attract support from the less politically aware elements within the Kurdish community and from international parties which may have intentions in the region other than Kurdish rights.[1] Kurdish nationalists use existing regional inequalities to prove their argument that the policies of the Turkish State have been exploitative, assimilationist and discriminatory and that an independent Kurdish state should therefore be established. On the other hand, the Turkish State, while accepting that regional inequalities may have been behind the recent ethnic conflict, categorically rejects any deliberate policy to keep the Kurdish region underdeveloped. In recent decades the state's official position has been to detach the Kurdish problem from its ethnic, cultural and international contexts and present it as a question of terrorism and misplaced development strategies. The dominant view in Turkish politics considers the ethnic problem as something that will disappear in the light of economic progress and nation state building. There is an implicit acceptance of Kurdish ethnicity in this, despite the explicit denial of the existence of a Kurdish problem. Implicitly it is assumed that sub-national identities and loyalties will give way to a coherent national identity once economic problems are resolved, as people will be transferring their loyalties from the ethnic community to the nation or social classes. This view is persistently emphasised by Bülent Ecevit, the many times Prime Minister of Turkey, who considers ethnic conflict to be a kind of myth generated by the failure of Turkish economic modernisation. Uneven regional development stemming from the state's negligence of eastern and south-eastern Anatolia is seen to be the breeding ground for dissatisfaction, social tension and conflict. The official position is premised upon the assumption that high economic growth does not necessarily translate into equitable wealth distribution within the country. Economic policies since the establishment of the Republic have generated both economic growth in Turkey as a whole, and increasing regional and socio-economic inequalities. As the most underdeveloped regions, namely eastern and south-eastern Anatolia, coincide with the areas with the greatest concentration of Kurdish population, socio-economic tensions take an ethnic form. When social development fails to take place in spite of overall economic development, and when regional differences in social and human development are severe, then ethnic conflict becomes a strong possibility where such regional divisions also coincide with different concentrations of ethnic populations.

To a certain degree the official explanation seems plausible, considering that in most ethnic conflicts inequalities between the conflicting groups do exist. In most countries where severe ethnic conflicts have taken place, such as Tigrai and Eritrea, there is a high correlation between the lack of social development and long-term violent ethnic conflicts. On this count Turkey is no exception. It is evident that the east and south-east are the least developed areas of Turkey and that it is therefore only natural that the inhabitants will demand better living conditions. Yet the demands of the Kurdish population in the least developed regions are not limited to economic betterment. This raises the question of whether the main determinants in ethnic conflict can be reduced to economic inequalities. In the conflict in Turkey, cultural, political and human rights are high on the agenda, which is indicative of the existence of other dimensions as important to underprivileged groups as the economic one. The fact that the release from prison of the four DEP (Democracy Party) parliamentarians in July 2004, in reaction to pressure from the EU and the US, prompted large-scale support in the form of rallies and demonstrations throughout the areas populated mostly by Kurds is a testimony to the fact that the problem is far from purely economic. Only after more than 30,000 deaths on both sides has the Turkish Government decided to give serious attention to the development of the underdeveloped regions. It seems that economic development alone may not resolve the tension in the region, and that the return to true democracy in the region should be high on the agenda. Economic development of the east and south-east regions is a necessary but probably insufficient for achieving peace in the region. The importance of freedom of expression, freedom to participate in political processes, including the freedom to form political parties, should not be underestimated. However, attempts to develop the region economically remain an essential part of the process as they will deliver the conditions under which lasting peace can be established. As they stand, the two regions are far behind the rest of Turkey in every socio-economic index conceivable.

It should be realised that the Kurdish question in Turkey is multi-dimensional and requires a multi-dimensional analysis which pays attention to cultural as well as economic factors. The Kurds are a divided nation mostly living in Turkey, Syria, Iraq, Iran and ex-Soviet states. In recent years thousands of Kurds have also found their way to western Europe as political and economic refugees. The treaty between the Ottoman Empire and Persia, following the Battle of Chaldiran in 1514, saw the first physical division of the Kurds as the borders were re-drawn. The great majority of the Kurds remained under the jurisdiction of the Ottomans until the First World War, at the end of which the biggest division of the Kurdish population took place with the Treaty of Sèvres which created the states of Syria and Iraq, thus leaving the Kurds under the jurisdiction of four different states.

The concessionary yet at the same time pacifying policies of the Ottoman State prevented the emergence of a unified Kurdish nationalism. The Ottoman State capitalised on the existence of many conflicting Kurdish tribal groups and alliances. By granting a semi-autonomous state to a selected number of prominent Kurdish tribal leaders and naming them as the local representatives of the state, the Ottomans established indirect control over the remote Kurdish regions. In the large territories granted to them under the title of mir-i miranlik (emirate), the tribal leaders, who are referred to as 'aghas' in the region, ruled the people liberally in return for their pledges of political loyalty on behalf of their respective clans or nomadic tribes. The divide and rule policies of the Ottoman State, which fanned the conflict and rivalries between *aghas* and within each tribal group, worked effectively as far as the subordiantion of the Kurdish tribal groups was concerned. While the Ottoman State set local *aghas*, clans and tribes against each other in order to maintain a balance of power, it also gained legitimacy among the dominant tribes by arbitrating in their disputes and distributing privileges to some (Van Bruinessen 1992:164–165).

The Kurds were only one of the tens of distinct national, ethnic and religious communities that existed within the Ottoman Empire under an institutionalised tolerance. All cultures and religions were tolerated and no force was used to achieve social conformity or religious conversion. The meritocratic nature of the state bureaucracy ensured that people from any social and religious background could achieve successful careers as long as they had the necessary talent. The Kurds belonged to a number of different Islamic sects and as such were not discriminated against in the Ottoman Empire. In short the Ottoman State's deliberate policy of actively encouraging conflict among Kurdish tribal groups prevented the formation of a Kurdish nationalist ideology and a unified Kurdish movement within the state. Kurdish nationalism and Kurdish separatism emerged after the establishment of the Turkish Republic in 1923 and gradually led to ethnically driven conflict.

The question of why the ethnically driven conflict in Turkey has emerged and reached the status of a civil war between the PKK (Kurdish Workers Party), the independence-seeking guerrilla group, and the Turkish State, needs to be answered. As the conflict is an ethnic one and ethnic as identity does not necessarily evolve into nationalism in all ethnically divided societies, it is crucial to evaluate the conditions under which ethnic identity becomes a national identity and propels a nationalist movement.

ETHNICITY AND IDENTITY

Despite the rapid process of globalisation, which tends to weaken the power of nation states, the world is still divided into states with recognised boundaries and peoples of the world are still under the jurisdiction of one state or another. Ideology plays an important role in ensuring the unity of the state. Once the unifying ideology of the state loses common acceptance among the populace living within that state's territories, the ethnic question emerges. It seems that a common language, religion and race are the main features that define an ethnic group. Preconditions for the existence of a nation are often cited as being a sense of solidarity, a common language, culture, religion, myth, descent, legal rights and duties, historic territory and national consciousness (Seaton-Watson 1977; Greenfield 1992; Smith 1991). Listing a number of traits and features, however, is one thing, but their acceptance by everybody concerned is quite another. There are no criteria to dictate which of these features people should perceive as being the defining feature of a nation. Instead, the self-perception of the people seems to be absolutely vital to how they define themselves as an ethnic group, distinct from others around them. In addition to self-awareness, acceptance by 'the other' is important in the development of a distinct group. In a given territory the self-definition and 'other' definition of an ethnic group can be crucial, as this will demarcate the unity of a nation as well as the nature of ethnic relations. As the boundaries between nation and ethnicity are blurred, the possibility of conflict between self-definition and 'other' definition is high. If such definitions also demarcate territorial boundaries and legal and economic rights, tensions and confrontations are likely to emerge. Unless there is an almost total juxtaposition of a nation and self-aware sense of ethnicity, there is a danger of conflict. 'Ethnies', as the distinguishing ethnic attributes of a group, are shaped by different historical processes, which may occur rapidly or may take a long time. Many internal and external factors contribute to the formation of ethnies and ethnic identities, thus some ethnic groups may owe their origins to ancient times and others may have been formed relatively recently. The emergence of nations or nation states from ethnies and ethnic identities is by no means an automatic process. The relative strengths of ethnies and ethnic identities as well as international processes are crucial factors in whether or not ethnies become nations and nation states. The failure of ethnies to become nation states does not necessarily bring about their disappearance; ethnies may continue to exist as strong entities and may even be referred to by external parties as nations. However, their acceptance by nations other than the one in which they exist may not be sufficient to force their home state to recognise them as such, as their imagined or real demands would pose the threat of secession.

Thus the nature of the ethnic question in a given territory is determined by state structures and policies, by the strength of particular ethnic identities and by the international processes at work. In other words, depending on the internal and external dynamics, ethnic identity may remain dormant or may be mobilised into attempts to convert the ethnic group into its own nation state. As we saw earlier, due to state policies Kurdish identity remained dormant during the Ottoman Empire as the Kurdish leadership did not encourage the people to campaign for the formation of an independent Kurdish State. The Ottoman State structure and policies were not discriminatory towards various ethnicities and thus were not conducive to generating ethnic consciousness as many ethnic groups were free to express themselves. There was no official ethnic policy to oppress various ethnicities as the unifying principle was religion. Under the wide umbrella of Islam many ethnic groups like

Laz, Gürcü, Pomak and Kurds maintained their distinctiveness, and as a result no ethnic group felt the need to defend its individual cultural attributes.

Ethnocentrism was never a serious problem during the Ottoman period as no ethnic group attempted to impose its cultural superiority on others. Therefore, there was not a situation in which 'the other' was rejected, despised, excluded, demonised, or dehumanised. There was no dominant cultural group to make a minority or subordinate cultural group feel undermined or threatened. The virtual non-existence of ethnocentrism prevented the development of a potential conflict situation.

In Turkey, regional inequalities and thus the asymmetrical economic, political and social relationships between ethnic groups within the country are blamed for the conflict in the Kurdish region. However, while there is no doubt that asymmetrical economic relations are crucial in the emergence of ethnic conflict they do not create sufficient conditions on their own. Both the structural context in which inter-ethnic relations emerge and the nature of the individual's internalisation of these relations must also be taken into consideration.

Ethnicity is not a concrete concept, but is invented and constructed as a result of political imperatives and ideological preferences. However, once an ethnic discourse is generated and legitimised it plays a powerful role in the dynamics of ethnic relations. As an intellectual construct, ethnicity feeds on historical cultural differences and on myths, conceptions and doctrines which have developed out of these differences. Although there are no clear-cut, commonly recognised criteria for delineating ethnic groups, it is possible to categorise some of the criteria which are used into two broad areas; objective and subjective. Objective criteria include externally observable elements which are independent of individual volition and tie the individual to a group at birth, for example, racial characteristics, the material culture, language, religion, territory and social organisation. Individual psychological, mental and emotional processes that determine behaviour and attitudes towards different groups constitute the subjective criteria. However, it must be emphasised that not all of the above criteria are significant in all circumstances.

The existence of differences in terms of language, religion, race and territorial concentration may not necessarily lead to the emergence of an ethnic conflict. In addition to the existence of these objective criteria the subjective feelings of the individuals play a significant part. Mobilisation to collective action will be determined to a large extent by how people feel (subjective criteria) about the significance of objective criteria. Different individuals will give different weight to various objective criteria in defining their own identity. People's feelings and beliefs about their identities are dynamic and tend to change over time. State policies and one's perception of others about one's worth can be effective in changing people's feelings about their identities. In an existing conflict situation, the nature of the conflict can change people's views about their own identity and their feelings towards the other by stirring up dormant feelings. New identity forms can even be constructed or activated during the course of conflict. It is not inevitable that the co-existence of multiple ethnicities will generate ethnic conflict. The way in which the nation states treat different ethnic groups within their territories is absolutely crucial in the emergence or non-emergence of ethnic conflict. If the political culture and practice and its ramifications in legislation, constitutional arrangements and electoral systems are not discriminatory then the possibility of ethnic conflict will be small.

The above discussion has continually emphasised the significance of the historically given social, economic and political factors in shaping ethnic identities and has stressed the fact that there is no automatic reason for ethnic conflict to emerge in places where ethnic groups co-exist. Instead, each ethnic conflict needs to be analysed as a historically specific case. In the light of what has been argued above, the following section will highlight the salient features of the Turkish-Kurdish problem by asking the question of how and why it emerged; what are the main factors behind the conflict which has cost more than 30,000 lives and billions of US dollars since 1984? In order to provide answers to these questions, the next section will adopt a historical approach to analysing the relationship between Turkish nationalism and Kurdish nationalism in Turkey.

THE EMERGENCE OF CONFLICTING TURKISH AND KURDISH ETHNIES

Turkish and Kurdish nationalism did not emerge as a result of internal dynamics, instead Turkish nationalism emerged in reaction to nationalist uprisings in the Balkans during the Ottoman period and Kurdish nationalism emerged in reaction to Turkish nationalism, taking root during the process of nation building masterminded by Kemal Atatürk, the founder of the Republic. Nationalism in Turkey emerged as a historical necessity fuelled by the rise of nationalism and nation states elsewhere in the Balkans in Europe. Under the Ottoman Empire, nationalist movements by non-Muslim minorities were actively encouraged and supported by western powers such as Britain and France, and in the late 1880s a multi-dimensional Ottoman nationalism was fostered to prevent the disintegration of the Empire. Despite the fact that outsiders referred to the Ottomans as Turks there was no collective Turkish identity, as the state encouraged its subjects to identify instead with the Community of Islam headed by the Caliph, who was also the Ottoman Sultan (Lewis 1962:2). The ideology of the Islamic Community and the notion of Ottomanness was only able to maintain the unity of the Empire until the beginning of the twentieth century, when the Ottoman 'millet system' lost its viability. By the turn of the nineteenth century most of the cultural groups in the Balkans had broken away from the Empire through the wave of nationalism. The First World War also saw the separation of Arabs from the Empire. It soon became clear that Islam alone could not keep the Empire together. As a last resort in the final years of the nineteenth century the influential Ottoman intelligentsia invoked Turkish nationalism to prevent the complete disintegration of the Empire. Nascent Turkish nationalism, introduced and fervently advocated by a group of people called the Young Turks, took some time to be established and accepted. The realisation that the idea of Ottomanism and Caliphate had penetrated deeply into popular consciousness led the leader of the war of independence (1918–23) and later founder of the modern Turkish Republic, Kemal Atatürk, to resort to using them extensively in order to mobilise different Muslim groups (Turks, Kurds, Laz, Circassians, among others) against the occupying Allied forces (Oran 1990; Tuncay 1981).

Turkish nationalism gradually matured after the establishment of the Republic in 1923 (Kutlay 1997:245). Following independence and the establishment of the new Turkish Republic, the leadership saw the unification of the nation around a civic notion of nationalism as imperative. Yet in the process of nation building since 1923, the Turkish state has oscillated between civic and ethnic nationalism; while the military and the intelligentsia on the one hand attempted to foster an ethnic Turkish nationalism for recognition by outsiders, attempts were made to avoid negative reactions from non-Turkish Muslim groups through the introduction of a civic nationalism based on citizenship. On many occasions the Kemalist regime diverged from the civic notion of nationalism, which accorded importance to the idea of living together within the same borders, under the same laws with a shared language and moral code. The first task Kemalism set for itself in the period between 1923 and 1940 was to reduce the significance of religion as a unifying principle by adopting secularism in its place. However, this was in no way a smooth process as the people would not voluntarily accept the abolition of centuries old Caliphate and religious institutions. The use of anti-democratic and oppressive methods undermined the seemingly civic nature of the nationalist ideology being introduced as a unifying principle in place of Islam. The discrepancy between the rhetoric of the new Turkish state based on a 'civic notion of nationalism' and the reality of the 'notion of ethnic nationalism' which was the main pillar of Kemalist ideology has carried through into the twenty-first century. The struggle between the Islamists and the army and secularists who see themselves as the vanguard of the Kemalist Republic and the fight between the PKK and the state since the 1980s lend support to the existence of the discrepancy between the civic and ethnic nationalism.

Basing her argument on the works of Smith (1991, 1995), Anderson (1991) and Kymlicka (1995) on nationalism and ethnicity, Cizre-Sakallıoğlu emphasises the fact that Turkish nationalism has been based on 'two contradictory elements: an ethno-cultural dimension highlighting the ethnic singularity of Turkishness and a modern civil component which essentially grants equal citizenship rights to all those living in Turkish territory regardless of ethnic origin' (1996:6). The two contradictory elements enshrined in the definition of Turkish nationalism give the state the flexibility to call upon either one of them according to the exigencies of the time and political situation. As in contemporary Turkey, the definition of Turkishness based on the concept of the citizenship of the Turkish Republic does not give much room for self-definition of any ethnicity other than the Turkish. Kymlicka describes the attitude of the Turkish State *vis-à-vis* the Kurds as assimilationist by stating that 'the problem is not that Turkey refuses to accept Kurds as Turkish citizens. The problem is precisely its attempt to force Kurds to see themselves as Turks' (1995:132). The state ideology emphasises the supremacy of Turkish language, culture, education and history to the exclusion of others. The attempt to combine civic and ethnic concepts of the nation in the single term 'Turkish citizenship' has not been persuasive as far as the Kurdish nationalists are concerned. The ideology of the Turkish State does not recognise the existence of other significant self-imagined culturally distinct communities. In order to highlight the irrelevance of ethnic differences and ethnic rights, official parlance has referred to the Kurds simply as 'mountain Turks'. It has been repeatedly stated that Turkish citizenship grants full rights to everyone; all Turkish citizens have equal rights to enjoy the same privileges and thus there is no need for the existence of a minority status. There is therefore no question of the assimilation of a Kurdish minority as the existence of minority groups is simply denied by the Turkish ideology.

Using the deliberations of the Lausanne Treaty (1923) official discourse considers non-Muslims to be Turkey's only minority, all other groups are seen to constitute the Turkish nation through common religion and citizenship. While it can be affirmed that Kurds are not a minority group in Turkey, it must also be recognised that they are the second largest group and have made a vital contribution to the establishment of the current state and society. Unfortunately, the Kemalists' insistence that Kurds in Turkey are treated equally and that anyone who claims otherwise is a traitor has not been helpful in the resolution of the problem. Since 1930 the centralised state has used its immense power to institutionalise the notion of a single language, a single culture and a single ideology. Kurds' hopes of being treated equally in the new Republic were very quickly dashed as the new regime continued to seek to unify the nation under Turkishness. The 1924 Constitution defined citizen and citizenship in terms of Turkishness, thus laying the foundations of the Turkish 'ethnie'. For Kurds to be treated as equals they had to deny their Kurdishness and declare themselves Turks. Expressions of Kurdishness, even in mundane everyday life, were punished (Kızılkaya and Nabiler 1991:36). Various Kurdish uprisings were crushed between 1925 and 1938, generating a fear of the Turkish State amongst the Kurds and eliminating the leaders of rebellions.

Considering the dissolution of the mighty Ottoman Empire and the division of its land into many ethnically based nation states, one can understand the new Republic's fear that the country may become further divided if multiculturalism is allowed to flourish. Therefore, the new state has abandoned Islam as a unifying principle and replaced it with a contradictory Turkish nationalism.

In order to build a nation around this ideology the state has not hesitated to have recourse to the assimilationist and iron fist policies against those who have refused to be assimilated (Güzel 1995:12). The army in particular has adopted a very determined and rigid stance on the Turkishness of the new state, although lip service has been paid to the motto that all citizens are equal.

TREATIES OF SEVRES AND LAUSANNE

The Ottoman Peace Treaties of Sèvres (1920) and Lausanne (1923) are largely responsible for the contradictory way in which the Kurds have been treated in Turkey. In the Treaty of Sèvres the victorious powers of the First World War forced the defeated Ottoman State first to grant local autonomy to Kurds and second to promise the possibility of independence in the future. However, in the Treaty of Lausanne, the West had to negotiate with the independence war heroes of the new Republic who categorically refused to accept the provisions of the Sèvres Treaty. During the negotiations the Turkish delegation insisted that the Kurds were not a minority group. The fact that in the 1920s religion was the main criterion in the characterisation of minority groups helped the Turkish delegation to defend their case. Another useful factor was that the Kurdish members of the Turkish delegation confirmed that they were in agreement with the Turks in that the new Republic was to provide universal equal rights. This convinced others at Lausanne that the Kurds did not need to be considered as a minority group along with the Christians, Armenians and Assyrians. However, since the Treaty was drawn up the Turkish State has failed to keep its promises and has pushed forward Turkish nationalism, and promoted a single Turkish language and culture. National boundaries redrawn in the 1920s divided the Kurds into five different states; Iran, Iraq, Syria, Turkey and the Soviet Union. Since then, many Kurdish uprisings in the nation states in which they live indicate that a common religion is not sufficient to prevent the desire for cultural and national rights.

THE EMERGENCE OF KURDISH NATIONALISM IN TURKEY

Just as the rise of Turkish nationalism was an oppositional reaction to the rise of nationalism in the Balkans, Kurdish nationalism in Turkey is an antithetical reaction to Turkish nationalism. Authors like Chailand (1994), Oran (1990), Kutlay (1997) and Van Bruinessen

(1992) argue that the emergence of Kurdish identity and nationalism has been a long process. Chailand and Van Bruinessen, in particular, highlight the fact that there was no unified Kurdish identity to speak of in the nineteenth century. This is explained in terms of the socio-economic realities of Kurdish tribes in the region. Kurdish society consisted of territorially segmented tribes which were divided into clans and extended families. The tribal kinship system allowed their feudal leaders (*aghas*) to control the resources and distribute welfare and justice to their tribal members. The land on which the Kurdish tribes lived belonged to the Ottoman State and thus the tribal leaders had to please the Palace in order to obtain the privilege of controlling resources on behalf of the Sultan. As a result there was immense competition and conflict between *aghas* for political influence and economic superiority and this continued well into the twentieth century (Chailand 1994).

The Palace capitalised on the fragmented nature of the Kurdish elite and the protracted conflict between various *aghas* as there were fears of Kurdish unification against the state in remote territories. Divide and rule policies worked well with the interests of some Kurdish tribal leaders who declared allegiance to the state. This prevented the development of national consciousness and unity among the Kurdish people prior to the establishment of the Turkish Republic in 1923 (Oran 1990). This was exacerbated by the fact that Kurds belonged to different religious sects and that the areas in which they lived were also populated by Armenians and other indigenous peoples which did not help the creation of a Kurdish identity. The first significant signs of Kurdish nationalism in Turkey appear to have emerged at the beginning of the twentieth century.[2]

The Kurds fought alongside the Turks during the Turkish War of Independence (1918–22) against the 'infidels' who had invaded Muslim land. Until then a shared religion had been sufficient reason for the Kurds to identify with a common cause, thus they were not too occupied with the concept of their own Kurdish identity. Being different seemed to them to be normal, as the Empire consisted of a large number of different cultures and ethnic groups. Given the basic level of technology and communications in the region, nationalistic ideas did not travel fast. When they did begin to improve at the turn of the century, the way in which the Islamic State manipulated religion and religious sects did not allow the Kurds to develop a sense of identity. The state made sure that different tribal leaders had differing kinds of relationships with state power and with each other. The state often set the local *aghas* against each other or used their tribal groups in the persecution of the Armenians. After the establishment of the Republic in 1923, most *aghas* felt the need to remain close to the state in order to keep the properties they had confiscated from the departing Armenians and to be granted the private ownership of the tribal lands they had controlled throughout Ottoman times. The first serious signs of disenchantment with the new Kemalist State started to emerge in the early years of the Republic as many Kurdish tribal leaders felt betrayed by the fact that the new state took a very firm stand against expression of any identity other than Turkish. They expected to be granted Kurdish autonomy in the East, as envisaged by the Sèvres Treaty. Some Kurdish leaders were led to believe by the Lausanne Treaty that their allegiance to the Kemalist State and their indispensable contribution to the War of Independence would be rewarded by the Kemalist regime through the recognition of Kurdish identity and autonomy in the East (Kutlay 1997:151). Many commentators, including Barkey and Fuller (1995) state that during the years of the War of Independence (1920–23) Atatürk deliberately misled the Kurds by giving the impression that once the war was won he would be willing to negotiate with them on the matter of Kurdish nationhood. The adoption of Turkish nationalism as a unifying ideology prevented the new regime from giving other ethnic and religious groups the equal rights they used to enjoy under the Ottoman State. Kemalism was determined 'to assimilate the Kurds into a Turkish nation through the use of education and military force' (Barkey and Fuller 1995:63). However, ordinary Kurdish people were not concerned about the ideology of the new state, they were struggling to make ends meet in the harsh conditions after the First World War. On the other hand, a few of the Kurdish intelligentsia, some tribal leaders and some charismatic religious leaders had reason to show strong opposition to this exclusive Turkish nationalism. It was beyond the great majority of the mostly illiterate ordinary Kurds to understand the new notion of nationalism that opposed the all-embracing notion of the millet system, nor was it a priority for them to fight for the such complex and abstract concepts as Islam, Turkishness and Kurdishness.

Some charismatic leaders like Sheikh Said used religion and their religious charisma to mobilise the Kurds around the notion of Kurdishness. Their limited success in organising rebellious movements was due to the propaganda claiming that the secularist principles of the Kemalist State were tantamount to infidelity and blasphemy. However, while various rebellions in the 1920s and 1930s represented the emergence of Kurdish nationalism, they also attracted the wrath of the Turkish State which showed no tolerance of the existence of any identity other than Turkish. A vicious circle involving an increasing consciousness of Kurdish identity and ethnicity and the state's iron-fist policies has continued into the twenty-first century.[3]

The development of Kurdish nationalism in Turkey has been a slow process. The rebellions in the 1920s and 1930s did not have a systematic and well-worked out ideology, as demands for religious rule were mixed with nationalistic aspirations (Mumcu 1996; Rambout 1947:27; Van Bruinessen 1992:370). The Kemalist State's rejection of Islam as the main principle and its replacement with Turkish nationalism played into the hands of the Kurdish rebel leadership. The state's systematic assimilation policies exerted the superiority of nationalism over other ideologies and gradually provoked and nourished social movements emphasising other identities. Clashing Turkish and Kurdish identities found expression in Kurdish political movements such as Sheikh Said (1925), Ağri or Khoybun (independence) (1930) and the Dersim (1937) uprisings. These rebellions did find some supporters who sought to express their own Kurdish identity, however unsystematic they may have been (Van Bruinessen 1992; Kendal 1980).

There is a dialectical relationship between Kurdish nationalism in Turkey and the efforts of political modernisation to generate a nation state where primary importance is given to Turkish nationalism. The speed and intensity of the Kemalist modernity project has generated an antithesis in the form of a Kurdish narrative or discourse emphasising the distinctiveness of a Kurdish ethnicity. The 'mass politics' of Turkish modernisation which is enshrined in the struggle for resources, power and wealth has been influential in generating a Kurdish identity in Turkey. The grand development project aiming to industrialise the country, to develop modern communication and transportation facilities and to educate the people was instrumental in the growth of a sense of Kurdishness, even in the least developed areas. The socio-economic and political transformations in Turkey since the 1920s have paved the way for the emergence of 'Kurdish identity' as a modern phenomenon, as opposed to tribal and sectarian identities. The gradual development of Kurdish consciousness and the construction of the Kurdish 'imagined community' have been aided by advancements in modern communication facilities, such as the media, radio and television (Gellner 1992:279). The demands for Kurdish ethnic rights have run parallel with the modernisation of Turkish society as the educated Kurdish youth began to question the assimilationist policies of the state. In particular, the relatively free atmosphere created by the introduction of the multi-party system created breathing space for the educated Kurds to organise themselves and their demands for ethnic rights. However, the army has not been as tolerant as the political parties towards demands for democratic conditions in which Kurdish ethnic rights would be met and the Kurdish identity would be recognised. The military coups which occurred at regular ten-year intervals cracked down on Kurdish nationalists and the people and organisations which were considered to be their helpers. In this vein the leadership of the Democrat Party, which had relaxed its assimilationist policies in the Kurdish region after the 1954 elections, was punished by the military government which came to power following the 1960 coup. In order to prevent the rise of Kurdish consciousness, 55 Kurdish notables who were believed to be the driving force behind Kurdish identity consciousness were deported to western Turkey and all Kurdish village names were changed to Turkish ones (Beşikçi 1969; Entessar 1992; Van Bruinessen 1993). The ethnically based Kurdish movement became stronger and stronger in proportion to the intolerance shown to even simple demands for the development of Kurdish culture, for example to speak and publish in the Kurdish language. The military regimes in the 1960s, 1970s and 1980s did not hesitate to persecute anybody who showed even slight sympathy with these Kurdish aspirations, dubbing them enemies of the state. The traditional heavy-handed state policies against Kurdish self-expression led to the emergence of the PKK, whose members resorted to violence which in turn led to counter-violence on the part of the state (Barkey and Fuller 1998:17; White 2000:135). The indivisibility of Turkey and the unitary nature of the state has been the highest priority of the army which considers itself protector of the Republic and regards any threat to the national integrity as an act of treason. It was perceived that the demands for cultural rights, including education in one's mother tongue and broadcasting in ethnic languages were likely to gradually lead to demands for secession. Thus in 1983 the use of the Kurdish language in publications and the dissemination of ideas was banned with the introduction of Law number 2932.

The period between 1960 and 2000 witnessed both increasing state intolerance for demands for ethnic rights and the rise of identity consciousness amongst the Kurds in reaction to heavy-handed state policies. The state of emergency in the south-east, which was declared in the early 1980s and only lifted in 2002, contributed to the rise of Kurdish ethnic consciousness. The treatment of the south-east region's population as potential terrorists, the curtailment of their basic human rights and the state's counter-violence are all contributory factors in the people's heightened desire for the recognition of a Kurdish identity. One of the most significant outcomes of the military solution sought by the army has been to facilitate a transition for a large number of people from just being a member of an ethnic group due to common roots, myths, culture and territory, to what Smith (1986) calls an 'imagined community' characterised by an unifying common consciousness.

KURDISH NATIONALIST DISCOURSE IN TURKEY

The European Union and some commentators like White (2000) lay the blame for the Kurdish crisis in Turkey largely on the Turkish State's nationalistic policies. Without delving into the unanswerable question of whether Kurdish nationalism would have emerged if the Turkish State had not been following its nationalist policies, it is necessary to recognise that militarism is not a solution and that Kurdish identity is here for good. The European Union-engineered palliative reforms introduced in 2004 (in the form of lifting the ban on education in ethnic languages, and broadcasting in Kurdish) are certainly steps in the right direction. However, the PKK's decision to cancel its unilaterally declared ceasefire in 1999 and its attacks on military targets in June 2004 may endanger any possibility of resolving the problem. Solutions other than violence and counter-violence will have to be found if Turkey is to resolve the problem which has cost more than 30,000 lives and billions of US dollars. What then is a realistic solution to the Kurdish question and can Kurdish nationalist discourse provide any guidance? Has Kurdish nationalism in Turkey been consistent in its demands and coherent in its ideology?

The answer to this last question is a simple no, as the PKK's demands have oscillated between the establishment of an independent Marxist-Leninist state and claims for cultural rights such as broadcasting in Kurdish and educating in the mother tongue. The incoherence of the Kurdish nationalist discourse in Turkey can be explained by the prerogatives of 'realpolitik', as it has been reflective of changing political circumstances. The realisation that it was impossible to gain the open support of the US and the West, which considered Turkey an indispensable ally, and the fact that in the aftermath of September 11 the West included the PKK in their list of terrorist organisations, led the PKK to rename itself KONGRA-GEL. Furthermore, the heavy defeat of the PKK by the Turkish army and the capture of its leader Abdullah Öcalan intensified the belief among the PKK and subsequently the KONGRA-GEL leadership that it was more logical for them to strive for ethnic and cultural rights than for full independence. This was a major shift from the PKK's initial ideology which sought self-determination and demanded an independent Kurdish state based on the principles of Marxism and Leninism. There seems to be a parallel between what the PKK (KONGRA-GEL) has been saying since the late 1990s and the claims of Hatip Dicle, a member of the defunct DEP (Democracy Party), who was released from the Ulucanlar Prison on 9 June 2004 after eleven years of imprisonment along with three other DEP parliamentarians, Leyla Zana, Orhan Doğan and Selim Sadak, all of whom had been asking for ethnic and cultural rights for Kurds within the Turkish Republic.[4]

Some elements within Kurdish nationalist circles are now talking about 'constitutional citizenship' based on the concept of 'primary founders' of the Republic. In this conception, the Kurds consider themselves equal to the Turks insofar as the ownership of the state is concerned. As one of the two co-founders of the state, they position themselves in opposition to the 'other', whoever that might be. Belonging to the same motherland is the overarching identity under which Kurdish and Turkish sub-identities will flourish equally. The concept of 'constitutional citizenship' as a new pillar is invoked to overcome the difficulties posed by the concept of 'Turkish citizenship'. Kemalist and Kurdish nationalist ideologies are to control the state at the expense of the 'other'. Here the intention is to share power without antagonising Turkish nationalism by eliminating the superiority of Turkish nationalists and establishing equality with it at the expense of other ethnic groups. Time will tell if the Turks will concede power and strive for a pluralistic society and democracy based on shared authority. However, the concept of constitutional citizenship represents a fundamental shift from the *raison d'être* of the PKK and reflects the tenets of 'realpolitik'.

UNCOMPROMISING NATIONALISM

'Realpolitik' has also coloured the policies of the Turkish State since the Justice and Development Party (JDP) came to power in 2002. In order to improve Turkey's chances of joining the EU the JDP has issued a series of bold reforms. The reforms include the abolition of the death sentence, the complete removal of the state of emergency in Diyarbakir and Tunceli in 2002, and broadcasting in Kurdish for a few hours once a week on state television (TRT) since 9 June 2004. However, Kurdish nationalists see these as necessary but insufficient steps towards the resolution of the conflict (*Özgür Politika*, 11 June 2004). They insist that a general amnesty is required to establish the long awaited peace and persuade the PKK guerrillas to lay down their arms. They maintain that the Turkish army has been following an extermination policy towards the Kurdish fighters despite the unilateral ceasefire declared by the PKK in 1999 (*Özgür Politika*, 11 June 2004).

It is not surprising that the Turkish State has not been interested in any political deal with the PKK, as it sees it as a terrorist organisation and denies the very existence of a Kurdish question. According to the state, if there is a problem in the east and southeast, it is a problem of underdevelopment and economic backwardness, not an ethnic problem, thus those who talk about a Kurdish question are not to be tolerated. Official intolerance is enshrined in the 1980 Constitution which forbids any opinion which endangers Turkish national interests and prohibits the publication of any text in a language forbidden by law (articles 26 and 28). Until the recent surge of reforms since 2000 no language other than the officially recognised ones could be used in the expression and dissemination of thought (Special Law Decrees 1926, 1967 and 1983). The 1980 Constitution also made it illegal for any political party to recognise the existence of minorities or ethnic groups in Turkey, let alone to form a political party based on religious, racial, linguistic, cultural or national criteria other than those of Turkish nationalism.

Given the international pressure on Turkey to recognise the existence of Kurds and their cultural and political rights, and given that any political movement that promotes human rights and ethnic and political rights finds a large number of supporters in areas where Kurds are concentrated, it has become evident that the Kurdish question will not go away or be suppressed by militaristic approaches. The Kurdish movement has become a political movement since the establishment of the Republic in 1923. Following the speeches made by Leyla Zana, Hatip Dicle, Orhan Doğan and Selim Sadak in rallies in south-eastern provinces, the Kurdish nationalists regret some of the past events which have cost many lives on both sides, but they remain determined in their pursuit of their political demands, which receive both internal and external support. The fact that, despite the state's harsh militaristic policies, nationalistic aspirations have re-surfaced periodically indicates that unless the ethnic and cultural nature of the problem is addressed the state will come under increasing pressure, both internal and external, to resolve the Kurdish question.

In the twenty-first century the Kurdish problem has become an international problem as more than half a million Kurds now live in western Europe, particularly in Germany, and conflicts between the Turkish and Kurdish residents of European states affect the law and order there. Turkey's eagerness to secure a date for accession negotiations with the EU has increased the urgency of fulfilling both the political and economic conditions of the Copenhagen Criteria, which emphasise human rights issues, including cultural rights. What kind of political and ethnic rights will satisfy the KONGRA-GEL is a question for debate. However, simple measures to prevent the security forces from violating basic human rights in the Kurdish region might stop persistent reports by international agencies like the Helsinki Watch and Amnesty International about widespread human rights violations in the region (Amnesty International 1991, 1994, 1995; Helsinki Watch Report 1988; Human Rights Watch 2000).

Internally pressure from the Turkish Businessmen Association (TÜSİAD) and the Turkish Union of Chambers of Commerce and Industry (TOBB) since the early 1990s to find a political solution to the Kurdish question has put a very difficult choice in front of the army, which has taken a hawkish position on the issue (TOBB 1995; TÜSİAD 1997). The liberal attitude of business people stems from their very pragmatic concerns that the military campaign has been a significant drain on the nation's budget, fanning the already high rate of inflation, and that Turkey's accession into the EU hinges upon meeting the Copenhagen Criteria. The long-term international and internal pressures seem to have had some impact on the army, which has acquiesced on the matter of the recent reforms allowing broadcasting and teaching of the Kurdish language. This is a huge step as far as the army is concerned as it would not previously allow anybody to talk about a western-style, multi-ethnic and multi-cultural democracy for fear of encouraging separatism.

CONCLUSION: THE EUROPEAN UNION AND THE KURDISH QUESTION

The pressure on Turkey over the Kurdish question and human rights issues from the EU and the US has largely been determined by 'realpolitik'. They have not been forceful enough in their insistence as they have tacitly agreed with the Turkish official view that the Kurdish problem is one of underdevelopment and terrorism. Yet at the same time they have pursued the political conditionalities of the Helsinki Criteria for Turkey's accession to the EU, which has unnecessarily prolonged the process of negotiations between the two parties about setting a date to begin the accession negotiations (Brown 1995:128).

It seems that the JDP Government has the political will to explore other possibilities that might not be based on unity and uniformity around the notion of Turkishness. The notion of cultural pluralism gradually being introduced since 2000 and the granting of some cultural rights to the Kurds also serve the interests of the Islamists who want to guarantee the conditions for their own survival by joining the EU and by weakening the power of the army within the Turkish State. The reforms introduced by the JDP are a continuation of the process set in motion by Ecevit's Government in August 2000, passing a 14-article legislation package designed to harmonise Turkey's laws with those of the EU. The democratisation reforms concerning human rights were introduced mainly in reaction to internal pressures. The perception that entry to the EU will resolve the long-lasting cycle of economic crises in Turkey has intensified the demands of the business class and the majority of the population. In order not to endanger the possibility of Turkey's integration into the EU the Government introduced a democratisation package, which included the abolishment of the death penalty in peacetime, and the acceptance of broadcasting and education in languages other than Turkish. Furthermore, the state of emergency was lifted in the eastern and south-eastern provinces, except for Diyarbakır and Şirnak, and DEHAP, an ethnically based political party, particularly powerful in the Kurdish region, was allowed to participate in the November 2002 elections. These reforms have been universally welcomed as necessary but insufficient steps towards peace and stability in the country. The fact that the Turkish State has never carried out any atrocities or ethnic cleansing policies, and that there have been so many intermarriages between Turks and Kurds are strong indicators that it is not too late to develop fraternal ties to put an end to all the suffering on both sides and to concentrate efforts on development issues in order to eliminate poverty and socio-economic and political exclusion.

7
Conclusion

Since the introduction of the multi-party system in 1946 both the economy and democracy in Turkey have been through considerable ups and downs. Although the country has experienced a relatively moderate overall economic growth in the last 50 years, the economy has become quite fragile and has suffered from cyclical crises. It is interesting to note that the deficiencies of the economic system have been accompanied by crises in democracy. The fact that economic growth has not been matched by an equitable income distribution[1] has had serious consequences for democratisation. Compared with western democracies the Turkish democracy is still in its infancy and the process of eliminating neo-patrimonialist political culture and clientelism have been slow and painful. In some periods procedural democracy has actually intensified its entrenchment in that democratically elected governments have used their positions to provide economic privileges to their supporters. Given the limited state resources it has not been possible to sustain populist policies without severe balance of payment problems accompanied by high inflation. The austerity measures that have been implemented periodically in close co-operation with the IMF and the World Bank have in turn generated severe social tension which could only be controlled by oppressive policies either under military rule or civilian rule supported by the military. Consequently there is a strong connection between Turkey's economic crises and the crises of democracy which arose as the military took power in 1960, 1971 in 1980 and threatened to return to power in February 1997.

While military rule has been effective in ensuring macro-economic stability, it has, at the same time, provoked increased demands for better income distribution and thus forced democratically elected governments to resort to populist policies. In other words, a vicious cycle of economic growth, inequalities, populist policies, economic crises, political oppression and democracy has characterised Turkish economy and politics in the post-war period. However, the 1980s represent a turning point in the 'populist cycles', periodic fiscal crises of the state and periodic political crises (cf. Öniş 2003:1–5). While the demands of subordinate social classes have had some effect on government policies, the determining influence on major policy changes has come from the international economy. The demands of the world economy on less economically developed countries have been shaped by the changes in the nature of capitalism and in the methods it uses to overcome its crises. In Chapter 1 it was explained that in the post-war period 'developmentalism' and technological rents were used as the main mechanisms to meet the accumulation needs of the centre. The expansion of capitalism into peripheral areas between 1950 and 1970 was ensured through international capital flows and the expansion of direct investment by TNCs. Developmentalism in less economically developed countries like Turkey ensured the penetration of national economies by the TNCs through ISI policies. Populist policies were vital for the entrenchment of TNCs in Turkey through joint ventures involving state and private capital. Populist policies, which can be described as the use of state resources to provide support for certain social groups or classes in order to ensure support for the elite which controls the state, were essential for the expansion of the internal market, a *sine qua non* of the ISI, through high wages and farm gate prices.

The expansionary phase of global capitalism came to an end in the 1970s, and it was replaced by the 'incorporatist phase of capitalism' which did not necessitate developmentalism in less economically developed countries. From the 1980s onwards, capitalism attempted to resolve its crises not through further relocation of industry to the periphery, the main characteristic of the post-Fordist New International Division of Labour, but through the movement of speculative capital. The developmentalist state, while very useful in the Fordist and post-Fordist expansionary stages of capitalism, has been seen as an obstacle in the phase of incorporatist capitalism which has characterised the world economy since 1980. Therefore, since the 1980s both the core capitalist countries and the IFIs have been advocating the rolling back of the state. They insist that states should only provide the necessary conditions for the operations of the free market. The IFIs play a vital role in persuading less economically developed countries, through economic and political conditionalities, to liberalise their economies in order to ensure global financial openness. Since 1980 the tolerance shown or active encouragement given to state intervention in the economies of less economically developed countries during the expansionary phase of capitalism has been replaced by a strict adherence to liberalisation, democratisation and good governance. For Turkey and other less economically developed countries, submission to economic and political conditionalities has meant the restructuring of the economy, politics and society. Populist distributional policies are not only no longer tolerated, but are also blamed for some economic and political ills. As a result of their gradual phasing out since 1980, income distribution in Turkey has worsened very rapidly. However, the heightening social tension in the country due to decreasing standards of living and the increasing income gap has not led to a direct military take-over since the middle of the 1980s. The resentment over liberalisation polices which found strong expression in the rise of political Islam in the mid 1990s was only pacified with a military ultimatum in February 1997 and no serious breakdown was created in the democratic order. The governing elite was extremely careful not to endanger the country's relations with the IFIs and the EU which have been adamant about political conditionalities that include the further expansion of civil and human rights. Strict adherence to both economic liberalisation and procedural democracy has created severe economic and political crises in Turkey: while the complete liberalisation of the capital account in August 1989 increased the country's fragility and led to successive financial crises in 1994, 2000 and 2001, being unable to use authoritarian solutions led to the crises of governance. The existing party and electoral system led to a mushrooming of political parties and weak and unstable governments incapable of resolving the economic, political and social crises. Yet the IFIs and neo-liberals have been vehemently arguing in chorus that liberalism and liberal democracy is the only solution to the development impasse in Turkey. The debates on the relationship between democracy and development are not new. What is significant about the recent attempts to link democracy and development is their insistence to operate with a limited definition of democracy, i.e. the procedural democracy, and to insist on institutional reorganisation to ensure good governance.

The concept of good governance has been popularised to persuade less economically developed countries to restructure their economies and politics in such a way as to speed up their integration into the global economy. The good governance parlance, with its emphasis on democratisation and respect for human rights, at best aims to introduce elements of democracy without striving to consolidate it. As argued in Chapter 3, the procedural or minimalist approach to democracy tends to enhance structural inequalities and thus serves to entrench the status quo. The austerity measures and economic and financial liberalisation that accompany the minimalist approach to democracy fail to improve living standards for the majority or to reduce social tension in countries like Turkey. Political intervention by the IFIs in the process of democratisation in Turkey has served to strengthen the position of dominant classes and international capital at the expense of the wage earners, the salaried and the farmers. The minimalist approach to democracy and good governance parlance are based on a false assumption that democratisation and good governance will necessarily lead to economic growth. Yet evidence shows that there is no direct relationship between democracy and economic development; the highly complicated relationship cannot simply be inferred from observing the correlation of the occurrences of the two. What determines the course of development is not the type of regime but the nature of the state. The precondition for the co-occurrence of democracy and development in less economically developed countries is that the state itself has to be both democratic and developmental. Good governance parlance puts a high premium on institutional changes in less economically developed countries without taking into consideration the nature of the state and entrenched crony-ism and corruption. Without challenging the root causes of inequalities taking into consideration the nature of politics in less economically developed countries, the neo-liberalist good governance parlance cannot achieve democracy and development in these countries. What is needed is a democratic strategy which is fundamentally different to the SAPs imposed on less economically developed countries like Turkey. Democratisation of economic affairs tops the list of priorities of the democratic strategy which aims to increase economic growth while improving standards of living for the majority of people, ensuring an equitable income distribution and promoting broad participation in decision-making. This would necessitate a strong state that would regulate private capital and the economy as a whole in order to serve the needs of the majority. By leaving everything to the market, neo-liberal policies simply prevent the implementation of democratic development programmes by the state.

Neo-liberal policies in Turkey and other less economically developed countries have served the interests of the powerful elite and international capital. The implementation of economic and political conditionalities, which include the good governance rhetoric, have refashioned the Turkish State by slowly destroying its developmentalist features since the 1980s. While economic liberalisation policies have undermined the power and autonomy of the state and made nationalist policies and national capital accumulation redundant, they have not been receptive to local needs and priorities. Furthermore, the promotion of abstract democratic rights and procedural democracy has not provided a platform for the people to influence economic decisions so as to ensure economic growth, equity and social welfare.

The formation and maturation of the Turkish developmental state took about three decades (1930–60) during which time a nationalistic development strategy that aimed to create a Turkish bourgeoisie was followed. Contrary to the neo-liberal contention, represented by Akat (1994), Heper (1985, 1996) and Rodrik (1991a), that the cyclical crises in Turkey since the 1950s and particularly since 1980 are due to the ever present dirigiste state, I would argue that it is the gradual watering down and final abandonment of developmentalism and its replacement with a neo-liberal state that is mainly responsible for the fragility of the economy and the ensuing economic and social crises. This is clear from the fact that the most important industrial establishments were created during the developmentalist period (1930–60). In the period between 1960 and 1970, while state guidance was still important, the nascent bourgeoisie was gradually strengthening its grip on the economy. Between 1930 and 1950 the developmentalist state was very successful in mobilising national resources for economic development, but quite unsuccessful as far as democratisation was concerned. Economic growth and democracy did not develop in parallel to each other. Although the country's productive capacity improved considerably, the demands of the masses were not equally met. While paying some attention to the demands of farmers and workers, the state did not hesitate to use its power to ensure their acquiescence. The introduction of the multi-party system in 1946 and the entrenchment of electoral politics were not inevitable outcomes of economic development but largely the results of realpolitik. The single-party state introduced some elements of democracy in order to counteract the Soviet threat by persuading Turkey's western allies that the country was in the process of becoming a western-style democracy. Therefore the prerogatives of realpolitik, such as Turkey's desire to receive Marshall Aid and US military aid and to join NATO, were vital in the abandonment of the authoritarian single-party system. Obviously, external influences were not the only factors in the introduction of democratic processes. Democracy is a process of struggle to control and distribute national resources. Given the scarcity of resources it was impossible to meet the conflicting demands of the nascent commercial and industrial bourgeoisie, the landlords, the workers and the farmers. Multi-party politics and the electoral system meant that it was largely the state elite, the political elite and the economic elite who were involved in the struggle for power. In practice this meant the gradual dissolution of the developmental state and the liberalisation of the economy and politics. However, this process has not been smooth, as the political class has acted paradoxically: while preaching about the virtues of liberalism and the free market economy it has used populist income distribution policies to ensure its own legitimacy.

The more economically developed world and the IFIs, which represent the interests of corporate capital, tolerated this to a certain extent because Turkey's legal and institutional structures were not suitable for the export of speculative finance capital into the country. The West and the IFIs capitalised on Turkey's increasingly serious debt crisis by using aid money as a carrot to ensure rapid changes in Turkey's legal and financial systems. The establishment of the Istanbul Stock Exchange, the privatisation of the state economic enterprises, the abolition of agricultural subsidies and the liberalisation of the capital account were all the necessary building blocks in the transformation of the Turkish economy.

The liberalisation of the capital account in 1989, which complemented the liberalisation of trade, extended and consolidated the process of liberalisation by ensuring that the conditions for the liberalisation of international capital movements were established. Contrary to the expectations of the IMF, the World Bank and the Turkish Government, complete liberalisation of the economy has not resolved the cyclical crises that the country has been experiencing since 1977. The cycles of crises in 1983, 1988, 1994, 1998, 2000 and 2001 inevitably led to serious questions about the validity and usefulness of liberalisation as a policy option for overcoming economic and financial difficulties in Turkey. Questions were also raised about the negative impacts of liberalisation on the Turkish economy and society. The analysis of the recent crises in Turkey, provided in Chapter 3, suggests that the cause of the long-term crisis and entrenched recession in Turkey cannot be reduced to mismanagement, as claimed by the IFIs and the West. I argue that the Turkish economic crises cannot be analysed in isolation from the structural crises of global capitalism, and that the way in which Turkey has been integrating into the global economy is largely responsible for the current problems. The long-term policies which aim to establish the hegemony of the 'free market' economy, deified by the IMF and the World Bank, have created structural weaknesses and serious bottlenecks in the Turkish economy. Each time the Turkish State attempted to overcome an economic crisis by following the IMF/World Bank prescriptions, Turkey sank deeper and deeper into further crises. In order to overcome the bottlenecks of the ISI policies of the 1960s and 1970s, the Turkish State, under the control of the bourgeoisie, moved towards greater integration into the world economy under the directives of the IFIs. By accepting the SAPs, the state and the bourgeoisie dramatically changed in their attitude towards state intervention in the economy. Throughout the 1960s and 1970s industrial capital flourished on protectionist rents, yet suddenly in the 1980s it turned its back on them by labelling them as irrational and wasteful market distortions (Yeldan 1995). The disposition of the state enterprises, which were considered outmoded and backward, and the implementation of austerity measures were carried out under the auspices of the military. The SAPs were instrumental in the restructuring of the Turkish economy throughout the 1980s and in the establishment of a new mode of capital accumulation in which both Turkish and international capital strengthened their position.

The state apparatus was used to transfer resources to the industrial and financial sectors. However, as internal capital formation was not capable of fuelling this rapid accumulation process, heavy borrowing was resorted to. Most of the money was obtained under the tutelage of the Bretton Woods institutions. Continuous borrowing was maintained only on the condition that certain 'structural reforms' were carried out under the tutelage of the IMF and the World Bank. In recent years, what may be called the Turkish economic bureaucracy has also been a staunch supporter of such 'structural reforms'. Equipped with the new liberal ideology, the economic bureaucracy sees structural reforms as the saviour in the avoidance of regular economic crises. Populist policies are blamed for the continuation of the crises and the mismanagement of public funds. Post-1980, the social state was eroded as a consequence of the abandonment of Keynesian policies in favour of monetarist policies. The state's increasing public sector borrowing requirements were met through internal and external borrowing which in turn enhanced the fragility of the economy. Financial liberalisation and the establishment of domestic capital markets furnished Turkey's successive governments with easy mechanisms to meet the public deficit quickly. The governments' insatiable financial requirements coupled with the limited size of the domestic financial system led to very high real interest rates. This in turn further increased the public borrowing requirements as increasing interest payments worsened the budget deficits.

The liberalisation of the capital account was quite timely as far as international finance capital was concerned. Turkey provided a very lucrative emerging market for the over-abundant financial capital in advanced capitalist countries which was in search of new investment outlets that would guarantee high returns in a short period. However, the inflows of finance capital increased the fragility of the Turkish economy. The liberalisation of the capital account could have been beneficial for the country if the many coalition governments had been capable of effecting fiscal stabilisation and regulation of the banking sector. Instead, although the changes introduced in the 1990s generated economic growth, such growth was dependent on the inflows of highly volatile short-term capital. Consequently, investments in the productive sector have become less attractive and both domestic and foreign capitals have shied away from it. Contrary to neo-liberal assumptions, the liberalisation of capital markets does not necessarily lead to economic diversification and stability. The cyclical capital flows which followed the 1989 capital account liberalisation exacerbated economic fluctuations and that in turn brought about greater economic instability. The debt-dependent and highly fragile economic growth throughout the 1990s made the country extremely vulnerable to successive crises and the chickens came home to roost in 2000 and 2001. The 2001 crisis is considered to be the severest of all the crises suffered by Turkey since the 1950s (Öniş and Rubin 2003; Özatay and Sak 2002; Yeldan 2001a, 2001b). It had far reaching impacts on the economy and society: unemployment increased sharply, GNP and per capita income dropped considerably, a large number of small and medium-sized businesses collapsed, and living standards of the urban and rural poor declined severely. Bewildered by the depth and speed of the crisis, the public lost all faith in the political parties that had been in power in recent decades and punished them by electing the Justice and Development Party (JDP) into power in November 2002. The JDP Government put an end to the succession of ineffective coalition governments that had come and gone since 1991. They managed to attract votes from all sections of society despite having Islamic roots. They used a social democratic propaganda campaign to attract votes from the poor and the small business community which felt the impact of the crisis more severely than any other group. Furthermore, the JDP managed to attract some Kurdish votes by preaching for cultural pluralism. The fact that the 10 per cent national threshold in the elections made the chances of DEHAP, a political party popular among the Kurds, being elected into the Parliament quite slim, was a crucial factor in the election success of the JDP.

While the JDP's intention to work in close co-operation with the EU and the IFIs may not be conducive to delivering social equity in the future, it has certainly mobilised support from the West. Despite severe criticism from the opposition parties claiming that the JDP has a hidden agenda of instituting an Islamic state based on Shariat, the JDP has been doing its best to try to persuade the public, and the army in particular, that the JDP respects secularism and is committed to the principles of Atatürk's Republic. The deeds of the JDP so far indicate that they do not present a severe rupture with past policies. The party has shown strong signs that it will adhere to the economic policies recommended by the IMF and the World Bank and the political modernisation demanded by the EU. Whether the adherence to economic and political conditionalities will please the JDP's electorate is yet to be seen. However, it is necessary to highlight that on the cultural front Islamists are not very happy with the JDP's new centre-right stance and the concessions it has made to secularist forces within Turkish society. The Kurdish nationalists are also protesting that the changes so far made in the move towards multiculturalism are far from satisfactory and the laws introduced to please the EU have not been properly implemented. The farming community too is bitter about the way the agricultural sector is being restructured under the guidance of the Bretton Woods institutions and the West.

The economic reform package introduced in 2000 represents the pinnacle of neo-liberalist agricultural policies, which are being implemented at an alarming pace. The almost complete elimination of support prices, the introduction of direct income support in 2002, the withdrawal of support for the unions of agricultural co-operatives, the promulgation of the Sugar Law (2001) and the Tobacco Law (2002) have all been put into practice under the strict control of the IMF, the World Bank, the WTO, the US and the EU. A number of letters of intent submitted to the IMF since 1999, the 2000 Economic Reform Loan (ERL) agreement and the 2001 Agricultural Reform Implementation Project (ARIP) agreement signed with the World Bank are indicative of the impact of external forces on the Government's decision to restructure Turkish agriculture in accordance with the interests of transnational agribusiness firms. The implementation of the above-mentioned policies reflects the determination of both the Turkish State and the West to move away from developmentalism. The internationalisation of agricultural production and trade and the global hegemony of the TNCs in world agriculture have meant the end of the old division of labour. In the new international division of labour in agriculture US agribusiness firms have become a dominant power, forcing less economically developed countries to produce luxury foods for export and durable food components such as oils and sweeteners. The increasing debt of less economically developed countries is used as the main mechanism to persuade them to accept the role of providing labour-intensive off-season fruits and vegetables, beef, poultry, fish and flowers. This necessitates the abandonment of the production of the traditional crops for both export and domestic markets. The production of crops like wheat, barley, cotton, tobacco, hazelnuts and sugar beet is discouraged through the withdrawal of financial support for their producers. Such policies will have serious implications for food security and the agricultural sector as a whole in Turkey. In the face of increasing cuts in state subsidies and rising input prices since 1980, household agricultural producers had to develop survival strategies; however, by the end of the 1990s they had exhausted all such strategies. The latest liberalisation policies, implemented since 2000, have accelerated the processes of de-peasantisation and de-agrarianisation already at work since the 1980s. The resemblance of these policies to Mexico's Second Agrarian Reform arouses fears of similar repercussions. Mexico's agriculture has been transformed by its entry into the GATT and NAFTA and by the implementation of the extensive Second Agrarian Reform since 1992. The process of de-agrarianisation, reflected in the decline of grain production in the *ejidal* sector, has created food security problems for the rural masses. In the newly structured agricultural industry, international companies have established indirect control over fresh fruit and vegetable production. Small producers who lack the investment capital needed to go into joint ventures with international capital are pushed away from the land and agriculture. It seems that a similar scenario is unfolding in Turkey, and policies implemented in conjunction with the ERL and the ARIP are leading to the impoverishment and marginalisation of the rural masses and increasing their dependence on international companies. There are strong signs that the agricultural sector is shrinking, the production of traditional crops is declining, unemployment in rural areas and migration to urban areas are increasing and worst of all Turkey is becoming more and more dependent on food imports. These are all signals of the new wave of social and political tension in both rural and urban areas.

We saw that disenchantment with economic and political problems finds expression in social movements coloured by ethnicity and religion. Ethnically oriented protestation in recent years showed itself in the form of the PKK movement which emerged in 1978 as an independence seeking Marxist-Leninist guerrilla movement and recently reinvented itself as KADEK (Kurdistan Freedom and Democratic Congress), supposedly a political organisation, due to mounting international opposition to its violent tactics. Though Kurdish nationalism emerged in reaction to Turkish nationalism following the establishment of the Republic in 1923, it has only been an influential organisation since the 1980s. The ascendance of Kurdish identity politics in the 1980s was not accidental; the contradictory tendencies of globalisation provided ideal conditions for the nourishment of Kurdish ethnic identity. While globalisation has led to homogenisation in certain areas, such as similar tastes in food and clothes, it has also generated inequalities globally, nationally and regionally. In the emergence of Kurdish ethnic politics, the policies of the Turkish State and global processes played a mutually reinforcing role. Feeling threatened by the rapidity of changes and socio-economic inequalities, some of the Kurds in Turkey started to pay attention to the ideas which emphasised their distinctiveness. Their demands for ethnic and cultural rights received active support from the IFIs, which insisted on democratisation, and from the US and the EU which pushed for pluralistic policies with an emphasis on cultural rights as a constituent element of human rights. The

Islamists also jumped onto the bandwagon in demanding pluralistic policies allowing cultural liberties. The demands of Islamic parties for democracy, freedom of expression, human rights and integration into Europe should not, however, be dismissed as simply an act of hypocrisy using democracy as a tool to come to power in order to work towards the establishment of the Shariat. The fact that the Virtue Party, which carried the banner of political Islam, split up into two new political parties, the Felicity Party and the Justice and Development Party, is indicative of the complicated processes at work. There is a need to go beyond the identity politics which have been dominated by political elites. An analysis of political Islam must also take into consideration the significance of other classes and groups. The rise of political Islam cannot be reduced to the desires of the professional middle class struggling to assert an alternative identity. The inclusion of historico-conjunctural factors in the analysis will provide better insights into the growth of the social base of political Islam among different social classes.

The Islamic political movement has been a broad-based movement binding together a variety of social groups including the poor and destitute in both rural and urban areas as well as intellectuals, professionals and businesspeople who have felt excluded from the dominant power basis in society. The rise of political Islam in Turkey cannot simply be explained by the reactions of the poor to the forces of globalisation. There is no doubt that Islam plays a binding role among the marginalised of various class backgrounds and that the moral argument used by Islamists emphasising equity hides the divergence of interests among the supporters of political Islam. Despite the sense of being excluded experienced by both poor and rich supporters of the Islamic movement, in reality the stakes are very different. While for the marginalised supporters of Islamic politics the issue is to make ends meet, for the so-called Islamic bourgeoisie the issue is to increase their share of the benefits of globalisation and integration into the world economy. The Islamic bourgeoisie has mainly been interested in promoting its own interests through Turkey's further integration into the world economy. While not in power it has been possible for the Islamic bourgeoisie to maintain a close alliance with the poor and disadvantaged on the one hand and the rising Islamic elite on the other. However, time will show whether this alliance, formed within a protest movement will continue once the Islamic bourgeoisie is in power.

The rise of political Islam in the 1980s and 1990s occurred within the context of the decline of the state power brought about by globalisation. The vacuum this created provided the conditions for the emergence of competing claims to national, religious and ethnic identity. Sub-national separatist movements taking ethnic or tribal forms and supra-national revivalist movements taking religious and civilisational forms flourished as manifestations of globalisation. The Islamist bourgeoisie in recent years neglected the role of Islam as a meaningful system and used it as a populist ideology to mobilise the exploited alienated masses for its own cause. The Islamic bourgeoisie organised itself under the Welfare Party to pursue its class interest. Globalisation of production in particular played an important role in the consolidation of the Welfare Party's support among the small to medium-size business sector in provincial towns. The global shift from Fordism to post-Fordism has allowed the proliferation and strengthening of small and medium-scale businesses in Turkey, particularly in provincial cities like Denizli, Gaziantep, Kahramanmaraş, Konya, Çorum, Urfa and Kayseri. These businesspeople resent the cosy relationship which developed between the state authorities and some privileged businesspeople during the developmentalist era guided by the Kemalist modernisation project. The fact that the failure of the Kemalist nationalist project to ensure an equitable distribution of economic benefits had resulted in the social and economic exclusion of a significant proportion of the population was the main factor behind the success of the Islamic Welfare Party and its successors. Furthermore the Islamist parties' unconventional door-to-door method in political campaigns has gained them a considerable number of votes. This has been possible not only because they give the impression of caring for the people and respecting their views and values, but also because of the food and other consumption items they distribute, especially in poor shantytown areas.

Intentionally or unintentionally, the military has played a significant role in the rise of political Islam in Turkey. The policies followed in the aftermath of the 1980 military take-over deserve particular scrutiny. The September 1980 intervention was the third of its kind since 1960, and was justified by the long-lasting social, economic and political instability throughout the 1970s. The succession of weak coalition governments had not been able to resolve the crises as they failed to move away from the economic stalemate created by import substitution, or to put an end to widespread violence and terrorism, and did not manage to form a stable government. The army's main intention in September 1980 was to clear all obstacles to the establishment of a 'free-market economy' which would speed up Turkey's integration into the global economy. For this, political and economic stability were considered to be the *sine qua non*. In the so-called transitional period leading up to democracy, the army changed the Constitution (1982), curtailed civil liberties and workers' rights, and limited trade union activities. Furthermore, the military used Islam as a counter-force against the left, which was considered to be the main culprit in the social and political instability of the late 1970s. The 10 per cent national threshold in elections introduced under the auspices of the military in the 1980s, seems to have benefited mainly the Islamic parties, as many political parties, both on the right and on the left, with very similar party programmes, fought one another to capitalise on the gap left by the two most powerful parties closed down by the military: the Justice Party and the Republican People's Party.

Given the inevitability of globalisation and the still powerful influence Kemalism and the army exert over Turkish society, it is not surprising that some elements within the Islamic Virtue Party have started to adopt the language of pluralism and use concepts like democracy, multiculturalism and even secularism. The pluralistic parlance of the JDP during and after November 2002 played a vital role in its election success, which in turn has given the party the opportunity to put into practice its Islamisation from below. The JDP's success is remarkable in that it achieved a landslide victory despite the army. The JDP's victory indicated an almost complete wiping out of the parties of the September 12 regime. Despite the fact that most of the JDP's leadership originates from the Islamic movement, the party's programme is not specifically Islamic but conservative and democratic. Although there has not been any research about the composition of the JDP's voters, some commentators claim that the JDP represents the votes of the conservative middle class with democratic tendencies (Insel 2002). For some the success of the JDP should be attributed not only to its attempt to distance itself from anti-secularist radical Islam but also to recent economic and political crises. The JDP represents a synthesis of conservatism and liberalism, its political and economic discourse promising to remain faithful to the free market economy, to promote the interests of small businesses and to bring social justice both in terms of economy and identity. The JDP's victory should be interpreted as a civil liquidation of the entire Parliament and all the parties within it, i.e. the DSP, MHP, ANAP, DYP and SP. The JDP presented itself as a party capable of solving problems; as a democratic party aiming to restructure the centre-right, as opposed to the political Islam represented by the SP and Erbakan; as a party striving to combine conservative values with liberalism and to use the state to ensure development and social justice (Keyman 2002). However, early signs suggest that such a combination may not be able to achieve the development, social justice and equitable income distribution Turkey's people have been waiting for.

The economic and political reform programme which has been on the agenda since the 2000 crisis represents a major rupture with the developmentalist strategy which nourished clientelism and corruption. On the other hand, complete liberalisation of the economy has generated fragility and created conditions for further instability. Economic growth based on the short-term inflow of volatile capital and internal borrowing is not sustainable. What is needed is to increase the productive capacity and international competitiveness of the Turkish economy; only then may it be possible to achieve some sort of political and social stability. There is a need to progress from production based on fewer skills, agriculture and natural resource exploitation to production based on more advanced skills, technology and capital-intensive activities. This structural transformation needs to be accompanied by a rapid capital accumulation based on domestic savings, investments and increased exports. These are the *sine qua non* of Turkey's recovery from crisis. Economic growth, structural change and productive upgrading would necessitate an imitation and adaptation of internationally available technologies. The state should play a central role in this process by controlling the process of integration into the global economy. The policy of unconditional surrender to international forces through liberalisation needs to be re-evaluated. The opening-up of the economy to imports and external capital should not be carried out without serious thought about how it would benefit the national interest. If necessary, liberalisation should be introduced gradually without undermining the productive capacities of national enterprises. Similar caution should be applied to capital account liberalisation to ensure that capital inflows do not undermine domestic capital formation and that they support domestic investment rather than consumption. Foreign capital should be encouraged as long as it helps to build domestic production capabilities and exports.

There is no need to be afraid of state involvement in the economy. On the contrary, the state should play an active role in forming various ties with business circles and in consultation with them it should develop policies which will increase the competitiveness of the productive sector. The private sector should be supported by the state through human resource development, physical infrastructure development and policies addressing technology, finance and the organisation and competitiveness of industry. However, the temporary support and protection given to the private sector should be conditional on investment, export and productivity targets. All these suggestions are based on the premise that without production there cannot be healthy distribution. The post-1980 period has witnessed an unsustainable distribution policy based on borrowing and debt. A small group of rent-seeking people amassed wealth through speculative activities and the state provided the necessary conditions for this. Contrary to the belief held by the proponents of the Washington Consensus, liberalisation in Turkey has not reduced the role of the state in the economy, it has simply given it a new role: that of an agent of international capital. In this role the Turkish State has been the main cause of the current crisis. Turkey's recovery may be very difficult, but it certainly necessitates a re-evaluation of the role of the state in the economy and the re-instatement of a developmental state genuinely concerned with the enhancement of the economy's productive capabilities as well as the expansion of productive employment. As suggested by Stiglitz (1998a, 1998b) there is an urgent need to go beyond the Washington Consensus. The complete liberalisation approach should give way to an approach that will emphasise the importance of a long-term development strategy in which the state will play a significant role.

Notes

INTRODUCTION

1 For instance trade between industrial countries accounted for 37.1 per cent of international trade while trade with non-industrial countries was 43.2 per cent of total world trade. This changed significantly as time passed and in 1990 trade between industrial countries reached 55 per cent of world trade while trade between industrial and non-industrial countries declined to 26.6 per cent of world trade.

2 Until the 1960s about 50 per cent of the total direct investment had gone to the Third World and this percentage had dropped to 16.5 per cent by 1988–89. More than half of this went to only a handful of East, South and South East Asian countries.

3 Net inflows of equity capital rose sharply from US$3.2 billion in 1990 to between US$32 billion and US$48 billion in the 1993–97 period (World Bank 1998).

CHAPTER 1

1 The report was prepared by M. W. Thornburg, G. Spray and G. Sorke who were sent in 1946 on a mission by the US to decide whether aid should be given to Turkey.

2 For various aspects of the stabilisation policies see Boratav 1991; Kazgan 1988; Oyan 1987 and Türel 1984.

3 Some of the encouragement funds given to exporters are: rebate of indirect taxes, cheap credit through Eximbank, duty free imports, premium paid from the 'export encouragement fund' and from the 'price stability fund', and exemption from 'institutions tax'. For instance, export tax rebate has increased from 6 per cent of the value of the total exported manufactured goods in 1980 to 19.2 per cent in 1984.

4 Most internal borrowing has been of a short-term nature and came to maturity in January 1996. In January 1996, in order to raise funds to meet debt obligations the Government issued 128 trillion Turkish Lira (£142 billion) worth of bonds with an average 221.63 per cent interest. Most bonds were either for the duration of 100 days or 144 days.

CHAPTER 2

1 The concept of hegemony was popularised by Antonio Gramsci. In its simplest form, hegemony refers to consent as opposed to coercion or physical force. In a Gramscian fashion, Chantal Mouffe (1979) identifies hegemony with the process of a collective will or general interest by the hegemonic class. Although, in reality, there is no such thing as general or

collective will, the hegemonic class makes the dominated classes believe that its own interest is the interest of everyone by using its economic and political position and cultural institutions such as religion, school, media, architecture and value systems. Through these institutions, the hegemonic class integrates, assimilates, articulates and neutralises particular interests in society and nationalises itself.

CHAPTER 3

1 Crony capitalism and excessive government intervention, speculative financial liberalisation, lack of government supervision on foreign debts of domestic companies and IMF bail-out packages are among the often cited causes of the 1998 Asian crisis (Rivera-Batiz 2001).
2 The rate of growth in the private manufacturing sector was 2.1 per cent per annum in the 1980–88 period.
3 The wage policy of the 1980–88 period led to the reduction of the domestic demand on the one hand and to the lowering of wage costs in industry on the other. The share of wage labour in both private and public manufacturing value added declined from 26.5 per cent to 15 per cent in this period.
4 High interest rates were maintained as a result of the fear of currency substitution under a convertible currency regime and as a result of the state's active involvement in the domestic asset markets through the issuing of bonds.
5 For instance, the rate of interest on the government debt instruments (GDI) was dropped to the US$30–40 range in the early days of the programme. This was a huge change from the 100–120 per cent interest rate on GDI throughout the post-1994 crisis period. Consequently, fiscal expenditures on interest dropped 3.5 per cent below the target. Tax revenues also exceeded the target programme by 10.5 per cent during 2000 (Yeldan 2001a, 2001b Tables 1 and 2, Figure 3).
6 In the 'casino capitalism' established as a result of financial liberalisation since the 1980s the financial sector has been the arena in which investments in state shares and bonds have been made. Consequently the banking sector has become characterised by an unhealthy growth due to speculative capital accumulation. The ratio of total activities of the banks to national income has increased from 35 per cent in 1990 to 41 per cent in 1995 and 65 per cent in 2000. This financial deepening was due to high rates of real interest on valuable state papers, which were used to finance public deficits. The domestic debt accumulated through state shares and bonds jumped from being equal to 7 per cent of the national income in 1990 to 29.3 per cent at the end of 1999. The total interest paid on domestic debt reached a staggering 638 per cent of public investment in 1999 (Bağımsız Sosyal Bilimciler İktisat Grubu 2001:4, hereafter BSBIG).

CHAPTER 5

1 The distribution of votes among political parties in the 1995 elections were as follows: Welfare Party 21.4 per cent; True Path Party 19.2 per

cent; Motherland Party 19.7 per cent; Democratic Left Party 14.6 per cent; Republican People's Party 10.7 per cent; National Action Party 8.2 per cent and People's Democracy and Labour Party 6.1 per cent. The last two parties were not represented in Parliament as their votes were below the 10 per cent national threshold.

2   The percentage of votes and the number of seats in the 550 member Parliament in the 1999 elections were: Democratic Left Party 22.19 per cent (136 seats); National Action Party 17.98 per cent (117 seats); Virtue Party (Fazilet Party, the successor to the Islamist Welfare Party) 15.41 per cent (111 seats); Motherland Party 13.2 per cent (86 seats); True Path Party 12.01 per cent (85 seats). Other parties were not represented in Parliament due to their failure to reach the 10 per cent national threshold.

3   Some claim that the democratic discourse of the Justice and Development Party is nothing more than a ruse (*Takiyye*) to gain time to consolidate its power and to work towards an Islamic state.

4   The percentage of votes for the main political parties in the November 2001 elections were as follows: Justice and Development Party 34.27 per cent; People's Republican Party 19.39 per cent; True Path Party 9.55 per cent; National Movement Party 8.33 per cent; Young Party 7.24 per cent; Pro Kurdish DEHAP 6.21 per cent; Motherland Party 5.12 per cent; Felicity Party 2.48 per cent; Democratic Left Party 1.14 per cent; Socialist Workers Party 0.51 per cent. Smaller parties and independent candidates shared the rest of the votes.

5   According to Toprak's (1993:244) classification, the West is defined in a variety of ways by the Islamic discourse: technological and industrial development, Christianity and Christian culture and democracy are the most significant factors used in their definitions.

6   For a detailed account of this process see Hakan Yavuz (1998), 'Islamic Political Identity in Turkey: Movements, Agents, and Processes', Unpublished PhD dissertation, University of Wisconsin-Madison.

7   Kemalist hegemony was interrupted between 1950 and 1960 when the Democrat Party ruled and in the 1983–93 period when Turgut Özal's Motherland Party was in power. Both periods are characterised by the rule of relatively better democracy.

8   For various assessments of Said Nursi and Nurcu Movement see Kara (1998), Ocak (1999), Dumont (1986), Yavuz (1999).

9   The National Security Council consists of five generals, the President, the Prime Minister, the Foreign Minister, the Defence Minister, and the Minister of Internal Affairs.

10   There is a huge debate within the theoretical-conceptual literature concerning the direction of change and transition within the capitalist system. The notions of post-Fordism, post-industrialism, post-modernism and Fifth Kondratiev constitute the centre of the discussions. Some of the topics discussed within the debate include the following far-ranging and diverse issues: the organisation of manufacturing systems; the political problems resulting from regulatory issues regarding the global world order; the future of the nation state; and the introduction of potential political solutions ranging from revolutionary socialism to neo-liberal conservatism.

11   The number of small and medium-scale production units that have sub-contracting arrangements with international companies has been on the rise since 1980. A survey carried out in Denizli, Gaziantep, Konya, Çorum and Edirne indicates that more than half of the small to medium-sized firms established since 1980 had sub-contracting arrangements with international companies operating mainly in the garment insustry (Kişoğlu *et al.* 1997). Şahin (1997), Nichols and Sungur (1996) and Oyan and Konukman (1997), looking at various aspects of subcontracting firms, highlight the fact that KOBIs (small to medium size firms) established in the so-called Anatolian Tigers have had little help from the state and would welcome more help. KOBIs tend to rely heavily on the exploitation of non-unionised labour including a significant amount of female and child labour. For a detailed analysis of labour relations in sub-contracting firms see Demiriz (2000).

12   For instance White (1994) shows that in poor neighbourhoods of Istanbul where domestic piecework and family workshops are integrated into the global economy the relations between female labourers and the employers are governed by fictive and actual kinship.

13   For various aspects of post-Fordism and flexible specialisation see Lash and Urry (1987), Piore and Sabel (1984) and Arrighi (1995).

14   For the concept and the process of informalisation see Portes *et al.* (1989).

15   Boratav's (1995) survey carried out in 1993 reveals that the Islamists were more successful than the social democrats in convincing the working class and recent migrants in Istanbul that uniting under Islamic identity and fighting against corruption may be the solution to economic and political ills.

16   For a detailed account of MÜSİAD's vision of Islamic economy and society see MÜSİAD (1994), and numerous articles published in *Çerçeve* quarterly and *Bülten* published by MÜSİAD.

17   For a detailed analysis of the process of informalisation see Portes, Castells and Benton (1989).

18   The number of companies that joined the MÜSİAD members has increased to more than 5000 since its establishment in 1990 (Buğra 2002).

CHAPTER 6

1   There are no reliable figures about the number of Kurds living in Turkey and estimates range from 15 to 20 million people. This is about one fourth of the population and there is an increasing demand for ethnic recognition among them.

2   It is ironic that it was the Ottoman State itself that paved the way for the emergence of the seeds of Kurdish nationalism. Fearing that the Armenians in the Kurdish region might follow in the footsteps of the Balkan peoples, in 1891 Sultan Abdulhamid ordered the establishment of the Hamidiye Regiments, which consisted of Kurdish tribal armies under the leadership of their tribal *aghas*. The Hamidiye Regiments both heralded the emergence of a Kurdish identity and acted as an obstacle to the strengthening

of such an identity. They were very influential in keeping under control the nationalistic aspirations of the Armenians who were stirred up by the Russians and the British. The state played the Hamidiye Regiments card very well by choosing them from Sunni Muslim Kurds in rural areas and using them against both the urban bourgeoisie, who were disenchanted with the oppressive regime, and against rebellious nationalistic non-Muslim elements such as the Armenians and the Assyrians as well as against Shiite Kurds. It could be said that the formation of the Hamidiye Regiments was conducive to the unification of various tribal groups under the banner of Hamidiye Regiments, thus contributing to the process of identity formation. However, the way in which they were used stirred up competition and religious rivalries between various religious sects, which worked against the formation of a Kurdish identity (Kutlay 1997:80–95).

3   The consolidation of Kemalism as the state ideology over the years meant the gradual disappearance of the relative tolerance to Kurdish identity in the new Parliament (Kutlay 1997:152). Until the introduction of the multi-party system in 1946 most Members of Parliament representing Kurdish provinces were selected from non-Kurdish regions and ethnic backgrounds (Kutlay 1997:152). Since the 1950 elections, Kurdish feudal and semi-feudal notables (*aghas, beys, sheiks*) used their economic and political power in Kurdish regions to get into Parliament.

4   In an interview with the daily newspaper *Özgür Gündem* on 11 June 2004, Hatip Dicle claimed that KONGRA-GEL's approach to the solution of the Kurdish question was similar to his own. He pleaded with the Turkish Government to pay attention to the cultural and political aspirations of the Kurds in Turkey and to establish the conditions under which the Turks and Kurds will be able to co-exist peacefully. He openly advocated a pluralistic society within a unified state of Turkey. He raised serious concerns about the Turkish Government's sincerity on the issue of ethnic rights and true democracy. He interpreted the release of the four DEP parliamentarians as an act of political expediency to persuade the Council of Europe Parliamentary Assembly to end the monitoring of Turkey's human rights practices. It is ironic that within a week of the interview the Council of Europe Parliamentary Assembly endorsed a report on 22 June 2004 to drop Turkey from the list of countries to be monitored (*Turkish Daily News*, 23 June 2004).

CHAPTER 7

1   For a recent account of the relationship between economic crises and income distribution see Şenses (2003).

Bibliography

Adelman, I. (1999) 'Editorial: Financial Crises–Causes, Consequences and Remedies', *Working Paper* No. 889 (Department of Agricultural and Resource Economics and Policy: University of California).

Ahmad, F. (1981) 'The Political Economy of Kemalism', in Kazancıgil, A. (ed.) *Atatürk Founder of a Modern State* (London: C. Hurst and Co.).

Akat, A.S. (1994) '1994 Bunalımı Üzerine Çeşitlemeler (Interpretations of the 1994 Crisis), *Görüş*, No. 15 (İstanbul: TÜSİAD Publication).

Akman, C. (2001) 'Devletin "Borç Çukuru"' (The Deep Hole of State Debts), *Birikim*, Mayıs: 32–45.

Akşit, B. (1991) 'Islamic Education in Turkey', in Tapper, R. (ed.), *Islam in Modern Turkey* (London: I.B. Tauris).

———. (1993), 'Studies in Rural Transformation in Turkey 1950–1990', in Stirling, P. (ed.), *Culture and Economy in Turkish Village* (London: Eothen Press).

Alavi, H. (1972) 'The State in Post-colonial Societies: Pakistan and Bangladesh', *New Left Review*, No. 74: 59–81.

Allison, L. (1994) 'On the Gap between Theories of Democracy and Theories of Democratisation', *Democratisation*, 1(1): 9–19.

Alpay, S. (1991) *2020 Yılında Türkiye* (Turkey in the Year 2020) (İstanbul: AFA Yayınları).

Altunkemer, M. and Ekinci N. (1992) 'Capital Account Liberalization: The Case of Turkey', *New Perspectives on Turkey*, Fall, No. 8: 89–108.

Amin, S. (1980) *Class and Nation Historically and in the Current Crisis* (New York: Monthly Review Press).

Amnesty International (1991) *Report 1991* (London: Amnesty International Publications).

———. (1994) *Turkey: A Time for Action*, February (London).

———. (1995) *Turkey: A Political Denial*, February (London).

Anand, R., Chibber, A. and van Winjbergen, S. (1990) 'External Balance and Growth in Turkey' in Aricanli, T. and Rodrik, T. (eds), *The Political Economy of Turkey: Debt, Adjustment and Sustainability* (London: Macmillan).

Anderson, B. (1991) *Imagined Communities: Reflections on the Origin and Spread of Nationalism* (London: Verso).

Apter, D. (1965) *The Politics of Modernisation* (Chicago, IL: University of Chicago Press).

Arıcanlı, T. and Rodrik, D. (eds) (1990), *The Political Economy of Turkey: Debt, Adjustment and Sustainability* (London: Macmillan).

Arın T, (1986), 'Kapitalist Düzenleme, Birikim Rejimi ve Kriz (II): Azgelişmiş Kapitalizm ve Türkiye (Capitalist regulation, Accumulation and Crisis (II): Underdeveloped Capitalism and Turkey), *Onbirinci Tez*, Kitap Dizisi 3, (İstanbul: Uluslararası Yayıncılık).

Arrighi, G. (1995) *The Long Twentieth Century* (London: Verso).

Avcıoğlu, D. (1968) *Türkiye'nin Düzeni: Dün-Bugün-Yarın* (The Order of Turkey: Yesterday-Today-Tomorrow) (Ankara: Bilgi Yayınları).

Ayata, S. (1990) 'The Rise of Islamic Fundamentalism and Its Institutional Framework', in Eralp, A., Tünay, M. and B. Yeşilada (eds), *The Political and Socioeconomic Transformation of Turkey* (Westport, Connecticut, London: Praeger).

Aydın, Z. (1986) *Underdevelopment and Rural Structures in Southeastern Turkey* (London: Ithaca Press).

——. (1993) 'The World Bank and the Transformation of Turkish Agriculture' in Eralp, A., Tünay, M. and Yeşilada, B. (eds), *The Political and Socioeconomic Transformation of Turkey* (Westport, Connecticut, London: Praeger).

——. (2002) 'The New Right, Structural Adjustment and Turkish Agriculture: Rural Responses and Survival Strategies', *European Journal of Development Research*, 14(2): 183–208.

Baffes, J. and Meerman, J. (1997) 'From Prices to Incomes: Agricultural Subsidization without Protection', *Word Bank Papers* (Washington D.C.: World Bank).

Bağımsız Sosyal Bilimciler İktisat Grubu, (2001) <bagimsizsosyalbilimciler. org>, 'The Evaluation of the Transition to a Strong Economy Programme', downloaded 19 September 2001.

Bağımsız Sosyal Bilimciler, (2003) 'Evaluations on the Turkish Economy at the beginning of 2003 and the JDP's Government Programme' (in Turkish), <www.bagimsizsosyalbilimciler.org>, downloaded 15 August 2003.

Bağımsız Sosyal Bilimciler, (2004) 'Macroeconomic Developments in Turkey' at <www.gpn.org> downloaded 29 June 2004.

Balassa, B. (1979) *Growth Policies and Exchange Rate in Turkey*, World Bank Reprint Series, No.181.

Barkey, J.H. (1990) *The State and Industrialisation Crisis* (Boulder: Westview Press).

Barkey, J.H. and Fuller, G.E. (1995) 'Turkey's Kurdish Question: Critical Turning Points and Missed Opportunities', *Middle East Journal*, 51(1): 59–79.

——. (1998), *Turkey's Kurdish Question* (New York: Rowman and Littlefield Publishers Inc).

Barington Moore, Jr (1966) *Social Origins of Dictatorship and Democracy: Lord and Peasant in the Making of the Modern World* (Boston: Beacon Press).

Barkin, D. *et al.* (eds) (1990) *Food Crops vs. Feed Crops: The Global Substitution of Grains in Production* (Boulder: Lynne Rienner).

Beetham, D. (1992) 'Liberal Democracy and the Limits of Democratization', *Political Studies*, XL: 40–53.

Beetham, D. and Boyle, K. (1995) *Introducing Democracy: 80 Questions and Answers* (Oxford: Polity Press in Association with Blackwell Publishers).

Berkes, N. (1965) *Batıcılık, Ulusçuluk ve Toplumsal Devrimler* (Westernism, Nationalism and Social Revolutions) (Istanbul).

Berksoy, T. (1982), *Azgelişmiş Ülkelerde İhracata Yönelik Sanayileşme* (Export Oriented Industrialisation in Underdeveloped Countries) (İstanbul: Belge Yayınları).

Bernstein, H. (1994) 'Agrarian Classes in Capitalist Development', in Sklair, L. (ed.), *Capitalism and Development* (London: Routledge).

——. (2000) '"The Peasantry" in Global Capitalism Who, Where, Why?' in Panitch, L. and Leys, C. (eds) *The Socialist Register 2001* (London: Merlin Press).

——. (2001) 'Agrarian Reform after Developmentalism?' Paper presented at Development Studies Association Annual Conference, 10–12 September.

Beşikçi, I. (1969) *Doğu Anadolu'nun Düzeni* (The Structure of Eastern Anatolia), Development Studies Association Annual Conference, 10–12 September (Ankara: E Yayınları).

Bhagwati, J. (1995) 'The New Thinking on Development', *Journal of Democracy*, 6(4): 50–64.

Binswanger, H. and Deininger, K. (1999) 'Towards a Political Economy of Agriculture and Agrarian Relations', unpublished manuscript, Washington D.C.: World Bank.

Birnie, P. (1993) 'The UN and the Environment' in Roberts, A. and Kingsbury, B. (eds), *United Nations, Divided World* (Oxford: Clarendon Press).

Black, C.E. (1967) *The Dynamics of Modernisation: A Study in Comparative History* (New York).

Boratav, K. (1974) *Türkiye'de Develetçilik* (Etatism in Turkey) (İstanbul: Gerçek Yayınevi).

——. (1988) 'Giriş' (Introduction), in Bulutay, T. (ed.) *Türkiye'de Tarımsal Yapı ve İstihdam* (Agricultural Structure and Employment in Turkey) (Ankara: DIE).

——. (1990) 'Inter-Class and Intra-Class Relations of Distribution Under Structural Adjustment: Turkey During the 1980s', in Aricanli, T. and Rodrik, T. (eds), *The Political Economy of Turkey: Debt, Adjustment and Sustainability* (London: Macmillan).

——. (1991) *1980 li Yıllarda Türkiye'de Sosyal Sınıflar ve Bölüşüm* (Social Classes and Distribution in Turkey in the 1980s) (İstanbul: Gerçek Yayınları).

——. (1993) 'State and Class in Turkey: A Study in Capitalist Development', *Review of Radical Political Economics*, 25(1): 129–147.

——. (1994) 'Contradictions of "Structural Adjustment": Capital and State in Post-1980 Turkey', in Öncü, A., Keyder, Ç. and Ibrahim, S.E. (eds) *Developmentalism and Beyond: Society and Politics in Egypt and Turkey* (Cairo: American University in Cairo Press).

——. (1995) *İstanbul ve Anadolu' da Sınıf Profilleri* (Class Profiles in Istanbul and Anatolia) (İstanbul: Türk Tarih Vakfı Yurt Yayınları).

——. (2001) '2000–2001 Krizinde Sermaye Hareketleri' (Financial Movements in the 2000–2001 Crisis), *İktisat, İsletme ve Finans*, 186: 7–18.

Boratav, K., Türel, O. and Yeldan, E. (1994) 'Distributional Dynamics in Turkey under "Structural Adjustment" of the 1980s', *New Perspectives on Turkey*, Fall, No. 11: 43–69.

Boratav, K. and Türkcan, E. (1991) *Türkiye'de Sanayileşmenin Yeni Boyutları ve KİTler* (New Dimesions of Industrialisation and State Economic Enterprises in Turkey) (Istanbul: Tarih Vakfı Yayınları).

Boratav, K., Yeldan, A.E. and Köse, A.H. (2000) 'Globalization, Distribution and Social Policy: Turkey 1980–1998', *CEPA Working Paper Series 1* (New School University, New York).

Boratav, K. and Yeldan, E. (2001) 'Turkey, 1980–2000: Financial Liberalisation, Macroeconomic (In)-Stability and Patterns of Distribution', CEPA and New School for Social Research, mimeo.

Boyer, R. (1988) 'Technical Change and the Theory of "Regulation"', in Dosi, G. *et al.* (eds), *Technical Change and Economic Theory* (London: Printer).

Bratton, M. (1994) 'International versus Domestic Pressures for "Democratisation" in Africa', paper presented at the conference '*The End of Cold War: Effects and Prospects for Asia and Africa*' (London: SOAS, UCL).

Bratton, M. and van de Walle, N. (1992) 'Popular Protest and Political Reform in Africa', *Comparative Politics*, No. 24: 419–442.

Braudel, F. (1982) *The Wheels of Commerce* (New York: Harper and Row).

Brenner, R. (1998) 'The Economics of Global Turbulence', *New Left Review*, No. 229: 1–264.

Brown, J. (1995) 'The Turkish Imbroglio: Its Kurds', *Annals*, AAPSS, No. 541, September.

Bruinessen, M.V. (1978) *Agha, Sheikh and State. On the Social and Political Organisation of Kurdistan* (Rijswick: Enroprint).

Bryceson, D., Kay, C. and Mooij, J. (eds) (2000) *Disappearing Peasantries? Rural Labour in Africa, Asia and Latin America* (London: IT Publications).

Buğra, A. (1994) *State and Business in Modern Turkey: A Comparative Study* (New York: State University of New York Press).

——. (1998) 'Class Culture and State: An Analysis of Interest Representation by Two Turkish Business Associations', *International Journal of Middle Eastern Studies*, 30: 521–39.

——. (1999) *Islam in Economic Organisations* (Istanbul: The Turkish Economic and Social Studies Foundation).

——. (2001) 'Bir Krize ve Ahlâki Ekonominin Çöküşüne Dair' (On a Crisis and Collapse of Moral Economy), *Birikim*, May, No. 45: 46–59.

——. (2002a) 'Labour, Capital, and Religion: Harmony and Conflict among the Constituency of Political Islam in Turkey', *Middle Eastern Studies*, 38(2): 187–204.

——. (2002b) 'Political Islam in Turkey in Historical Context: Strength and Weaknesses', in Balkan, N. and Savran, S. (eds), *The Politics of Permanent Crisis: Class, Ideology and State in Turkey* (New York: Nova Science Publishers).

Bulutoğlu, K. (1967) 'Financing Turkey's Development Plan', in İlkin, S. and İnanç, E. (eds), *Planning in Turkey* (Ankara: METU).

——. (1970) *Türkiye'de Yabancı Sermaye* (Foreign Capital in Turkey) (İstanbul).

Burmeister, L.L. (1986) 'Warfare, Welfare and State Autonomy: Structural Roots of the South Korean Developmental State, *Pacific Focus*, 1(2): 121–146.

Cammack, P. (1994) 'Political Development Theory and the Dissemination of Democracy', *Democratisation*, 1(3): 353–372.

Castells, M. (1992) 'Four Asian Tigers with a Dragon's Head', in Applebaum, R.P. and Henderson, J. (eds) *States and Development in the Asian Pacific Rim* (Newbury Park, CA.: Sage).

——. (1996) *The Rise of Network Society* (Cambridge: Cambridge University Press).

——. (1997) *The Power of Identity* (Oxford: Blackwell).

Castells, M., Portes, A. and Benton, L. (eds), (1989) *The Informal Economy: Studies in Advanced and Less Developed Countries* (Baltimore: The Johns Hopkins University Press).

Celasun, M. (1990) 'Fiscal Aspects of Adjustment in the 1980s', in Arıcanlı, T. and Rodrik, D. (eds), *The Political Economy of Turkey: Debt, Adjustment and Sustainability* (London: Macmillan).

——. (1991) 'Trade and Industrialisation in Turkey: Initial Conditions, Policy and Performance in the 1980s', Paper Presented at the UNU/WIDER Conference, Paris, 1–3 September.

Celasun, M. and Rodrik, D. (1989) 'Debt, Adjustment and Growth', in Sach, J. (ed.), *Developing Country Debt and Economic Performance*, Vol. III (Chicago: University of Chicago Press).

Central Bank of Turkey (2004) *2003 Yıllık Rapor* (2003 Annual Report) (Ankara).

Chailand, G. (1994) *The Kurdish Tragedy* (London and New York) in association with UNRISD.

Chalker, L. (1991) *Good Government and the Aid Programme* (London: ODA).

Chase-Dunn, C. (1989) *Global Formation, Structures of the World Economy*, (Oxford: Basil Blackwell).

Cizre-Sakallıoğlu, Ü. (1996) 'Historicizing the Present and Problematizing the Future of the Kurdish Problem: A Critique of the TOBB Report on the Eastern Question', *New Perspectives on Turkey*, Spring, 14: 1–22.

Cizre-Sakallıoğlu, Ü. and Yeldan, E. (2000) 'Politics, Society and Financial Liberalization: Turkey in the 1990s', *Development and Change*, 31: 481–508.

Clapham, C. (1993) 'Democratisation in Africa: Obstacles and Prospects', *Third World Quarterly*, 14(3): 432–438.

Clarke, S. (1991) 'State, Class Struggle, and the Reproduction of Capital' in Clarke, S. (ed.), *The State Debate* (London: Macmillan).

Cohen, R. and Kennedy, P. (2000) *Global Sociology* (Basingstoke and New York: Palgrave).

Commission of the European Communities (1991) *Human Rights, Democracy and Development Cooperation Policy*, Commission Communication to the Council Parliament, SEC (91) 61 final, 25 March, Brussels: CEC.

Cornelius, W.A. and Myhre D. (eds) (1998) *The Transformation of Rural Mexico: Reforming the Ejido Sector* (San Diego, La Jolla: Center for U.S–Mexican Studies, University of California).

Cox, D., Eser, Z., and Jimenez, E. (1998) 'Motives for Private Transfer over the Life Cycle: Analytical Framework and Evidence from Peru', *Journal of Development Economics*, 55(1): 57–81.

Çelebi, I. (1991) *Dışa Açık Büyüme ve Türkiye* (Outward Orientated Growth and Turkey) (Istanbul).

Çınar, M. (1997) 'Mission Impossible', *Private View*, 1(2): 72–78.

Dahl, R.A. (1956) *A Preface to Democratic Theory* (University of Chicago Press).

——. (1971) *Polyarchy, Participation, and Opposition* (New Haven: Yale University Press).

——. (1982) *Dilemmas of Pluralist Democracy* (New Haven: Yale University Press).

Derviş, K. and Petri, P. (1987) 'The Macroeconomics of Successful Development: What are the Lessons?' *NBER Macroeconomics Annual*.

Diamond, L. (1993) 'The Globalization of Democracy', in Slater, R., Schutz, B. and Dorr, S. (eds) *Global Transformation and the Third World* (Boulder: Lynne Rienner).

Diamond, L., Linz, J.J. and Lipset, S.M. (1989) 'Preface', in Diamond, L., Linz, J.J. and Lipset, S.M. (eds) *Democracy in Developing Countries, Vol.4, Latin America* (Boulder, CO: Lynne Rienner).

Di Palma, G. (1990) *To Craft Democracies: An Essay on Democratic Transition* (Berkeley: University of California Press).

Doğruel, S. and Yeldan, E. (2001) 'Macroeconomics of Turkey's Agricultural Reforms: An Intertemporal Computable General Equilibrium Analysis', mimeograph, June 2001.

DPT (1996) *VII. Beş Yıllık Kalkınma Planı, 1996–2000* (VII. Five-Year Development Plan, 1996–2000) (Ankara: DPT).

Dumont, P. (1986) 'Disciples of the Light: the Nurcu Movement in Turkey', *Central Asian Survey*, No. 2.

Dunleavy, P. and O'Leary, B. (1987) *Theories of the State* (Basingstoke: Macmillan).

Eickelman, D.F. (1999) 'Qur'anic Commentary, Public Space, and Religious Intellectuals in the Writings of Said Nursi', *Muslim World*, LXXXIX, nos. 3–4: 260–269.

Eisenstadt, S.N. (1966) *Modernisation, Protest and Change* (Englewood Cliffs, NJ: Prentice Hall).

Ekinci, N. (1996) 'Financial Liberalisation Under External Debt Constraints: The case of Turkey', *METU-ERC Working Paper*, 96/05.

——. (1998) 'Türkiye Ekonomisinde Gelişmenin Dinamikleri ve Kriz' (Growth and Crisis Dynamics in the Turkish Economy), *Toplum ve Bilim*, No. 77: 7–27.

Elster, J. (1985) *Making Sense of Marx* (Cambridge: Cambridge University Press).

Entessar, N. (1992) *Kurdish Ethnonationalism* (Boulder CO: Lynne Rienner).

Erdilek, A. (1986) 'Turkey's New Open Door Policy of Direct Investment: A Critical Analysis of Problems and Prospects', *METU Studies in Development*, 13(1–2): 171–191.

Evans, P.B. (1995) *Embedded Autonomy: States and Industrial Transformation* (Princeton, NJ: Princeton University Press).

Evans, P. B., Rueschemeyer, D. and Skocpol, T. (eds) (1985) *Bringing the State Back* (Cambridge: Cambridge University Press).

Featherstone, M. and Lash, S. (2001). 'Introduction', *Theory, Culture & Society*, 18(2–3): 1–19.

FAO (1996) The World Food Summit (Rome: FAO).

——. (2000) *Agriculture, Trade and Food Security: Issues and Options in the WTO Negotiations from the Perspective of Developing Countries*, Vol. II: Country Case Studies (Rome: FAO).

Frank, A.G. (1967) *Capitalism and Underdevelopment in Latin America* (New York: Monthly Review Press).

Fraser, N. (1995) 'From Redistribution of Recognition? Dilemmas of Justice in a "Postsocialist" Age', *New Left Review*, 212: 68–93.

——. (1997) *Justice Interrupts: Critical Reflections on the 'Postsocialist' Condition* (London: Routledge).

Friedland, W. (1994) 'The New Globalisation: The Case of Fresh Produce' in Bonno, A. *et al.* (eds) *From Columbus to Conagra* (Lawrence: The University of Kansas Press).

Friedmann, H. (1978) 'World Market, State and Family Farm: Social Basis of Household Production in the Era of Wage Labour', *Comparative Studies in Society and History*, Vol. 20.

——. (1982) 'The Political Economy of Food: The Rise and Fall of the Postwar International Food Order, *American Sociological Review*, Vol. 88 (annual supplement).

——. (1993) 'The Political Economy of Food: A Global Crisis', *New Left Review*, No. 197.

——. (1994) 'Premature Rigor', *Review of International Political Economy*, 1(3): 552–561.

Friedmann, H., and McMichael, P. (1989) 'Agriculture and the State System: The Rise and Decline of National Agricultures, 1870 to the Present' *Sociologica Ruralis*, 29(1).

Fukuyama, F. (1992) *The End of History and the Last Man* (London: Hamish Hamilton).

Gellner, E. (1992) *Uluslar ve Ulusçuluk* (Istanbul: Insan Yayınları).

Giddens, A. (1990) *The Consequences of Modernity* (Cambridge: Polity Press).

Green, R.H. (1986) *Sub-Saharan Africa: Poverty of Development, Development of Poverty*, IDS Discussion Paper (Brighton: Institute of Development Studies).

Greenfield, L. (1992) *Nationalism: Five Roads to Modernity* (London and Cambridge MA: Harvard University Press).

Gülalp (1980) 'Türkiye'de İthal İkamesi Bunalımı ve Dışa Açılma (The Crisis of Import Substitution and Liberalisation), *METU Studies in Development*, 7(1–2): 127–149.

——. (1983) *Gelişme Stratejileri ve Gelişme Ideolojileri* (Development Strategies and Development Ideologies) (Ankara: Yurt Yayınları).

——. (1992) 'A Postmodern Reaction to Dependent Modernisation: The Social and Historical Roots of Islamic Radicalism', *New Perspectives on Turkey*, 8: 15–26.

——. (1997) 'Globalizing Postmodernism: Islamists and Western Social Theory', *Economy and Society*, 26(3): 419–433.

——. (2001) 'Globalization and Political Islam: The Social Base of Turkey's Welfare Party, *International Journal of Middle East Studies*, 33: 433–448.

Güzel, Ş. (1995) *Devlet-Ulus* (Istanbul: Alan Yayıncılık).

Gwynne, R.N. and Kay, C. (2000) 'Views from the Periphery: Features of Neoliberalism in Latin America', *Third World Quarterly*, 21(1): 141–156.

Habermas, J. (1989) *The Structural Transformation of the Public Sphere: An Inquiry into a Category of Bourgeois Society* (Cambridge, MA: MIT Press).

Hadenious, A. (1992) *Democracy and Development* (Cambridge: Cambridge University Press).

Hall, S. (1991) 'The Local and the Global: Globalization and Ethnicity', in King, A.D. (ed.) *Culture, Globalization and the World System: Contemporary Conditions for the Representations of Identity* (Basingstoke: Macmillan).

——. (1992) 'The Question of National Identity', in Hall, S., Held, D. and McGrew, T. (eds), *Modernity and its Features* (Cambridge: Polity Press).

Harvey, D. (1989) *The Condition of Postmodernity* (Oxford: Basil Blackwell).

Hathaway, D. (1987) *Agriculture and the GATT* (Washington D.C.: Institute for International Economics).

Hazine Müsteşarlığı, (2000a) *Enflasyonla Mücadele Programı Politika Metinleri, Cilt I: Niyet Mektubu, Para Politikası, Ekonomik Kararlara İlişkin Mevzuat* (Documents on Anti-inflationist Polices, Vol. I: the Letter of Intent, Monetary Policy, Regulations on Economic Decisions), Ocak (Ankara: Hazine).

——. (2000b) *Enflasyonla Mücadele Programı Politika Metinleri, Cilt II: Niyet Mektubu, Para Politikası, Ekonomik Kararlara İlişkin Mevzuat* (Documents on Anti-inflationist Polices, Vol. II: the Letter of Intent, Monetary Policy, Regulations on Economic Decisions), Temmuz (Ankara: Hazine).

Held, D. (1984) *Modern State and Social Theory* (Stanford: Stanford University Press).

——. (1989) 'Central Perspectives on the Modern State', in Held, D. *Political Theory and the Modern State* (Cambridge: Polity Press).

Held, D., McGrew, A., Golblatt, D. and Perraton, J. (1999) *Global Transformations: Politics, Economics and Culture* (Cambridge: Polity Press).

Helsinki Watch, (1988) *Destroying Ethnic Identity: The Kurds of Turkey* (New York-Washington: Helsinki Watch Report).

Heper, M. (1977) 'Negative Bureaucratic Politics in a Modernising Context', *Journal of South Asia and Middle Eastern Studies*, 1(1).

——. (1985) *The State Tradition in Turkey* (Walkington: Eaton Press).

—— (1992) 'The Strong State as a Problem for the Consolidation of Democracy', *Comparative Politics*, 25(2): 169–194.

Hershlag, Z. (1968) *Turkey: The Challenge of Growth* (Leiden: E.J. Brill).

Hirst, P. (1994) *Associative Democracy* (Oxford: Polity Press).

Hirst, P. and Thompson, G. (1999) *Globalization in Question* (London: Routledge).

Hoogvelt, A. (2001) *Globalization and the Postcolonial World*, Second Edition (Basingstoke: Palgrave).

House of Commons Debates, (1990) *House of Common Debates*, Vol. 182. No. 28, cols 1235–99 (London: House of Commons).

Human Rights Watch, (2000) *Report on Turkey* (<www.hrw.org/reports/2000/turkey2/turk09.htm>).

Huntington, S.P. (1991) *The Third Wave: Democratisation in the Late Twentieth Century* (Norman and London: University of Oklahoma Press).

Hurd, D. (1990) 'Promoting Good Government', *Crossbow*, Autumn.

IMF (1999) *World Economic Outlook*, October (Washington D.C.: IMF).

Insel, A. (2002) '12 Eylül'den Çıkış Kapısı' (The Exit Door form 12 September), *Radikal*, 10 November.

Islamoğlu-Inan, H. (1994) *State and Peasant in the Ottoman Empire* (Leiden: E.J. Brill).

ISO (1995) *A Survey of the 500 Biggest Manufacturing Enterprises* (in Turkish), Istanbul: ISO.

Işıklı, E. and Abay, C. (1993) 'Destekleme Uygulamalarının Tarımsal Yapıya Etkisi' (The Impact of Support Policies on Rural Structures), in TMMOB, *Tarımsal Destekleme Politikaları, Sorunlar-Çözümler* (Ankara: TMMOB Ziraat Mühendileri Odası).

Jaffee, S. (1994) *Exporting High Value Food Commodities* (Washington D.C.: The World Bank).

Jayasuriya, K. (1999) *The Emergence of the Regulatory State in Post-crisis Asia* (Perth: Murdoch University Asia Research Centre).

Jessop, B. (1982) *The Capitalist State* (Oxford: Basil Blackwell).

———. (1990) *State Theory: Putting the Capitalist State in its Place* (Oxford: Polity Press).

Johnson, C. (1981) 'Introduction: The Taiwan Model', in Hsiung, J.S. (ed.), *Contemporary Republic of China: The Taiwan Experience, 1950–1980* (New York: Praeger Press).

———. (1982) *MITI and the Japanese Miracle* (Stanford CA: Stanford University Press).

———. (1995) *Japan: Who Governs?* (New York: W.W. Norton and Co).

———. (1999) 'The Developmental State: Odyssey of a Concept', in Woo-Comings, M. (ed.), *The Developmental State* (Ithaca, NY: Cornell University Press).

Kadıoğlu, A. (1996) 'The Paradox of Turkish Nationalism and the Construction of Official Identity', *Middle Eastern Studies*, 32(2): 177–193.

Kara, D. (1998) *Bediüzzaman Örneği: şeyh Efendinin Rüyasındaki Türkiye* (Turkey in the Dreams of the Shaikh: The Example of Bediüzzaman) (İstanbul).

Karaosmanoğlu, A.L. (1993) 'Officers: Westernization and Democracy' in Heper, M. Öncü, A. and Kreimer, H. (eds), *Turkey and the West: Changing Cultural Identities* (London, New York: I.B. Taurus & Co Ltd Publishers).

Kasaba, R. and Bozdoğan, S. (2000), 'Turkey at a Crossroad', *Journal of International Affairs*, 54(1): 1–20.

Karl, T.L. (1990) 'Dilemmas of Democratization in Latin America', *Comparative Politics*, 23(1): 1–21.

Kazgan, G. (1988) *Ekonomide Dışa Açık Büyüme* (Outward Oriented Growth in the Economy) (İstanbul: Altın Kitapları Yayınevi).

———. (1999) *Tanzimattan XXI. Yüzyıla Türkiye Ekonomisi* (The Turkish Economy from Tanzimat to the XXI Century) (İstanbul: Altın Kitapları Yayınevi).

Kendal [Nezan], (1980) 'Kurdistan in Turkey', in Chailand, G. (ed.), *People without a Country: The Kurds and Kurdistan* (London: Zed Press).

———. (1999) 'No Justice for the Kurds', *Le Monde Diplomatique*, March 3.

Kepenek, Y. and Yentürk, N. (1994) *Türkiye Ekonomisi* (Turkish Economy) (Ankara: Remzi Kitabevi).

Keyder, Ç. (1983) 'Paths of Rural Transformation in Turkey', *Journal of Peasant Studies*, 11(1): 34–49.

———. (1981) *The Definition of a Peripheral Economy, Turkey 1923–1929* (Cambridge: Cambridge University Press).

———. (1987) *State and Class in Turkey: A Study of Capitalist Development* (London: Verso).

Keyman, F. (1995) 'On the Relations Between Global Modernity and Nationalism', *New Perspectives on Turkey*, No. 64.

———. (2000) 'Modernite Sorunsalı ve 21.Yüzyıla Girerken Türkiye' (The Question of Modernity and Turkey at the Door of the Twenty First Century), *Doğu Batı*, 3(10): 49–62.

Keyman, F. (2002) 'AKP ve Muhafazakar-Liberal Sentez' (AKP and the Conservative-Liberal Synthesis), *Radikal Daily*, 17 November.

Kıraç, C. (1995) *Anılarımla Patronum Vehbi Koç* (My Memoirs of My Boss Vehbi Koç) (İstanbul: Milliyet).

Killick, T. (1995) *IMF Programs in Developing Countries: Design and Impact* (London: Routledge).

Kişoğlu, S. *et al.* (1997) 'Anadolu Sanayisi Araştırma Raporunun Sunulması' (Anatolian Industry Research Report) in *1997 Sanayi Kongresi* (ed.) (Makine Mühendisleri Odası: Ankara).

Kızılkaya, M. and Nabiler, H. (1991) *Dünden Yarına Kürtler* (Kurds from Yesterday to Tomorrow) (Ankara: Yurt Kitap-Yayın).

Kohli, A. (1991) *Democracy and Discontent: India's Growing Crisis of Governability* (Cambridge: Cambridge University Press).

Konukman, A., Aydin, A. and Oyan, O. (2000) 'Restructuring of the Turkish Public Finance Organisation' (in Turkish), *Proceedings of the V. Turkish Fiscal Symposium*, May, Antalya.

Köse, A. and Öncü, A. (1998) 'Anadolu Sermayesi Üzerine Gözlemler' (Observations on the Anatolian Capital), Proceedings of the 9th Congress on Industry (Ankara: Chamber of Engineers).

Köymen, O. (1998), 'Cumhuriyet Döneminde Tarımsal Yapılar ve Tarım Politikaları' (Rural Structures and Agricultural Policies in the Republican Era), *75. Yılda Köylerden şehirlere* (From Villages to Cities in the 75 Year), (Istanbul: Tarih Vakfı Yayınları).

Krueger, A. (1990) 'The Importance of Economic Policy in Development: Contrasts Between Korea and Turkey', in Krueger, A. (ed.), *Perspectives in Trade and Development* (Hemel Hempstead: Harvester Wheatsheaf).

Krueger, A. and Aktan, O. (1992) *Swimming against the Tide: Turkish Trade Reforms in the 1980s* (International Center for Economic Growth, ICS Press).

Krueger, A. and Turan, I. (1993) 'The Politics and Economics of Turkish Policy', in Bates, R. and Krueger, A. (eds), *Political and Economic Interactions in Economic Policy Reform* (Oxford and London: Blackwell).

Kubicek, P. (1999) 'Turkish European Relations at a Crossroads', *Middle Eastern Policy*, 6(4): 157–172.

Kuniholm, B. (2001) 'Turkey's Accession to the European Union: Differences in European and US Attitudes, and Challenges for Turkey', *Turkish Studies*, No. 2: 25–53.

Kuran, T. (1995) 'Islamic Economics and the Islamic Subeconomy', *Journal of Economic Perspectives*, No. 9: 155–177.

Kuruç, B. (1963) *İktisat Politikasının Resmi Belgeleri* (Official Documents of Economic Policies) (Ankara: AÜ Yayını).

Kutlay, N. (1997) *Kürt Kimliğinin Oluşum Süreci* (Process of the Kurdish Identity) (İstanbul: Belge Uluslararası Yayıncılık).

Kymlicka, W. (1995) 'Misunderstanding Nationalism', *Dissent*, Winter.

Lash, S. and Urry, J. (1987) *The End of Organised Capitalism* (Cambridge: Polity).

Laver, M. (1997) *Private Desires, and Political Action* (London: Sage).

Leftwich, A. (1993) 'Governance, Democracy and Development in the Third World', *Third World Quarterly*, 14(3): 605–625.

——. (1996) 'Two Cheers for Democracy? Democracy and Developmental State', in Leftwich, A. (ed.), *Democracy and Development* (Cambridge: Polity Press).

Leftwich, A. (2000) *States of Development* (Cambridge: Polity Press).

Lerner, D. (1958) *The Passing of Traditional Society* (New York).

Levine, D.H. (1986) 'Religion and Politics in Comparative and Historical Perspective', *Comparative Politics*, 19(1): 95–122.

Lewis, B. (1962) *The Emergence of Modern Turkey* (London: Oxford University Press).

Lipset, S.M. (1960) *Political Man* (London: Heinemann).

Llambi, B. (2000) 'Global-Local Links in Latin America's New Ruralities', in Bryceson, D., Kay, C. and Mooij, J. (eds), *Disappearing Peasantries? Rural Labour in Africa, Asia and Latin America* (London: IT Publications).

MacEwan, A. (1999) *Neo-Liberalism or Democracy?* (London and New York: Zed Books).

Maffesoli, M. (1996) *The Time of Tribes: The Decline of Individualism in Mass Society* (London: Sage).

Magatti, M. (1999) 'Globalization as Double Disconnection and its Consequences: An Outline', in Kennedy, P. and Hai, N. (eds), *Globalization and Identities Conference*, Vol. 2 (Manchester: Metropolitan University).

Mardin, Ş. (1969) *Din ve İdeoloji* (Religion and Ideology) (Ankara).

——. (1973) 'Centre-Periphery Relations: A Key to Turkish Politics?' *DAEDALUS*, 102(1).

——. (1978) 'Youth and Violence in Turkey', *Archives Européens de Sogiologie*, 1(19).

——. (1980) 'Turkey: The Transformation of Economic Code', in Özbudun, E. and Ulusan, A. (eds), *The Political Economy of Income Dsitribution in Turkey* (Holes and Meier).

——. (1990) *Türkiye'de Toplum ve Siyaset* (Society and Politics in Turkey) (İstanbul: İletişim Yayınları).

Marsh, R.R. and Runsten, D. (1998) 'Smallholder Fruit and Vegetable Production in Mexico: Barriers and Opportunities', in Cornelius, W.A. and Myhre D. (eds.), *The Transformation of Rural Mexico: Reforming the Ejido Sector* (San Diego, La Jolla: Center for U.S–Mexican Studies, University of California).

Marty, M. and Appleyby, S. (eds) (1991) *Fundamentalisms Observed* (Chicago: Chicago University Press).

Marx, K. (1859/1958a) 'The Eighteenth Brumaire of Louis Bonaparte', in Marx, K. and Engels, F. *Selected Works*, Vol. 1 (Moscow: Foreign Languages Publishing House).

——. (1859/1958b) 'Preface to a Contribution to the Critique of Political Economy', in Marx, K. and Engels, F. *Selected Works*, Vol. 1 (Moscow: Foreign Languages Publishing House).

Marx, K. and Engels, F. (1888/1958c) 'Manifesto of the Communist Party', in Marx, K. and Engels, F. *Selected Works*, Vol. 1 (Moscow: Foreign Languages Publishing House).

McMichael, P. and Myhre, D. (1991) 'Global Regulation vs. the Nation-State: Agro-Food Systems and the New Politics of Capital', *Capital and Class*, No. 43.

Migdal, J.S. (1988) *Strong Societies and Weak States: State-Society Relations and State Capitalism in the Third World* (Princeton: Princeton University Press).

Milliyet Daily, 5 December 1997. 'Yılmazdan Rejim Uyarısı' (Warning by Yılmaz on the Regime).

Milliyet Daily, 4 November 2002. 'Dünya Bizi Konuşuyor' (The World is Talking about Us).

Ministry of Agriculture (2003) 'Tarımsal Politikalar ve Hedefler' (Agricultural Policies and Targets), <www.tarim.gov.tr/arayuz/5/icerik.asp?efl= tari...\tarim_sektor&fl=tarim_politika.html>, Downloaded 18 December 2003.

Morrison, T. (1984) 'Cereal Imports by Developing Countries: Trends and Determinants', *Food Policy*, 9(1).

Mortimer, E. (1982) *Faith and Power: The Politics of Islam* (London: Faber and Faber).

Mouffe, C. (1979) *Gramsci and Marxist Theory* (London: Routledge and Kegan Paul).

Mumcu, U. (1996) *Kürt İslam Ayaklanması* (Kurdish Islamic Rebellion), 21st edition (Ankara: Umag Vakfı Yayınları).

Muradilhan, S. (2001) 'Opening the Floodgates', *Frontline*, April 2001.

MÜSİAD (1994) *İş Hayatında İslam İnsanı* (Homo Islamicus in Business Life) (Istanbul).

——. (1997) *MÜSİAD Bülteni*, No. 22, August–September.

Myrdal, G. (1968) *Asian Drama: An Inquiry into the Poverty of Nations*, 3 Vols (New York: Pantheon).

——. (1970) 'The "Soft State" in Underdeveloped Countries', Streeten, P. (ed.), *Unfashionable Economics: Essays in Honour of Lord Balogh* (London: Weidenfeld and Nicolson).

Nas, T. and Okedon, M. (eds), (1992) *Economics and Politics of Turkish Liberalisation* (Betlehem: Leigh University Press).

Nichols, T. and Sungur, N. (1996) 'Small Employers in Turkey: The OSTIM Estate at Ankara', *Middle Eastern Studies*, 32.

Nozick, R. (1974) *Anarchy, State, Utopia* (Oxford: Basil Blackwell).

Ocak, A.Y. (1999) *Türk Sufiliğine Bakışlar* (Views on Turkish Sufism) (İstanbul: Iletisim).

O'Connor, J. (1989) 'An Introduction to Theory of Crises Theories', in Gottdiener, M. and Komninos, N. (eds), *Capitalist Development and Crisis Theory: Accumulation, Regulation and Spatial Restructuring* (London: Macmillan).

O'Donnel, G., Schmitter, P. and Whitehead, L. (eds) (1986) *Transition from Authoritarian Rule: Prospects for Democracy*, Vols 1–4 (Baltimore MD and London: Johns Hopkins University Press).

OECD (1989) *Development Cooperation in the 1990s* (Paris: OECD).

Offe, C. (1999) 'How Can We Trust Our fellow Citizens? in Warren, M.E. (ed.) *Democracy and Trust* (Cambridge University Press).

Ohmae, K. (1994) *The Borderless World: Power and the Strategy in the International Economy* (London: Collins).

Olson, M. (1982) *The Rise and Fall of Nations* (New Haven, CT: Yale University Press).

Oran, B. (1990) *Atatürk Milliyetçiliği: Resmi İdeoloji Dışı Bir İnceleme* (Atatürk Nationalism: An Investigation of non-Official Ideological Nature) (Ankara: Bilgi Yayınevi).

Oyan, O. (1987) *24 Ocak Ekonomisimde Dışa Açılma ve Maliye Politikaları* (Liberalisation and Financial Policies in the 24 January Economy) (Ankara: Verso Yayıncılık).

——. (1997) 'Tarımsal Desteklemeye Alternatif Arayışları' (Searches for Alternatives for Agricultural Support), *Ekonomide Durum* 2: 78–96.

——. (1999) 'Tarımsal Destekleme Politikaları ve Doğrudan Gelir Desteği' (Agricultural Support Policies and the Direct Income Support), *TÜRK-İŞ Yıllığı*, Vol. 1: 187–200.

——. (2003) 'From Agricultural Policies to Agriculture without Policies', in Balkan, N. (ed.), *The Ravages of Neo-Liberalism: Economy, Society and Gender in Turkey* (New York: Nova Science Club).

Oyan, O. and Konukman, A. 1997. 'Esnek İşgücü Piyaysaları, Anadolu Kaplanları ve Sendikalaşma', in *1997 Sanayi Kongresi* (ed.) (Makine Mühendisleri Odası: Ankara).

Öniş, Z. (1992a) 'The East Asian Model Development and the Turkish Case: A Comparative Analysis', *METU Studies in Development*, 19(4).

——. (1992b) 'The Dynamics of Export-Oriented Growth in a Second Generation NICs: The Political Economy of the Turkish Case', *Bophorous University Research Papers*.

——. (1995) 'International Context, Income Distribution and the State Power in Late Industrialisation: Turkey and Korea in Comparative Perspective', *New Perspectives on Turkey*, No. 13.

——. (1996) 'Globalization and Finacial Blow-ups in the Semi-Periphery: Perspectives on Turkey's Finacial Crisis of 1994', *New Perspectives on Turkey*, Fall 15: 1–23.

——. (1997) 'The Political Economy of Islamic Resurgence in Turkey: The Rise of the Welfare Party in Perspective', *Third World Quarterly*, 18(4): 743–766.

——. (2001) 'Political Islam at the Crossroads: From Hegemony to Co-existence', *Contemporary Politics*, 7(4).

——. (2003) 'Domestic Politics versus Global Dynamics: Towards a Political Economy of the 2000 and 2001 Financial Crises in Turkey', in Öniş, Z. and Rubin, B. (eds), *The Turkish Economy on Crisis* (London: Frank Cass).

Öniş, Z. and Aysan A.F. (2000) 'Neoliberal Globalisation, the Nation State and Financial Crises in the Semi-Periphery: A Comparative Analysis', *Third World Quarterly*, 21(1): 119–139.

Öniş, Z. and Riedel, J. (1993) *Economic Crisis and Long-Term Growth in Turkey* (Washington D.C.: World Bank Publications).

Öniş, Z. and Rubin, B. (eds) (2003) *The Turkish Economy in Crisis* (London: Frank Cass).

Özatay, F. and Sak, G. (2002) 'The 2000–2001 Financial Crises in Turkey', Paper Presented at the Brookings Trade Forum 2002: Currency Crises (Washington D.C. May 2002).

Özbudun, E. (1991) 'The Post-1980 Legal Framework for Interest Group Associations' in Heper, M. (ed.), *Strong State and Economic Interest Groups* (Berlin: De Guyer).

——. (2000) *Contemporary Turkish Politics: Challenges to Democratic Consolidation* (Boulder, London: Lynne Rienner).

Özgür Politika, 25 February 2002, Daily Newspaper 'Çiftçi Destek Bekliyor' (Farmers are Hoping Support).

——. 11 June 2004, Daily Newspaper, 'Operasyonlar Durursa Çatışmalar da Durur' (Contlics Will Stop if Operations Stop).

Özkaya, T., Oyan, O., Işın, F. and Uzmay A. (2000) 'Türkiye'dekı Tarımsal Destekleme Politikaları, Dünü, Bügünü – Geleceği' (The Yesterday Today and Tomorrow of Agricultural Support Policies in Turkey) Unpublished paper prepared for TÜSES.

Parekh, B. (1993) 'Cultural Particularity of Liberal Democracy' in Held, D. (ed.), *Prospects for Democracy* (Oxford: Polity).

Pempel, T.J. (1999) 'The Developmental Regime in a Changing World Environment', in Woo-Comings, M. (ed.), *The Developmental State* (Ithaca, NY: Cornell University Press).

Pfaff, W. (1999) 'Between the Turks and Kurds, a History of Tension', *International Herald Tribune*, 3 April.

Phillips, A. (1999) 'Who Needs Civil Society? A Feminist Perspective', *Dissent*, 46(1): 56–61.

Piore, C. and Sabel, C. (1984) *The Second Industrial Divide: Possibility for Prosperity* (New York).

Poulantzas, N. (1973) *Political Power and Social Classes* (London: New Left Books).

Przeworski, A. (1991) *Democracy and the Market: Political and Economic Reform in Eastern Europe and Latin America* (Cambridge: Cambridge University Press).

——. (1992) 'The Games of Transition' in Mainwaring, S., O'Donnell, G. and Valenzuela, A. (eds), *Issues in Democratic Consolidation: The New South American Democracies in Comparative Perspective* (Notre Dame, IN: University of Indiana Press).

Raikes, P. (1988) *Modernising Hunger* (London: Catholic Institute of International Relations).

——. (2000) ' "Globalisation" and African Export Crop Agriculture', *Journal of Peasant Studies*, 27(2).

Rambout, L. (1947) *Les Kurdes et le Droit* (Paris).

Raynolds, L. (1997) 'Restructuring National Agriculture, Agro-food Trade, and Agrarian Livelihoods in the Caribbean', in D. Goodman and M. Watts (eds), *Globalising Food: Agrarian Questions and Global Food Restructuring* (London: Routledge).

Raynolds, L., Myhre, D., McMichael, P., Carro-Figueroa, V. and Buttel, F. (1993) 'The New Internationalization of Agriculture', *World Development*, 21(7): 1101–1121.

Refah Partisi (1992) *Adil Düzen: 21 Soru Cevap* (The Just Order: 21 Questions Answers) (Ankara).

Riesebrodt, M. (1993) *Pious Passions: The Emergence of Modern Fundamentalism in the United States and Iran* (Berkeley, CA: University of California Press).

Rivera-Batiz, F.L. (ed.), (2001) *The Political Economy of the Asian Crisis and its Aftermath* (Cheltenham: Edward Elgar).

Robertson, R. (1992) *Globalization* (London: Sage).

Robinson, M. (1996) 'Economic Reform and the Transition to Democracy', in Luckham, R. and White, G. (eds), *Democratization in the South: The Jagged Wave* (Manchester: Manchester University Press).

Rodrik, D. (1990a) 'Some Policy Dilemmas in Turkish Macroeconomic Management', in Aricanli, T. and Rodrik, T. (eds), *The Political Economy of Turkey: Debt, Adjustment and Sustainability* (London: Macmillan).

Rodrik, D. (1990b) 'Premature Liberalisation, Incomplete Stabilisation: The Özal Decade in Turkey', Centre for Economic Policy Reform, Discussion Paper No. 402.
——. (1990c) 'How Should Structural Adjustment Programs be Designed?', *World Development*, 18(7).
——. (1991a) 'Comment on Turkey' in Thomas, V. *et al.* (eds), *Restructuring Economies in Distress* (Oxford: Oxford University Press).
——. (1991b) 'Policy Uncertainty and Private Investment in Developing Counties', *Journal of Development Economics*, 36.
——. (1998) 'Who Needs Capital Account Convertibility', *Essay in International Finance*, 20–27 May.
——. (1999) *The New Global Economy and Developing Countries: Making Openness Work*, Policy Essay No. 24. Overseas Development Council.
Rouleau, E. (2000) 'Turkey's Dream of Democracy', *Foreign Affairs*, 79, November–December, 100–113.
Rueschemeyer, D., Stephens, E.H. and Stephens, J.D. (1992) *Capitalism Development and Democracy* (Cambridge: Polity Press).
Ruggie, J.G. (1993) 'Territoriality and Beyond: Problematizing Modernity in International Relations', *International Organization*, 47(1): 139–174.
Rustow, D.A. (1973) 'The Modernisation of Turkey in Historical and Comparative Perspective' in Karpat, K.H. (ed.), *Social Change and Politics in Turkey* (Leiden: E.J. Brill).
Sadoulet, E. and de Janvry A. (2001) 'Income Strategies among Rural Households in Mexico: The Role of Off-farm Activities', *World Development*, 29(3): 467–80.
——. (2002) 'Cash Transfer Programs with Income Multipliers PROCAMPO in Mexico', *World Development*, 29(6): 1043–1056.
Sandbrook, R. (1992) *The Politics of Africa's Economic Recovery* (Cambridge: Cambridge University Press).
Sanderson, S. (1986a) *The Transformation of Mexican Agriculture* (Princeton, New Jersey: University of Princeton Press).
——. (1986b) 'The Emergence of the "World Steer": Internationalization and Foreign Domination in Latin American Cattle Production', in Tullis, F.L. and Hollist, W.L. (eds), *Food, the State and International Political Economy* (Lincoln: University of Nebraska Press).
Saul, J.S. (1974) 'The State in Post-colonial Societies', in Miliband, R. and Saville, J. (eds), *Socialist Register, 1974* (London: Merlin Press).
Sayarı, S. (1996) 'Turkey's Islamist Challenge', *Middle East Quarterly*, 3(3): 35–43.
Saybaşılı, Kemali (1992) *İktisat, Siyaset ve Türkiye Economics* (Politics, State and Turkey) (Istanbul: Bağlam).
Scholte, Jan-Aart (1995) 'Construction of Collective Identity', paper presented at the conference on The Organization Dimensions of Global Change: No Limits to Co-operation (University of Cleveland, OH).
Schraeder, J.P. (1995) 'Political Elites in the Process of Democratisation in Africa, in Hippler, J. (ed.), *The Democratisation of Disempowerment: The Problem of Democracy in the Third World* (London: Pluto Press).
Schumpeter, J.A. (1942) *Capitalism, Socialism and Democracy* (New York: Harper Torchbooks).

Seaton-Watson, H. (1977) *Nations and States: An Inquiry into the Origins of Nations and the Politics of Nationalism* (Boulder: Westview).

Sencer, Muammer (1971) *Toprak Ağalığının Kökeni* (The Origins of Landlordism) (İstanbul: Tel Yayınları).

Shepard, W.E. (1987) 'Islam and Ideology: Towards a Typology', *International Journal of Middle East Studies*, Vol. 19.

Shiva,V., Holla, R., and Menon, K. (1997) 'Globalization and Agriculture in India' unpublished conference paper presented at an international conference on *Globalisation, Food Security*, New Delhi, 30–31 July.

Short, C. (1997) *Democracy, Human Rights and Governance*, speech given at the University of Manchester, 30 June 1997 (London: Department of International Development).

Sirman-Eralp, N. (1988) 'Pamuk Üretiminde Aile İşletmeleri (Household Production in Cotton Production) in Pamuk, Ş. And Toprak, Z. (eds) *Türkiye'de Tarımsal Yapılar* (Rural Structures in Turkey) 1923–2000, Ankara (Yurt Yayınları).

Sirowy, L. and Inkeles, A. (1990) 'The Effects of Democracy on Economic Growth and Inequality: A Review', *Studies in Comparative International Development*, 25(1): 126–157.

Smith, A.D. (1986) *Ethnic Origins of Nations* (Oxford).

——. (1991) *National Identity* (Harmondsworth, Middlesex: Penguin).

——. (1995) 'Gastronomy or Geology? The Role of Nationalism in the Reconstruction of Nations', *Nations and Nationalism*, 1(1): 3–23.

Solimano, A. (1999) *Globalisations and National Development at the end of the 20th Century* (Washington: World Bank, Policy Research Working Paper 2137, June).

Sönmez, M. (1980) *Türkiye Ekonomisinde Bunalım 24 Ocak Kararları ve Sonraları* (Crisis in the Turkish Economy: 24 January Decisions and their Aftermath) (İstanbul: Belge Yayınları).

——. (2002) 'Krizin Yıldönümü' (The First Anniversary of the Crisis) <sendika.org.belgeler.kriz>, downloaded 14 January 2002.

——. (2004) 'Bu Büyüme Sürdürülebilir mi?' (Is this Growth Sustainable?), <www.bagimsizsosyalbilimciler.org>, downloaded 26 June 2004.

Stanford, L. (1998) 'Opportunities under Privatizations Restructuring Commodity Systems in Michoacan', in Cornelius, W.A. and Myhre, D. (eds), *The Transformation of Rural Mexico: Reforming the Ejido Sector* (San Diego, La Jolla: Center for U.S–Mexican Studies, University of California).

State Planning Organisation (1963) *First Five-Year Development Plan* (Ankara: Prime Ministry, Republic of Turkey).

——. (1969) *Second Five-Year Development Plan* (Ankara: Prime Ministry, Republic of Turkey).

State Treasury (2001) 'Strengthening the Turkish Economy: Turkey's Transition Program', <www.hazine.gov.tr>, downloaded 14 November 2001.

Stavenhagen, R. (1996) *Ethnic Conflicts and Nation-State* (Basingstoke: Macmillan Press).

Stiglitz, J.E. (1998a) 'More Instruments and Broader Goals: Moving Toward the Post Washington Consensus', *The 1998 WIDER Annual Lecture*, 7 January, Helsinki.

Stiglitz, J.E. (1998b) 'Towards a New Paradigm for Development: Strategies, Policies and Processes', *Prebisch Lecture* given at UNCTAD, 7 October, Geneva.

——. (2000a) 'Capital Liberalization Economic Growth and Instability', *World Development*, 28(6): 1075–1086.

——. (2000b) 'What Learned from the Economic Crisis', *The New Republic*, April.

Stiles, K. (1991) *Negotiating Debt: The IMF Lending Process* (Boulder, CO: Westview).

Stokke, O. (1995) 'Aid and Political Conditionality: Core Issues and State of the Art', in Stokke, O. (ed.), *Aid and Political Conditionality* (London: Frank Cass).

Strange, S. (1996) *The Retreat of the State: The Diffusion of Power in the World Economy* (Cambridge: Cambridge University Press).

Sunar, I. (1974) *State and Society in the Politics of Turkey's Development* (Ankara: Ankara University Publication).

Sunar, I. and Toprak, B. (1983) 'Islam in Politics: The Case of Turkey', *Government and Opposition*, 31(3): 421–441.

Şahin, M. (1997) 'Türkiye'de Küçük ve Orta Boy İşletmelerin (KOBİlerin) Önemi' [The Importance of Small and medium Size Firms (KOBIs)], *MÜSİAD Bülteni*, No. 20 (Nisan-Mayıs).

Şenses, F. (1990) 'An Assessment of the Pattern of Turkish Manufactured Export Growth in the 1980s and Its Prospects', in Arıcanlı, T. and Rodrik, D. (eds), *The Political Economy of Turkey: Debt, Adjustment and Sustainability* (London: Macmillan).

——. (ed.) (1994) *Recent Industrialisation Experience in Turkey in a Global Context* (Westport, CT: Greenwood Press).

——. (2003) 'Economic Crisis as an Instigator of Distributional Conflict: The Turkish Case 2001', in Öniş, Z. and Rubin, B. (eds), *The Turkish Economy in Crisis* (London: Frank Cass).

Tan, D. (1999) *Kürt Ulusal Sorunu* (Istanbul: Devrimci Proleterya Yayınları).

Tandon, Y. (1999) 'Globalisation and Africa's Options', *Journal of Development Economics for Southern Africa*, 1(4&5), January–April.

Tekeli, İ., and İlkin, S. (1982) *Uygulamaya Geçerken Türkiye'de Devletçiliğin Oluşumu* (The Process of Etatism through Practice in Turkey) (Ankara: METU).

——. (1993) *Türkiye ve Avrupa Topluluğu* (Turkey and the European Community), Vol. II (Ankara: Ümit Yayıncılık).

Temel, A. (1999), 'Büyüme Ekonomik Yapı Değişmeleri (1946–1997)', *Bilanço 1923–1998 Ekonomi Toplum Çevre*, Cilt 2 (İstanbul: Tarih Vakfı Yayınları: 73–90).

Tezel, Y.S. (1994) *Cumhuriyet Döneminin İktisat Tarihi* (Economic History of the Republican Period) (İstanbul: Tarih Vakfı Yurt Yayınları).

Thornburg, M., Spry, G. and Soule, G. (1949) *Turkey: An Economic Appraisal* (New York: Twentieth Century Fund).

TOBB (1974) *İktisadi Rapor* (Economic Report) (Ankara: Union of Chambers of Commerce and Industry).

——. (1995) *Doğu Sorunu: Teşhisler ve Tepkiler* (Temmuz, TOBB Genel Yayın No. 302).

Toprak, B. (1981) *Islam and Political Development in Turkey* (Leiden).

Toprak, B. (1993) 'Islamist Intellectuals: Revolt Against Industry and Technology' in Heper, M., Öncü, A. and Kreimer, H. (eds), *Turkey and the West: Changing Cultural Identities* (London, New York: I.B. Taurus & Co Ltd Publishers).

Trimberger, E.K. (1978) *Revolution from Above: Military Bureaucrats in Japan, Turkey, Egypt and Peru* (New Brunswick: Transaction Books).

Tubiana, L. (1989) 'World Trade in Agricultural Products: From Global Regulation to Market Fragmentation', in Goodman, D. and Redclift, M. (eds), *The International Farm Crisis* (New York: St Martin's Press).

Tuncay, M. (1981) *Türkiye Cumhuriyeti'nde Tek-Parti Yonetiminin Kurulması (1923–1931)* (Ankara: Yurt Yayınları).

Tuğal, C. (2002) 'Islamism in Turkey: Beyond Instrument and Meaning', *Economy and Society*, 31(1): 85–111.

Türel, O. (1984) 'Ekonomik Istikrar Programlarına Genel Bir Bakış' (A General Consideration of Stabilisation Programmes) in Tekeli, I (ed.), *Türkiye'de ve Dünyada Yaşanan eEonomik Bunalım* (Economic Crises in Turkey and in the World) (TMMOB Makine Mühendisleri Odası 1984 Sanayi Kongresi Bildirileri).

——. (1999) 'Restructuring the Public Sector in Post-1980 Turkey: An Assessment' (Middle East Technical University, ERC Working Papers, No. 99/6).

Turkish Daily News, 23 June 2004, 'Council of Europe Ends Turkey Monitoring'.

TÜSİAD (1976) *Üçüncü Beş Yıllık Planın İlk Üç Yılının Değerlendirilmesi ve 1975 Yılının Uygulaması* (An Evaluation of the First Three Years of the Third Five Year Plan), January (İstanbul: TÜSİAD).

——. (1977) *1977 Yılına Girerken Türk Ekonomisi* (The Turkish Economy at the Beginning of 1977), January (İstanbul: TÜSİAD).

——. (1980) *The Turkish Economy* (İstanbul: TÜSİAD).

——. (1986) *Görüş*, October (İstanbul: TÜSİAD).

——. (1997) *Türkiye'de Demokratikleşme Perspektifleri* (Istanbul: TÜSIAD).

——. (1999) *Tarım Politikalarında Yeni Denge Arayışları ve Türkiye* (Searches for New Balances in Agricultural Policies and Turkey) (İstanbul: TÜSİAD).

TWN, <www.twnside.org.sg/title/food.cn.html> downloaded 3 May 2002.

UNCTAD (1990) *Trade and Development Report* (New York: UNCTAD).

UNDP (1991) *Human Development Report 1991* (New York: Oxford University Press).

Unvin, P. (1993) '"Do as I say, Not as I Do": The Limits of Political Conditionality', *European Journal of Development Research*, 5(1): 63–84.

US Department of Commerce (2000) *Survey of Current Business*, March.

US State Department (1948) *European Recovery Program: Country Studies*, Vol. 2, Chapter 15, Turkey.

Van Bruinessen, M. (1992) *Agha, Shaikh, and State: the Social and Political Structure of Kurdistan* (London: Zed Books).

——. (1993) *Kürdistan Üzerine Yazılar* (Essays on Kurdistan) (İstanbul: İletişim Yayınları).

Van Westering, J. (2000) 'Conditionality and EU Membership: The Cases of Turkey and Cyprus', European *Foreign Affairs Review*, 5(1): 95–118.

Wade, R. (1990) *Governing the Market: Economic Theory and the Role of Government in East Asian Industrialization* (Princeton: Princeton University Press).

——. (1996) 'Japan, the World Bank and the Art of Paradigm Maintenance: the East Asian Miracle in Political Perspective', *New Left Review*, 217: 3–37.

——. (2001) 'The US Role in the Long Lasting Asian Crisis', in Lukauskas, A.J. and Rivera-Batiz, F.L. (eds), *The Political Economy of the Asian Crisis and its Aftermath* (Cheltenham: Edward Elgar).

Wagstaff, H. (1982) 'Food Imports of Developing Countries', *Food Policy*, 7(1).

Walby, S. (2001) 'From Community to Coalition: The Politics of Recognition as the Handmaiden of the Politics of Equality in an Era of Globalization', *Theory, Culture & Society*, 18(2–3): 113–135.

Wallerstein E. (1979) *The Capitalist World Economy* (Cambridge: Cambridge University Press).

Walters, M. (1995) *Globalization* (London: Routledge).

Watts, M. (1994) 'Life under Contract', in Little, P and Watts, M. (eds), *Living Under Contract* (Madison: University of Wisconsin Press).

Watts, M. and Goodman, D. (eds) (1997) *Globalising Food: Agrarian Questions and Global Restructuring* (London: Routledge).

Weber, M. (1964) *The Theory of Social and Economic Organization* (New York: The Free Press).

——. (1965) 'Bureaucracy' in Gerth, H.H. and Mills, C.W. (eds) *From Max Weber: Essays in Sociology* (New York: Galaxy Books).

——. (1968) *Economy and Society*, Vol. 3 (New York: Bedminster Press).

Weiss, L. (1999) 'State Power and the Asian Crises', *New Political Economy*, 4: 317–342.

Weiss, L. and Hobson, J.M. (1995) *States and Economic Development* (Cambridge: Polity).

Weisskopf, T.E. (1981) 'The Current Economic Crisis in Historical Perspective, *Socialist Review*, 11(3): 4–5.

——. (2000) 'Left Perspectives on Long-Term Trends in Capitalism' in Pollin, R. (ed.), *Capitalism, Socialism and Radical Political Economy* (Cheltenham: Edward Elgar).

White, J.B. (1994) *Money Makes us Relatives: Women's Labour in Urban Turkey* (Austin: Texas University Press).

——. (1995) 'Islam and Democracy: The Turkish Experience', *Current History*, 94(588): 7–12.

White, P. (2000) *Primitive Rebels or Revolutionary Modernizers?, The Kurdish National Movement in Turkey* (London: Zed Books).

Winters, L.A. (1987), 'The Political Economy of the Agricultural Policies of Industrial Countries', *European Review of Agricultural Economics*, 14: 285–304.

Wiseman, J.A. (1995) 'Introduction: The Movement Towards Democracy: Global, Continental and State Perspectives', in Wiseman, J.A. (ed.), *Democracy and Political Change in Sub-Saharan Africa* (London: Routledge).

Wolff, P. (1987) *Stabilisation Policy and Structural Adjustment in Turkey, 1980–1985* (Berlin: German Development Institute).

Woo-Cumings, M. (ed.), (1999a) *The Developmental State* (Ithaca, NY: Cornell University Press).

——. (1999b) 'Introduction: Chalmers Johnson and the Politics of Nationalism and Development', in Woo-Cumings, M. (ed.), *The Developmental State* (Ithaca NY: Cornell University Press).

Wood, E.M. (1999) 'Global Capitalism in the World of Nation-States', *Monthly Review*, July–August.

Woodward, D. (2000) *The Next Crisis? Direct and Equity Investment in Developing Countries* (London: Zed Books).

Woodward, K. (ed.) (1997) *Identity and Difference* (London: Sage and Open University Press).

World Bank (1951) *The Economy of Turkey: An Analysis and Recommendations for a Development Program*, Report of a mission sponsored by the World Bank and Government of Turkey.

——. (1985) *World Development Report* (Washington D.C.: World Bank).

——. (1987) *World Development Report* (Washington D.C.: World Bank).

——. (1988) *Turkey: Towards Sustainable Growth*, Country Economic Memorandum (Washington D.C.: World Bank).

——. (1990) *Turkey: A Strategy for Managing Debt, Borrowings and Transfer under Macroeconomic Adjustment, Country Case Study*, June.

——. (1991) *World Development Report 1991* (New York: Oxford University Press).

——. (1992) *Governance and Development* (Washington D.C.: World Bank).

——. (1993) *The East Asian Miracle*, World Bank Policy Research Report (Oxford: Oxford University Press).

——. (1997) *World Development Report 1997* (New York: Oxford University Press).

——. (1998) *Global Development Finance*, Vol. II P. 14 (Washington D.C.: World Bank).

——. (1999) 'Development Goals', at <www.worldbank.org/data/dev/devgoal.html>.

——. (2001) 'Project Appraisal Document on a Proposed Loan in the Amount of US$600 Million to the Republic Of Turkey for an Agricultural Reform Implementation Project/Loan', Report No: 21177-TU, 6 June 2001.

WTO (2000) 'United States Proposal for Comprehensive Long-term Agricultural Trade Reform', 23 June, Report no G/AG/NG/W/15.

Wuthnow, R. (1987) *Meaning and Moral Order: Explorations in Cultural Analysis* (Berkeley, CA: University of California Press).

——. (1991) 'Understanding Religion and Politics', *Daedalus*, 120(3): 1–20.

Yabut-Bernardino, N. (2000) *An Impact Study of Agricultural Trade Liberalisation in the Philippines*, International South Group Network Monograph, No. 3.

Yalman, G. (1984) 'Gelişme Stratejileri ve Stabilizasyon Politikaları: Bazı Latin Amerika Ülkelerinin Deneyimleri Üzerine Gözlemler' (Development Strategies and Stabilisation Policies: Observations on some Latin American Experiences), in Tekeli, İ. *et al.* (eds), *Uygulamaya Geçerken Türkiye'de Devletçiliğin Oluşumu* (The Process of Etatism through Practice in Turkey) (METU: Ankara).

——. (2001) 'Bourgeoisie and the State: Changing Forms of Interest Representation within the Context of Economic Crisis and Structural Adjustment: Turkey during the 1980s'. Unpublished PhD Thesis, University of Manchester.

Yalman, G. (2002) 'The Turkish State and Bourgeoisie in Historical Perspective: A Relativist Paradigm or Panoply of Hegemonic Strategies', in Savran, S. and Balkan, N. (eds) *The Politics of Permanent Crisis: Class Ideology and State in Turkey* (New York: Nova Science Publishers, Inc.).

Yavuz, H. (1998) 'Islamic Political Identity in Turkey: Movement, Agents and Processes'. Unpublished dissertation, University of Wisconsin, Madison.

——. (1999) 'The Assassination of Collective Memory: The Case of Turkey, *The Muslim World*, 99.

——. (2000a) 'Turkey's Fault Lines and the Crisis of Kemalism', *Current History*, January.

——. (2000b) 'Cleansing Islam from the Public Sphere', *Journal of International Affairs*, Fall.

Yeldan, E. (1994) 'The Economic Structure of Power under Turkish Structural Adjustment: Prices, Growth and Accumulation', in Şenses, F. (ed.), Recent Industrialisation Experience of Turkey in a Global Context (Greenwood Press).

——. (1995) 'Surplus Creation and Extraction Under Structural Adjustment: Turkey, 1980–1992', *Review of Radical Political Economics*, 27(2): 38–72.

——. (2001a) *Turkish Economy in the Process of Globalisation* (in Turkish) (İstanbul: İletişim Yayınları).

——. (2001b) 'IMF-Directed Disinflation Program in Turkey: A Program for Stabilisation and Austerity or a Recipe for Impoverishment and Financial Chaos' mimeograph (Department of Economics, Bilkent University, Ankara).

——. (2001c) 'Turkey Cannot Overcome the Crisis Due to Her Strict Adherence to the IMF Programmes' (in Turkish), *Tes-İş*, June–July, 27–34.

——. (2003) 'Büyümenin Kaynakları Üzerine' (On the Sources of Growth), <www.bagimsizsosyalbilimciler.org>, downloaded 10 August 2003.

——. (2004) 'Türkiye Ekonomisi'nde Dış Borç Sorunu ve Kalkınma Stratejileri Acısından Analizi' (The Foreign Debt Question in Turkish Economy and its Analysis from the Point of View of Development Strategies), <www.bagimsizsosyalbilimciler.org>, downloaded on 25 June 2004.

Yenal, Z.N. (2001) 'Türkiye'de Gıda Üretiminin Yeniden Yapılanması' (Restructuring of Food Production in Turkey), *Toplum ve Bilim*, 88: 32–55.

Yentürk, N. (1994) 'Import Dependence of Exports in Turkish Economy' (in Turkish), A report prepared for DEIK, May, Istanbul.

——. (2001) 'The Last 20 Years of the Turkish Economy: The Fire is out, We Have Saved the Plot (in Turkish), <www.bagimsizsosyalbilimciler.org>, downloaded 19 September 2001.

Yerasimos, S. (1975) *Azgelişmişlik Sürecinde Türkiye* (Turkey in the Process of Underdevelopment), 3 Vols. (İstanbul: Gözlem Yayınları).

Yılmaz, H. (1997) 'Democratisation from Above in Response to the International Context: Turkey, 1945–1950', *New Perspectives on Turkey*, Fall, 17: 1–37.

Yüksel, M. (1993) *Kürdistan'da Değişim Süreci* (The Process of Change in Kurdistan) (Ankara).

Zunes, S. (1999) 'Kurdistan Policy Critiqued', *The Progressive Response*, 3(7), <www.kurdish.com/articles/kwr-article-31.html>.

Index